The Westminster Confession of Faith

THE WESTMINSTER

CONFESSION OF FAITH.

With Introduction and Notes

BY

THE REV. JOHN MACPHERSON, M.A.,

EDINBURGH:
T. & T. CLARK, 38 GEORGE STREET.

PRINTED IN GREAT BRITAIN BY
MORRISON AND GIBB LIMITED

FOR

T. & T CLARK, EDINBURGH
NEW YORK   CHARLES SCRIBNER'S SONS

FIRST PRINTED 1881
TWELFTH IMPRESSION 1958

CONTENTS.

INTRODUCTION.

CHAP.		PAGE
I. THE PLACE AND PURPOSE OF CONFESSIONS OF FAITH,		1
II THE EARLIER CONFESSIONS OF THE SCOTTISH CHURCH,		7
III. THE WESTMINSTER CONFESSION,		11

THE CONFESSION OF FAITH.

		PAGE
I. OF THE HOLY SCRIPTURE,		29
II. OF GOD, AND OF THE HOLY TRINITY,		41
III. OF GOD'S ETERNAL DECREE,		46
IV. OF CREATION,		52
V. OF PROVIDENCE,		54
VI. OF THE FALL OF MAN, OF SIN, AND OF THE PUNISHMENT THEREOF,		60
VII. OF GOD'S COVENANT WITH MAN,		65
VIII. OF CHRIST THE MEDIATOR,		70
IX. OF FREE WILL,		78
X. OF EFFECTUAL CALLING,		82
XI. OF JUSTIFICATION,		87
XII. OF ADOPTION,		92
XIII. OF SANCTIFICATION,		94
XIV. OF SAVING FAITH,		97
XV. OF REPENTANCE UNTO LIFE,		100
XVI. OF GOOD WORKS,		104
XVII. OF THE PERSEVERANCE OF THE SAINTS,		110
XVIII. OF ASSURANCE OF GRACE AND SALVATION,		113
XIX. OF THE LAW OF GOD,		116
XX. OF CHRISTIAN LIBERTY AND LIBERTY OF CONSCIENCE,		122
XXI OF RELIGIOUS WORSHIP AND THE SABBATH DAY,		126
XXII. OF LAWFUL OATHS AND VOWS,		131
XXIII OF THE CIVIL MAGISTRATE,		135
XXIV. OF MARRIAGE AND DIVORCE,		138
XXV. OF THE CHURCH,		142
XXVI. OF COMMUNION OF SAINTS,		145
XXVII. OF THE SACRAMENTS,		147
XXVIII. OF BAPTISM,		150
XXIX. OF THE LORD'S SUPPER,		153
XXX. OF CHURCH CENSURES,		158
XXXI. OF SYNODS AND COUNCILS,		161
XXXII. OF THE STATE OF MEN AFTER DEATH, AND OF THE RESURRECTION OF THE DEAD,		165
XXXIII. OF THE LAST JUDGMENT,		166
INDEX,		169

PREFACE TO THE SECOND EDITION.

———◆———

IN sending forth a new edition of this Handbook, I have little to
say by way of preface. The announcement from the Publishers
that the first issue was nearly exhausted came upon me unexpectedly,
and I have not been able to give anything like a thorough revision
to the book Many friends have favoured me during the past yea·
with communications regarding my work, from which, had more time
been allowed, I might have profited more largely. I cannot forbear
expressing my special indebtedness to Principal Douglas,—my only
surviving divinity Professor,—who kindly called attention to certain
imperfections in my notes, some of which I have endeavoured to
correct in this new edition. The sale of a large issue within twelve
months is to me peculiarly encouraging, as it shows that this Handbook has been the means of awakening considerable interest in the
Westminster Confession, and giving a new impetus to its systematic
study

JOHN MACPHERSON.

FINDHORN, FORRES, 18th March 1882.

THE CONFESSION OF FAITH.

————◆————

INTRODUCTION.

CHAPTER I.

THE PLACE AND PURPOSE OF CONFESSIONS OF FAITH.

1. Confessions of Faith—Subordinate Standards.—The Confession of
Faith adopted by any church may be in certain respects compared
to a set of rules accepted by an ordinary association as a term of
membership. If these rules have been carefully and wisely drawn
up, they will make prominent those principles which are specially
to characterize the society ; and reluctance on the part of any one
to observe the fundamental articles of association would imply un-
willingness to join or to remain in its membership. Society rules,
however, may be purely arbitrary. Even if some reason may have
determined their original adoption, this reason may be unknown to
persons accepting them. It may not be a term of membership that
each one who adopts the rules of the association must have acquainted
himself with the grounds on which they rest, or the circumstances
under which they were originally framed. To the members of such
associations, the set of rules which they have adopted is their
supreme standard of reference, and they have nothing to do with
the source from which he who originally drafted them may have
drawn. A Confession of Faith, however, is accepted by members
of churches acknowledging it, simply as a subordinate standard.
This designation in no way modifies its authority or relaxes the
obligation of those who join the communion of the church by
which it is received. The subordination intended is that of derivation. The members of the church receive the Confession as a
statement of the truth contained in Scripture, and not as a document in itself authoritative apart from its scriptural ground. In
entering into the communion of a church holding by any particular
Confession, we not only agree to maintain the doctrinal positions
therein contained, as the members of an association promise to
observe the adopted rules, but we further make the affirmation that
we hold the statement of doctrine in that Confession to be in

A

accordance with the truth of Holy Scripture. To appeal from the Confession to Scripture on doctrinal points in the way of repudiating the confessional statement in favour of the scriptural, involves the abandonment of that communion of which the Confession is the bond. If any particular doctrine has been carefully formulated in the Confession, our adoption of that Confession is an expression of our belief that the doctrine thus formulated is the very truth revealed in Scripture. We must not therefore suppose that by calling our Confession of Faith a subordinate standard, we give ourselves liberty to set its exposition of doctrine aside in favour of any other interpretation of Scripture passages bearing on that doctrine. If ·ve feel compelled to do so, we repudiate the Confession as a standard altogether. While careful to avoid the Romish notion of the indefiniteness of Scripture, which led to the introduction of an infallible interpreter, we must guard against the abandonment of those definite views of Scripture truth to which the church has attained by painful discussion and sustained investigation. The demand for a return to Scripture is virtually a plea for individualism, and is inconsistent with Church organization. This has been a favourite resort of those who wished to introduce novelties of belief without sacrifice of position. The Remonstrants at the Synod of Dort, in the endeavour to render plausible their Arminian doctrine, were wont to disparage the authority of Covenants and Confessions under pretence of accepting Scripture only as their rule. To a similar pretext of the Erastian Coleman, we find George Gillespie making a very pointed rejoinder in his controversial tract *Male Audis.* 'It is in vain for them,' says he, 'to palliate or shelter their covenant-breaking with appealing from the Covenant to the Scripture, for *subordinata non pugnant.* The Covenant is *norma recta,*— a right rule, though the Scripture alone be *norma recti,*—the rule of right. If they hold the Covenant to be unlawful, or to have anything in it contrary to the Word of God, let them speak out.' We do acknowledge only one authoritative rule of faith—the Holy Scriptures. No church Confession is ever set forth as co-ordinate with Scripture in authority. The Confession simply expresses our view of the teaching of Scripture on important doctrines, and the acceptance of this basis of a common faith becomes a convenient bond of union, a fitting term of communion for those thus doctrinally agreed. In an Act of Parliament there is commonly a clause inserted for the purpose of interpreting the terms employed throughout. In the administration of that law, the meaning authoritatively given to terms occurring therein must be accepted. It will not avail to say that these terms may possibly convey certain other impressions. Now the Confession is an interpretative clause, which the particular church accepting it appends to the Scripture. We find in Scripture, for example, such terms as these,—counsel of God, sin, the wages of sin, justification, faith, etc. Various interpretations have been given of those terms, and they have been employed in the setting forth of doctrinal views diametrically opposed to one another. All claim the Bible as favouring their particular doctrinal opinions. The Confession authoritatively interprets such terms for our church, and definitely states what form of doctrine, in the use of these terms, may be maintained in the church.

2. What the Adoption of a Confession implies.—It is important to determine as nearly as possible what the acceptance of a Confession of Faith ought to be regarded as implying. All the great and influential church creeds have been produced in peculiar crises of the church's history, and each necessarily reflects to some extent the local colouring and the accidental circumstances of its origin. Without in the least impairing the integrity of the document, we may distinguish between that in it which is merely local and occasional, and that which is essential and characteristic. This is the distinction commonly made between the substance and the details of doctrinal formularies. The American formula of subscription explicitly limits the adoption of the authorized standards to an acceptance of the system of doctrine. It must be admitted that such a phrase is capable of being used in a very vague and uncertain way. It is also very evident that any such general distinction as that between the spirit and the letter, the substance and the particular details, is liable to great abuse, and has been often sadly misapplied. Yet that a difference must be made between divergencies from certain accidental modes of expression and view, and divergencies from points of doctrine fundamental to the general course of doctrine represented in the symbol, must be clear to every candid mind. This distinction between type and formula has been well expressed by Martensen; and what he says of Lutheran standards may, of course, be with equal truth applied to our own Calvinistic standards: ' By the *type* of Lutheranism we mean its ground form, its inextinguishable, fundamental, and distinctive features. As we recognise in a man or in a people an inward peculiarity, an impress, which belongs to them from eternity, never appearing in perfect clearness in time, and yet recognisable even amidst temporal imperfections; so we can detect in the Christian Confessions a church individuality, a fundamental abiding form, which, amidst change and growth, is constantly reproducing itself; whereas the theological *formulæ* in which this form is expressed are more or less characterised by relativity and transitoriness' (*Chr. Dogmatics*, p. 55). When this distinction is honestly made, room will be found under the same Confession for independent thinkers, who, while holding by the same general type of doctrine, have their own way of explaining the several points of the common faith. On a careful examination of the Westminster Confession, it is found that certain doctrines are therein maintained, no one of which may be denied without involving the overthrow, or at least a breach in the integrity, of the general system which they together constitute. Dr. Hodge has enumerated eighteen distinctive doctrinal statements from the Confession, in regard to each one of which the Confession maintains a specific form of doctrine which every one accepting the formulary is bound loyally to support.[1]

In the previous section we noticed how latitudinarians in doctrine, disliking the exactness of confessional utterances, make an illegitimate appeal from the Confession to Scripture, thinking to find apparent support for their views in a partial presentation of scriptural expressions. To maintain the view, however, just indicated in regard to the interpretation of a subscribed creed is, when rightly understood, not only not latitudinarian, but genuinely conservative. It is the conservation of the essential principles embalmed in the Confession. This implies the genuine spiritual appreciation of those principles, the hearty adoption of those doctrines as our own deepest spiritual convictions. Dr. Cunningham has clearly expressed this position of true liberalism, which distinguishes the fundamental from the occasional, that which belongs to the explanation or presentation of a doctrine from the doctrine itself. Towards the close of his essay on Calvin and Beza, in which he had been showing at length the theological developments of the latter divine, Dr. Cunningham maintains that, while he considers those additional determinations of Beza to be strictly in accordance with Scripture truth, and fair logical deductions from the principles laid down by Calvin, it would nevertheless be inexpedient that those precise and definite expressions should find a place in symbolical books, or be made a term of communion. The individual Christian is required to make diligent search in order to acquire all truth attainable in regard to details as well as to general principles; but the Church must only formulate those statements of truth to which the many individuals belonging to her community may yield assent, and in regard to which unity of belief may be expected and claimed. One who goes with Calvin might refuse to go with Beza. No formulary should occasion divisions of such a kind. 'Calvin probably would have made a difficulty about adopting precise and definite deliverances on some points, concerning the truth of which the great Calvinistic divines of the seventeenth century had no hesitation. But it will probably be admitted that he was qualified for the office of a minister in a Calvinistic church, even in this advanced nineteenth century.' (*Reformers and Theology of the Reformation*, p. 412.)

8. **A Confession should be, not vague, but definite.**—It has been necessary to show that theological refinements and explanatory theories should have no place in a church formulary, and that, so far as these do appear in such a document, a certain freedom may be exercised regarding them, which may not be extended to statements affecting the very substance and characteristic type of the

---

[1] 'What is meant by adopting the Westminster Confession?'—an article by Dr. Hodge in *Princeton Review* for 1867, reprinted as an Appendix to Dr. A. A. Hodge's *Commentary on the Confession of Faith*.

Confession. We must, however, guard against the notion that the interests of freedom are to be advanced by rendering the formulary short and vague in expression. It is quite a fallacy to suppose that greater liberty is enjoyed under a brief statement of beliefs than under a detailed enumeration of doctrines. When care is taken in admitting doctrinal statements only on leading and fundamental points, definiteness and fulness in a symbolical book will prove a high recommendation. What hampers is not the definiteness with which characteristic and essential doctrines are stated, but the unwise selection of materials to which this definite expression is given. Thus, for example, in regard to the Westminster Confession, containing, according to Dr. Hodge, express and definite statements in reference to eighteen characteristic doctrines of Calvinism, as the symbol of a Calvinistic Church, it is desirable that the position to be maintained on each of these points be clearly laid down. If vaguely expressed, one, interpreting some of these positions in a special way, might find himself in a communion, the members of which, interpreting those truths otherwise, were out of sympathy with him, and he might find his expressions of belief subjected to an interpretation of which he had not himself conceived. Now it is just to avoid such uncertainties that church Confessions are framed. The supreme standard of the Scripture is appealed to by all Christians, but by our own particular church creed it is authoritatively declared in what sense the doctrinal statements of Scripture are understood. If the expression given to such interpretation be vague, its right of existence cannot be vindicated. Granted, then, that into our Confession no doctrinal positions are put to which Confessional authority should not be given, it is impossible to state those positions with too great definiteness and precision.

The prime difficulty in compiling a Confession, and in vindicating one already compiled, lies in answering the question, What precisely are the doctrines that ought to be formulated? By some it has been thought that the number of these should be reduced to a minimum. Repeatedly the so-called Apostles' Creed has been proposed as most fit for a general church symbol. During the second quarter of the present century there was a remarkable movement conducted within the Danish Church, by Grundtvig, a vigorous and popular theologian, who insisted upon the adoption of this ancient and simple doctrinal formulary. He did so on very peculiar grounds. As the church owes its origin to Christ, and its continuance to His promise that the gates of hell shall not prevail against it, even so, he argues, must it have for all times one faith and one baptism, as well as one Lord. The authoritative expression of this one faith exists in the baptismal formula as slightly expanded in the Apostles' Creed. This Creed, on the basis of the baptismal formula, he supposes to have been dictated word for word by the risen Saviour to the apostles during the forty days. Grundtvig maintains that church power can be continued only while this bond between the living Saviour and the church endures ;—a peculiar fancy somewhat parallel to that of Apostolical Succession. This is utterly unhistorical, and evidently the simple formulary in question cannot be received as a divinely prepared and sanctioned creed. It must be judged of according to its doctrinal sufficiency and comprehensiveness. On examination, however, we find in it no doctrine of Holy Scripture, of divine decrees, or of divine Providence ; no statement of the doctrines of grace. It is simply a *resumé* of leading historical truths. The incarnation and suffering of Christ are related, but there is no reference whatever to the purpose for which He lived and died. The existence of the church is acknowledged, but there is no doctrine of the sacraments. Belief in the forgiveness of sins is expressed, but it is not said that this is in any way connected with the redemption wrought by Christ. The resurrection and everlasting life are confessed, but how the resurrection of the just is to be attained unto, we are not told. These characteristic doctrines of Christian faith were not among the special attainments of the post-apostolical age. Upon the whole, the Westminster divines assigned to this document its right place. At the end of the Shorter Catechism they printed the Ten Commandments, the Lord's Prayer, and the Creed. They appended the following explanatory note :—' Albeit the substance of that abridgment, commonly called the Apostles' Creed, be fully set forth in each of the Catechisms, so as there is no necessity of inserting the Creed itself ; yet it is here annexed, not as though it were composed by the Apostles, or ought to be esteemed canonical Scripture, as the Ten Commandments and the Lord's Prayer, but because it is a brief sum of the Christian faith, agreeable to the Word of God, and anciently received in the churches of Christ.' This is all that can be said of it. Certainly there is no heresy in it ; but of the heresies that have actually appeared throughout the history of the church, there are few which those adopting the Apostles' Creed as their symbol might not maintain. As a term of communion, acceptance of so general a formulary has no meaning. It would be just as well to say, ' I believe the doctrines of Scripture, interpreting these in my own fashion,' as to say, ' I subscribe to such a general statement of doctrine as is given in the Apostles' Creed.'

A question now arises as to the advantage or disadvantage afforded by such a summary presentation of doctrine as respects the liberty of the individual church member. Professor Macgregor has clearly shown, in an able and useful article on ' Revision of the Westminster Confession,' that a short creed may prove to the individual an instrument of great tyranny (see *British and Foreign Evang. Review* for 1877, pp 692-713). If such a short Confession as the Apostles' Creed, of which we have spoken, be adopted, whenever any member proclaims heretical views regarding those vital doctrines not formulated, he must be tried and convicted by means of laws laid down there and then. Entering a communion in which such a general formulary is received, one comes under, not only the Confession, but the unwritten understanding of the church in regard to all other doctrinal questions which have never been formally set before him. When one is asked to sign a document, a petition, a cautionary obligation, or the like, he requires that the statements in it be clear and express. He knows then what his obligation amounts to. Even so in regard to a church symbol. That which is expressly set down in it as an essential and necessary part of it,—to that should every one accepting it feel himself bound. As for matters unexpressed therein, he must not be held to these, notwithstanding the notion of some in the church that they are the proper and becoming complement of the doctrines expressed. Doctrines unexpressed may have more or less consideration shown them according as they receive the general consensus of belief in the church. When any such doctrine has actually gained universal acceptance in a church, it may be added to the church creed as a new theological attainment. Until thus formulated, however, it cannot be used as a legislative or disciplinary instrument. When, therefore, a church presents to one entering her communion a detailed exposition of her accepted doctrines, he may understand that so long as his convictions accord with those formulated beliefs, his freedom on other doctrinal points will not be interfered with ; whereas in the case of a church with a vague and too summary creed, a member never knows what point in his belief may one day be ruled unsound.

CHAPTER II.

THE EARLIER CONFESSIONS OF THE SCOTTISH CHURCH.

1. The Confession of Knox. — The earliest Confession of Faith adopted by the Scottish Reformed Church was that commonly called Knox's Confession. The five ministers who were appointed to draw up the Books of Discipline were apparently engaged upon the Confession, but it undoubtedly bears the special impress of the genius and individuality of Knox. It was presented to Parliament assembled at Edinburgh, on the 17th July 1560, read aloud article by article twice over, and adopted by the Three Estates of the realm as the authoritative doctrinal formulary of the Reformed Church of Scotland. It consists of twenty-five chapters. The arrangement of topics seems to have been mainly determined by an endeavour after simplicity of statement; yet there is also observable a certain system of historical sequence. It may be divided into two general portions. The first division embraces eleven chapters, and in the arrangement of these a purely historical development is observed :—(1) Of God ; (2) Of the Creation of Man ; (3) Of Original Sin (which treats of Adam's fall, hereditary guilt, and regeneration by the Spirit of Christ) ; (4) The Revelation of the Promises ; (5) The Continuance of the Church. (6) Incarnation of Jesus Christ ; (7) The Mediator,—very God and

very man ; (8) Election (our election in Christ, His brotherhood with
man, what the manhood and the Godhead in the Saviour, severally
and combined, effect); (9) Christ's Death, Passion, and Burial;
(10) Resurrection ; (11) Ascension. The second division embraces
fourteen chapters, and may be described as in its arrangement mainly
doctrinal rather than historical. Here the opposition to Romanism
is specially apparent :—(12) Faith in the Holy Ghost ; (13) The Cause
of Good Works ; (14) What Works are reputed good before God ;
(15) The Perfection of the Law and Imperfection of Man ; (16) Of
the Church; (17) On the Immortality of the Soul (evidently suggested
by what was said of the Church triumphant); (18) Notes of the
True Church (owing to the circumstances of the nation and age,
this subject is treated with great care and unusual minuteness);
(19) Authority of Scripture ; (20) General Councils ; (21–23) Of the
Sacraments (their administration, and admission to partake of them) ;
(24) Of the Civil Magistrate; (25) Of Gifts freely given to the Church.

From the titles of the chapters it will be seen that there is less
appearance of any attempt to secure an outward or formal unity in
the formulary as a whole than is evident in the preparation of subsequent Confessions. This circumstance has been insisted upon of
late in a most superficial manner. Some of those who are never
weary of reiterating the popular objections to the exactness of doctrinal definition which characterizes the Westminster Confession, are
pleased to refer approvingly to this old Scottish Confession in a way
which suggests their acquaintance with its chapter headings rather
than with its contents. Considering the auditory which Knox had
to address, consisting indeed of the highest nobles of the land, but
most of them rude and untutored, though proud and dignified
enough, and considering that the whole document had to be received
after a hearing merely, and not after careful and minute study, we
may easily understand how indispensable it was, not only that the
leading doctrines should be very simply stated, but also that, as far
as possible, each article might be viewed by itself as a separate proposition. If this need for the detachment of the articles be taken
into account, it may satisfactorily explain why special chapters are
not assigned to such theological commonplaces as are found in
almost all other Protestant symbols. Thus, for example, we have no
separate chapter on Justification, — *articulus stantis vel cadentis
ecclesiæ,*—and indeed we observe a characteristic avoidance of all
abstract theological terms. Had Justification been treated of in a
special section, it must have been closely articulated with doctrinal
statements going before, and so expressed as to be subsumed in the
treatment of doctrines following. The peculiar character, therefore,
of the age in which this Confession was prepared, and specially the
circumstances in which it was to be presented, rendered the method
adopted in its composition a necessity.

Yet if we pass from the mere chapter headings and the arrangement of sections to the contents of this old Scottish Confession, we

shall find that we have here the same type of doctrine fundamentally as that set forth in later and more detailed Reformed symbols. The peculiar form of Protestant doctrine originally introduced into Scotland was undoubtedly Lutheran, but the earlier Lutheranism is not to be distinguished from the strictest Calvinism. Indeed, it is interesting to notice that the three earliest influential teachers of the Reformed religion in Scotland, Patrick Hamilton, George Wishart, and John Knox, had respectively come under the influence of the three great continental teachers, Luther, Zwingli, and Calvin. The relation of Knox to Calvin, however, is not that simply of an admirer and follower, but rather that of a fellow-labourer in the same general line. The type of doctrine developed by Calvin and Knox was Augustinian, and it is well known that Knox was a diligent and admiring student of the great Latin Father. The thorough agreement of Knox with Calvin on fundamental doctrinal questions may be seen from his chief theological treatise—*Of God's Predestination.* That the Scottish Confession was regarded by those who adopted it as in harmony with the most pronounced formularies of the Reformed Church, is beyond all reasonable dispute. Attention has been called by Professor Mitchell to this important fact recorded by Knox himself, that Erskine of Dun, a well-known superintendent of that time, along with other superintendents and ministers, in 1566 acknowledged the later Swiss Confession, as fairly representing the doctrine, which for three years previously, under their own Confession, they had taught. This clearly shows how the Scottish Confession was understood, and how its doctrinal position was interpreted by some of the most intelligent of its original subscribers. To appreciate the importance of the parallel between the Scottish and the later Swiss Confession, it is necessary to state a few particulars concerning the latter formulary.

The *Confessio Helvetica Secunda* drawn up by Bullinger in 1562 is generally regarded as one of the most exact and detailed of all the Reformed Confessions. It has a peculiar interest, too, as originating not in any attempt to meet an ecclesiastical emergency, but as a calm and deliberate endeavour to satisfy the writer's own spiritual needs, and to give expression to his personal convictions of doctrinal truth. For four years it had lain aside in its author's desk, till circumstances of Church and State called it forth. Though not prepared in view of those circumstances, it was found admirably to suit the occasion. The Reformed type of doctrine represented in this formulary is in every respect at least as elaborate and advanced as that of the Westminster Confession, and, as we have seen, the most intelligent of the Scottish divines accepted it not as an advance upon their own Scottish Confession, but as setting forth the very same doctrine. They felt that those who honestly and intelligently accepted the one could not reasonably decline to receive the other. We may well regard the Swiss Confession as the doctrinal equivalent of both the Scottish Confession and the Westminster Confession. He who does not scruple to receive the doctrinal contents of Knox's Confession need have no scruples in adopting the doctrinal standards prepared by the Westminster divines.

2. The Aberdeen Confession.—The Confession of which we have spoken, continued to be recognised in the Church of Scotland, and there was no attempt to replace it by any other till 1616, when the Assembly met in Aberdeen, and drew up a series of articles, which were offered to the Presbyterian party as a compromise by those who had a leaning toward Prelacy. Speaking of this Assembly, Hetherington says : ' It is chiefly remarkable on account of a new Confession of Faith drawn up by the prelatic party, sufficiently orthodox in its doctrines, but meagre and evasive in respect of church government and discipline, for a very evident reason.' *(History of Church of Scotland,* p. 219.) This statement is not to be unreservedly accepted. The meagre character of its positions in reference to church government is evident enough, but besides this, a careful examination of its doctrinal utterances will show that, under an apparent reverence for the most strictly-expressed ortho-doxy, room is left for at least a variety of belief on questions of vital importance to the maintenance of a true and healthy Protestantism. It was evidently so understood by the Prelatists and those with Romish tendencies, who unhesitatingly subscribed the new Articles. The time chosen for drawing up such a Confession was most oppor-tune. The most capable and zealous of the Presbyterian party felt that Knox's Confession must now give place to a more exact and detailed representation of their characteristic beliefs. The Pre-latists, however, by a trimming policy sought to appear agreed with the Presbyterians on doctrinal points, without too far committing themselves. Thus, for example, the Aberdeen Confession gives forth vague and inconclusive statements regarding justification, which, while apparently laying down the Lutheran doctrine, by no means exclude the Romish view that confounds justification and sanctifica-tion. It was an attempt to deceive true Presbyterians in regard both to doctrine and to discipline. The projected *Formula Concordiæ* was unsuccessful, because it was hollow and untrue. The Aberdeen Confession exercised no real influence over the Church ; but the leading theologians of that time had their hearts still set upon the production of a Confession sufficiently minute and detailed to meet the requirements of the Church. Already the thought of having such a Confession prepared seems to have occupied the mind of Henderson, and as the most influential divine in the Scottish Church, he availed himself of every opportunity to keep the idea prominently before the Church Courts. In the Assembly of 1639, Henderson secured the appointment of a committee to prepare a full Confession of Faith. The unsettled state of affairs probably prevented much progress being made. In 1641, however, Hender-son was allowed to retire from pastoral work in order to give his whole attention to the framing of such a Confession. When in 1643 called, with like-minded brethren, to join the Westminster Assembly, undoubtedly these preliminary studies would be found most helpful.

CHAPTER III.

THE WESTMINSTER CONFESSION.

1. The Westminster Assembly—Its Appointment and its Purpose.— During the twenty years that preceded the meeting of the Westminster Assembly, Laud had been systematically and energetically labouring to enforce uniformity in the observance of certain outward ceremonies. Against the violence and persistency of this rule, not only pronounced Puritans, but generally even those other earnest and spiritually-minded men who were well content to maintain a moderate Episcopacy, entered, as opportunity allowed, a vigorous and decided protest. The Reforming party, to the members of which the name of Puritan was indiscriminately given, sought to secure, as far as possible, uniformity in the expression of their doctrinal beliefs; and only in subordination to this did they aspire after uniformity in discipline. While the High Church section, under the leadership of Laud, had directed its efforts to the attainment of external harmony, and from the enforcement of ceremonies proceeded to the uprooting of all doctrinal peculiarities that might discord with these, the Evangelical section within and without the Episcopal Church showed an interest primarily in doctrine, and took to do with questions of order and ceremonial only in so far as these were supposed to affect favourably or unfavourably the purity of doctrinal belief. 'In all the complex varieties of Puritanism, the heart of man is addressed through the intellect. Laud addressed it through the eye. External order and discipline, the authority of existing law and existing governors, were the tests to which he appealed.' (Gardiner, *Puritan Revolution*, p. 75.) The ceremonies contended for by the Prelatists were regarded by the more thoroughgoing and self-consistent of the Puritans as essentially popish. Their rejection was therefore sought on doctrinal grounds. Against their continuance George Gillespie argued most ably in his earliest published treatise, entitled *A Dispute against the English Popish Ceremonies* (1637). By some of those who urged their adoption, it was maintained that they were necessary; others were satisfied with maintaining their expediency; others ventured to say no more than that they were lawful. Gillespie shows elaborately that they are not necessary, nor yet expedient, nor even lawful. The most moderate of all the advocates of a modified Episcopacy argued that these ceremonies might be ranked among things indifferent, and therefore such ceremonial observances might be agreed to for the sake of uniformity. Of course, one who regarded the observance of these ceremonies as essentially unlawful, and calculated to influence the intellect for error through the senses, could not admit their indifferency.

The endeavour was now to be made to secure doctrinal uniformity among the several Protestant Churches of Britain and Ireland. This was the main object for which the Westminster Assembly was called. In addition to this, it was hoped that the result of the labours of its members would be to bring them into closer relations with the Reformed Churches on the Continent. The time for such a Convention, too, was most happily chosen, when, to use the words of Professor Mitchell, 'Conformist and Nonconformist were not yet formally separated, when men, trained in the study of the Fathers, yet familiar with the tendencies and principles of the Reformation, were not so rare as they now are, when the Church was still under the influence of a marvellous revival.' (*Minutes of Assembly*, Introd. lxxv.) Under the Commonwealth—when the sectaries, Nonconformists of the most extreme type, gained an overweening ascendency, and every one was forced to take a determined stand with one or other of the two parties in the State—such an assembly would have been impossible.

The arrangements connected with the calling of the Assembly bring us into full view of the unhappy relations in which King and Parliament then stood to one another. The Parliament, at a sitting held on the 12th day of June 1643, published an ordinance in which the 1st of July of that year was fixed for the meeting of 'an Assembly of learned and godly divines and others, to be consulted with the Parliament for the settling of the government and liturgy of the Church of England, and for vindicating and clearing of the doctrine of the said Church from false aspersions and interpretations.' As Hetherington shows, this Assembly was of necessity called by Parliament, for Prelacy had been already abolished, and no other constituted church system had yet taken its place. Some ten days after the issuing of the Parliamentary ordinance, the king, acting on what he regarded as his royal prerogative, issued a proclamation forbidding those to meet who had thus been summoned by the Parliament. When the 1st of July arrived, the Puritan section of those invited obeyed the summons, and met in Henry the Seventh's Chapel at Westminster. On the roll as originally fixed by Parliament there were 151 members, comprising 121 clergymen and 30 lay assessors. The first meeting for the special business of the Assembly was held on Thursday the 6th July. A considerable time was spent in revising the Thirty-nine Articles, as they had been ordered by Parliament to do. 'But being limited,' the revisers explain in their preface to these Articles, 'by the same orders, only to the clearing and vindicating of them, though we found ourselves necessitated for this end to make some, yet we made fewer alterations in them, and additions to them, than otherwise we should have thought fit to have done, if the whole matter had been left to us without such limitation, conceiving many things yet remaining to be defective. and other expressions also fit to be changed. And herein we proceeded only to the finishing of fifteen Articles, because it pleased both Houses, by an order bearing date October 12, 1643, to require us to lay aside the remainder, and enter upon the work of Church Government. And afterwards, by another order, to employ us in framing a Confession of Faith for the three kingdoms, according to our Solemn League and Covenant; in which Confession we have not left out anything, that was in the former Articles material, necessary to be retained.' Though these Articles were found unsuitable for an immediate basis of a national Confession, this work spent upon them undoubtedly helped to prepare the minds of members for their subsequent labours. At an early sitting it was agreed to ask the co-operation of representatives from the Scottish Presbyterian Assembly, in order that the design of their own meeting—to procure nearer agreement with the Church of Scotland—might be accomplished. On August 7, Commissioners appeared before the General Assembly of the Scottish Church met at Edinburgh, requesting aid in the work on which they were engaged. As a bond of union around which both Scotch and English Reformers might gather, the Solemn League and Covenant was drawn up. In the composition of this document, Alexander Henderson, who was Moderator of the Assembly, had a principal share. This was at once a league formed for the establishment and defence of civil liberty, and a covenant entered into for the maintenance of doctrinal purity and religious truth. The Solemn League and Covenant was adopted on the 17th August by the General Assembly, and ratified that same day by the Convention of the Estates of the realm. On the 15th September the Commissioners appointed took their places in the Westminster Assembly. These were—Robert Baillie, George Gillespie, Alexander Henderson, and Samuel Rutherford, ministers; Lord Maitland and Johnston of Warriston, elders. The Covenant was taken by all the members of the Assembly and of Parliament on September 25, and soon afterward subscription was required of all people both in England and in Scotland. Its terms are not violent and fanatical, as some seem to imagine. It consists of six articles, requiring every subscriber to endeavour to secure conformity in doctrine and discipline, to extirpate Popery, Prelacy, and everything opposed to sound doctrine, to preserve Parliamentary rights and the royal authority, to discover and bring to punishment all malignants causing faction between the king and the people, to maintain peace and preserve union between the two kingdoms, and to support one another in prosecuting the ends contemplated in the forming of that League and Covenant. The substance of it was summed up in the resolution to endeavour the reformation of religion according to the Word of God, and the example of the best Reformed Churches. A nobler end could not be sought than that which those divines had in view, when they accepted this Covenant as a common basis of operations, and in its phrases gave expression to those aspirations which they hoped to realize.

2. The Westminster Assembly—Its Composition.—Among the theologians who met together as members of this Assembly were men of great learning, and not a few of singular breadth and liberality of mind. Of those most celebrated for their learning may be named the Prolocutor or President, Dr. Twisse, distinguished very highly as a philosophic and systematic theologian; Drs. Lightfoot and Coleman, celebrated as Orientalists; Dr. Gataker, still remembered for his successful demonstration of the difference between New Testament and classical Greek; and such generally eminent divines as Gouge, Goodwin, Tuckney, and Burroughs. Among those whose praise is still in all the churches for their genial liberalism and catholicity of spirit, it may be enough to mention Reynolds, Calamy, and Arrowsmith. Without any exaggeration, it may be said that in no previous or subsequent Assembly has there been present such a galaxy of talent as in the Assembly of Westminster. Of the Scotch members, Henderson, Gillespie, and Rutherford were all singularly able and scholarly men, and all of them contributed largely to the debates and to the practical efficiency of the Assembly. The English members seem to have been originally chosen by the Parliamentary representatives according to a certain local distribution, so that two members were elected to represent each county. An honest endeavour was made to render the composition of the Assembly truly representative of all the varying shades of Protestant opinion. Royalist divines were chosen as well as Puritan; but when the king forbade their meeting, they preferred to obey the king rather than the Parliament. That the Prelatic party was not represented in the Westminster Assembly cannot, therefore, be fairly attributed to the partiality of Parliament, or to any sinister design carried through by the more powerful Puritans. As actually constituted, we find this Assembly singularly well chosen, and representative of varying opinions in a remarkable degree. The members certainly were not men who had stood neutral in the national and ecclesiastical struggles. The leading members had all been prominent in these controversies. But they were fair men, not fanatical; amenable to reason and open to conviction, though deeply exercised and already well established in the truth. Among the calmest and most judicial minds in that venerable Assembly, the Scotch members deserve a conspicuous and honourable place. They had very definite opinions of their own on points of doctrine as well as on points of discipline, yet we find them wisely using their influence to moderate disputes and heal differences, willing to secure agreement on points of importance by making ready accommodation on points of detail. For example, in debating about the decree of God, it appeared that some held that there were two decrees, one to life and the other to destruction, while others held that there was but one eternal decree. This seems really a difference only in terminology. Rutherford held that probably there was only one decree, but thought it not fit to enter this opinion in the Confession. Gillespie followed on the same side. The Scotch divines thus took a position alongside of Calamy and Reynolds, the most liberal and conciliatory of all the members of Assembly. Among these divines there were certainly men who had pet theories of their own on various heads of doctrine, but they did not obtrude their private views or seek for them symbolic recognition. Thus, for example, Dr. Twisse was the most celebrated defender of Supralapsarianism, and had written in its support a folio volume of 800 pages; yet no effort seems to have been made to secure for its expression a place in the Westminster formulary. Rutherford and Gillespie had asserted in their works the divine right of Presbytery, but they did not insist that their theory should have expression given to it in the Confession. In glancing over the list of English members, we do certainly miss some very eminent names, both on the Episcopal and on the Puritan side. Bishop Hall, Archbishop Usher, and such like, would certainly have been welcomed as most important aid by the divines; but though orthodox in doctrine, they were rendered ineligible by their persistent adherence to the cause of the king. Owen was yet a young man and comparatively unknown. Such a one as Baxter would be very likely, in depreciation of himself, to prevent his name from being put into the list. In his *Life and Times*, Baxter gives the following admirable account of the character and worth of this Assembly: 'The divines there congregate were men of eminent learning and godliness, and ministerial abilities and fidelity; and being not worthy to be one of them myself, I may the more freely speak that truth which I know, even in the face of malice and envy, that, as far as I am able to judge by the information of all history of that kind, and by any other evidences left us, the Christian world, since the days of the Apostles, had never a Synod of more excellent divines (taking one thing with another) than this Synod and the Synod of Dort were.'

8. The Westminster Assembly—Its Controversies.—During the first two years of its sittings the Assembly was mainly occupied with discussions regarding church polity and government. The great majority of the members of Assembly entertained strong convictions in favour of the Presbyterian form of church government, as both scriptural and peculiarly suited to the circumstances of the age and nation. The views of the Presbyterians, however, met with opposition from two parties in the Assembly. The Erastians, on the one hand, objected to the co-ordination of the ecclesiastical with the civil power. The Independents, on the other hand, objected to the institution of classical Assemblies or Presbyteries as courts of review, maintaining that each separate congregation was completely independent and under the control of no superior judicatory.

(1.) **The Erastian Controversy.**—In order to estimate aright the importance of the Erastian controversy carried on in the Assembly, we must not limit our view to the contention of the few Erastians among its members. The only thoroughgoing Erastian among the clerical members was Coleman, though Dr. Lightfoot supported these views to a certain extent. Of the lay assessors the only one who argued in the Assembly on behalf of these opinions was the learned Selden. We must remember, however, that these single champions of the supremacy of the civil power were backed up by the almost unanimous sympathies of the members of Parliament. The Liberal party, as liberalism was then understood, was in power; but while sincerely desirous to secure a general reformation in the doctrine and discipline of the church, the leaders in reform could not fail to remember what they had suffered from the tyranny of ecclesiastical courts and officers. They were therefore extremely jealous of clerical interference, and determined to resist every demand that savoured of clerical pretension. Selden had shown himself an earnest defender of the rights of Parliament in opposition to royal encroachments, and was now equally determined in opposing what he considered the illegitimate claims of the clergy. In his treatise *On Tithes* he had denied that these were levied, as the Bishops maintained, by any divine right, but only because imposed by the law of the State. Anti-royalist therefore as he was, Selden was also keenly anti-clerical. Erastianism may, of course, be maintained even by a republican in as pronounced a form as by an extreme supporter of the divine right of kings. Selden drew his argument for the sub ordination of the church under the state from the circumstances of the Jewish Commonwealth. His oriental studies had been wondrously extensive; but to a modern eye, his critical powers seem somewhat jejune, and his learning cumbrous and undigested. Dr. John Light-foot (1602–1675) is still remembered as having made solid contribu-tions to the advancement of Hebrew studies, and amid much that is purely fanciful, and even utterly absurd, his quaint illustrations of the New Testament from rabbinical sources furnish many valuable suggestions. Coleman, though now forgotten, had a great reputation in his own time, and was justly ranked with Selden and Lightfoot, as a most distinguished and erudite orientalist. His discussion was interrupted by illness, and when visited by members of Assembly, he expressed his wish to resume his argument on his return. He was never able to appear again in the Assembly, and died toward the end of March 1645. In their discussions in favour of the Erastian theory, all these scholars laid chief stress upon Jewish customs and traditions as illustrating the divine idea of government. One of the members of Assembly (Mr. Vines), replying to Lightfoot's arguments against the exercise of ecclesiastical power in excommunication, indicated the unsatisfactoriness of this mode of reasoning. 'I desire,' he says, 'he would not tell us how he finds in Jewish authors, but what he finds in the Word of God, whether judging finally (in regard to leprosy) and acting upon that judgment were not in the priests.' (*Minutes of Assembly*, p. 442.)

The defence of Erastianism by Coleman was not confined to his speeches in the Assembly. He gave great offence to his brethren by insisting upon Erastian principles in the most pronounced way in his sermon preached before the House of Commons. A pamphlet war was carried on between George Gillespie and Coleman, which resulted in a most triumphant vindication of the doctrine of spiritual independence. In the Assembly itself a keen debate followed the delivery of Coleman's sermon, and was closed by the expression of a conviction that all the Erastian arguments had been thoroughly answered. Immediately after this debate in the Assembly, a Parliamentary ordinance concerning church government was issued (see *Minutes of Assembly* for March 20, 1645). Against this the members of Assembly took exception, both for what it contained and also for the assumption of power in issuing it. Consequently a petition, respectful but firm in tone, was addressed to Parliament. The Ordinance proposed to appoint commissioners to judge of scandals and administer discipline. This, the petitioners maintain, would be to give the power of discipline to those to whom it does not belong, and to this, conscience would not allow them to yield. Parliament resented the presentation of the petition, and voted it a breach of privilege. The House of Commons thought it necessary to vindicate itself against the Assembly, the City, and the Scotch, assuring them of its sincerity in maintaining the Covenant, and its desire to maintain the peace of the country, but at the same time declaring that to accede to the views of the Assembly would be to grant an arbitrary and unlimited power to ecclesiastical courts which rightly belonged to the jurisdiction of Parliament. Gillespie admirably answered this charge in his *Aaron's Rod Blossoming* (1646), where he shows that Presbyterian church government is the least arbitrary and most fitted for a limited monarchy of all forms of ecclesiastical rule (see Book ii. chap. 3). The Anti-Erastian views of the Assembly have been clearly expressed in the Confession in the special chapter on Church Censures (xxx.), and will be found more in detail in the Form of Presbyterial Church Government, usually bound up with the Confession.

(2.) **The Independent Controversy.**—Among the original members of the Assembly there were certain very staunch opponents of the Presbyterial form of church government, who argued most persistently on behalf of congregational independency. These were known as the five dissenting brethren. Though few in number, their singular abilities and well-sustained reputation for piety and general worth secured for them respectful consideration and an honourable position in the Assembly. Some of their names are not yet forgotten. —Thomas Goodwin, Jeremiah Burroughs, William Bridge, Philip Nye, and Sydrach Simpson. Goodwin is now highly esteemed by all lovers of Puritan theology as one of the very ablest theologians of that eminently theological age. Bridge is a practical writer whose treatises are peculiarly fragrant and savoury, and show admirable skill in speaking words of tenderness to the weary and downcast. Burroughs is still known for his *Commentary on Hosea*, and exhibits

B

all the tenderness of Bridge with much greater force and strength. Nye, though most prominent of them all in debate, is in himself the least attractive. His worldly craft and cunning, his incessant intrigues with political dissenters, acted more injuriously than any other influence in retarding, and in some particulars frustrating, the work of the Assembly. Several names were added later until the Independents in the Assembly numbered ten or twelve. The only name among those who seem to have taken any part in the debates is that of William Greenhill, known by his *Commentary on Ezekiel.* He was Burroughs' colleague at Stepney ; Burroughs being known as the morning star, Greenhill as the evening star. The characteristic point for which they contended in the matter of church government was that the congregation or congregational eldership is to be regarded as the highest authoritative ecclesiastical court ; that from this session there can be no appeal, Synods, composed of ministers and elders from different congregations, having only power of consultation and advice. So far as church government is concerned, there is in Independency no gradation of courts, there is indeed no plurality of courts. The Congregational Union is an association of ministers and elders, which, like any other association, may show its disapprobation of the conduct or views of any individual member by ejecting him from its membership. The Independent controversy arose over such questions as the right and power of excommunication as an act proper to the church courts (Erastians denying wholly the ecclesiastical character of the office, and the Independents limiting its exercise to the particular congregation immediately interested), and also in regard to Courts of review, Classical Assemblies or Presbyteries, Synods and Church Councils, the Independents urging their special views against such judicatories. Unfortunately lending themselves, as it would seem, to the crafty influence of Nye, these dissenting brethren were too apt to take advantage of every possible occasion to dispute the position of the majority of the House, and so greatly hindered the Assembly's work. On reading the *Minutes of the Assembly* one is painfully struck with the readiness shown by those brethren to enter their dissent even on the most trivial points. The forbearance and extreme courtesy exercised toward them by the Presbyterian majority cannot be too highly praised.

4. **Preparation of the Westminster Confession.**—Special care was taken in making preliminary arrangements for the great work of the Assembly. Some of the most moderate and learned members were chosen to form a committee for drawing up an outline of doctrinal matter for the projected Confession. As originally constituted this small committee was entirely composed of men whose names are still remembered with honour. Dr. Gouge, one of the most highly esteemed of all the London preachers ; Dr. Temple ; Dr. Hoyle, an able divine and accomplished professor of theology ; Gataker and Arrowsmith, both celebrated for their scholarship ; Burroughs.

Burgess, Vines, and Goodwin—such were the distinguished men who were required to prepare material and sketch an outline for the Confession. Appointed on 20th August 1644, this committee on 4th September made a report to the Assembly, and asked that their number should be increased. Among those added at this time, we find such well-known names as these. Reynolds, Herle, Tuckney. And finally, on the 12th May 1645, we find that a report had been made of the progress gained by the committee in tabulating the heads of doctrine, and probably also in arranging the subdivisions of the work. Then, for the actual framing of a first draft of the Confession, a small committee was formed, comprising several leading members of the former committee. To these were added the Scottish Commissioners. We have no means for determining precisely the method pursued by these divines in carrying on the important work with which they had been entrusted. Their previous labours, however, in revising the English Articles, must have proved of signal service. Their judgments were formed and their minds were enriched by the doctrinal debates then carried on; the records of their discussions would undoubtedly contain abundant dogmatic material; and the tact so necessary to indicate what exactly should be included, and what should be passed over, must have been largely developed and refined by these previous laborious studies upon such carefully-prepared doctrinal articles. It is highly probable that, when revising the Thirty-nine Articles, they would engage in the comparative study of the Protestant Confessions. They would thus be warned by the incompleteness or over-minuteness of the earlier church symbols, and, most important of all, they would be in large measure delivered from that narrow sectarianism which, expecting no good outside of its own church, looks for none. When the actual preparation of the Confession was commenced, it was proceeded with most deliberately and with admirable considerateness. The committee of singularly gifted men, to which we have already referred, having first of all arranged a general scheme for the distribution of the doctrine under appropriate chapter headings, resolved itself into sub-committees, to each of which from time to time certain heads of doctrine were committed. No statement now appearing in our Confession can be regarded as the result of any rash and ill-considered judgment. Revision after revision took place. The several sub-committees laid their conclusions before the general committee, and those statements of doctrine which passed such review were next submitted to discussion and debate in the full Assembly. And these reviews were no mere formal affairs. We find that the original drafts of the committee, though upon the whole accepted in the form in which they were presented, were yet subjected in the Assembly to minute and careful criticism, certain phrases relating to points of detail were omitted, certain particulars added, and various modifications introduced. Thus an unusual amount of labour—skilled labour—was expended upon the Confession. Drafted by some of the ablest of the divir.es, each section was considered and separately voted upon by the whole Convention. On the 25th September 1646, nineteen chapters of the Confession, being then finished and finally revised, were sent up for approval to the House of Commons. On the 26th November of the same year, the Confession was completed, ordered to be transcribed, and then laid before both Houses of Parliament. It only secured a qualified approval, the anti-clerical and Erastian spirit which prevailed in the Commons showing itself jealous of such passages as seemed to claim for church officers a power such as Parliament insisted belonged to itself alone. Objections were specially made against certain expressions in the twenty-fourth chapter; while chapters thirty and thirty-one were condemned, and by the Parliament of 1659 these obnoxious chapters were re-committed. What is of special interest to us as Scottish Presbyterians is the adoption of this Confession by the Presbyterian Assembly in Scotland. When the General Assembly met at Edinburgh in August 1649, the Westminster Confession was presented, carefully examined, and solemnly ratified, as being agreeable to God's Word, and in nothing contrary to the received doctrine, worship, discipline, and government of the Scottish Kirk. Presbyterianism, however, being overturned in 1661, a period of thirty years followed, during which the Presbyterian Standards and the enactments authorizing them were completely ignored. In 1690 came the great Revolution Settlement, and an Act was passed in Parliament in June of that year ratifying the Confession of Faith, and settling Presbyterian Government. Since that time to this day, the Westminster Confession continues to be the avowed symbol of our church, acknowledged by English-speaking Presbyterians in every quarter of the globe.

5. **Doctrinal Characteristics of the Confession.**—When we compare the Confession with the Catechisms prepared by the same Assembly, we certainly find in the latter special elaborations of doctrinal points which are either omitted or expressed more vaguely in the Confession. On a careful examination it will appear that this was purposely done, for several of those points which are passed over in the Confession were fully debated during its preparation, and were excluded after mature deliberation. Such doctrinal statements as were afterwards set down in the Catechisms secured the almost unanimous approval of the divines, but to give them a place in the Confession they considered to be unwise. Almost a year passed between the completing of the Confession of Faith and the issuing of the Larger Catechism. Hence the latter has been commonly regarded as, in a sense, a higher authority in doctrine than even the Confession. Not unfrequently we find an appeal made from the Confession to the Catechism in such a way as to imply that the earlier document must be interpreted and supplemented from the later. Those who do so generally maintain that the Catechism is just as authoritative a standard of doctrine in our church as the Confession. This state-

ment, however, is not quite exact. The Free Church Assembly of 1851 passed an Act containing a declaration in reference to the publication of the Subordinate Standards and other authoritative documents; and in that declaration it is acknowledged that a difference in degree of binding authority must be made between these several documents. To the Confession of Faith every office-bearer must testify in solemn form his personal adherence. To the Catechisms, sanction is given simply as directories for catechising. These Catechisms, therefore, are to be our guides in imparting catechetical instruction; but, when we seek to describe the type of doctrine which is accepted by our church, this must be done by a simple reference to her Confessional utterances.

When we examine the Westminster Confession in the light of its own express statements, and in connection with the known views of those more immediately engaged upon it, we shall find its general doctrinal tone extremely moderate. Of all the Reformed formularies, it is perhaps not too much to say, the Westminster Confession is the most correct and balanced in its representation of genuine Calvinism,—not, as some, overlooking any essential truth, nor, as others, including what might well be omitted. Several doctrinal points which were not developed by Calvin himself were elaborated with great minuteness by Beza, his own immediate successor, and by Turretine and other great systematizers of the seventeenth century. It is in regard to these elaborations that differences have arisen among those who claim to call themselves Calvinists. Such an out-line of doctrinal truth as will admit of a diversity of view in regard to details and the adoption of explanatory theories, is just what a Confession of Faith ought to exhibit. Certain far-reaching truths, which must be held by all maintaining that general type of doctrine, ought to be laid down with minuteness and precision; theories in explanation of those central truths, which may or may not be ac-ceptable to men holding by those truths, ought to have no place in a general formulary. The moderate Calvinists accept the positions laid down by Calvin himself, but more or less demur to the detailed determinations of those who profess to have carried on his work. The Confession, as representing mainly the simple and original doctrine of Calvin, and leaving open those questions not precisely determined by him, should prove a rallying-point for all parties belonging to that school. Among those accepting the Westminster formulary, opinions on these points, varying from those of the most moderate to those of the most extreme type, may be entertained, so long as Confessional expression for them is not demanded. The church holding by this Confession may comprise those contrasted parties, just as the Assembly which framed it embraced such men as Twisse and Calamy.

Calvinism has been too often judged by the foolish extravagances of extreme men. It is possible so to state Calvinistic doctrine as to render it repulsive and inconceivable to thoughtful and cultured

minds. This may be done without importing any actually new
doctrinal element, but simply by the disproportionate treatment of
certain unquestionable and fundamental truths. A careful and dis-
passionate examination of the Westminster Confession will show
that while its type of doctrine is decided and pronounced Calvinism,
it has been so wisely drawn up that there is scarcely a doctrinal
statement made which could have been omitted without destroying
its title to the name Calvinistic, and that, with singular propriety,
the several doctrines have had their due place assigned them in
the system. It is not unusual to speak of Calvinism as being
gradually toned down, and of its upholders as not venturing now to
maintain views which once on a time were fearlessly proclaimed.
Such language is extremely misleading. To say, as Dr. Schaff did
before the Pan-Presbyterian Council, that 'the five knotty points of
Calvinism have lost their point,' may be a smart saying, but, like
many other smart sayings, it is, to say the least, overdrawn. They
may not be stated now in exactly the same phraseology, but the
points themselves remain as theological attainments, constituting
the very essence of the Calvinistic creed. All true Calvinists cling
to those characteristic expressions of doctrine as tenaciously as
their precursors did in the Synod of Dort and in the Westminster
Assembly. He who renounces the doctrinal positions underlying
those so-called knotty points does not thereby pass from high to
moderate Calvinism, but actually passes over to the ranks of the
anti - Calvinists, and abandons the standpoint of the Reformed
Confessions.

By way of illustrating what we regard as the Calvinism of our
Standards,—a Calvinism that is at once moderate and genuine,—we
may take a hasty survey of the special teaching of the Confession
on these characteristic and testing doctrinal points :—1. Predestination. 2. Original Sin. 3. The Extent of Redemption.

1. The Calvinistic doctrine of Predestination is clearly set forth
in the Confession. Upon no point of doctrine perhaps has there
been so much discussion, accompanied by violence and exaggeration of statement. It is often urged as an objection against the
Westminster Confession, that so prominent a place is assigned in
it to the doctrine of Predestination. In answer to this objection,
we have to say, that a simple alternative is presented us. Either
this doctrine of Predestination is not true, and if so, ought to have
no place prominent or obscure ; or this doctrine is true, and if so,
then from the very nature of it, the place which it takes must be
conspicuous, and its presence must in large measure colour our
statement of other doctrinal positions. The danger lies, not in the
prominence given to it, but in its unguarded and inexact enunciation.
On the one hand, it may be so expressed as to appear identical with
the heathen doctrine of arbitrary fate. On the other hand, it may
be so expressed as to be evacuated of all theological importance ;
the name being retained, while the doctrine is really repudiated.

The Westminster divines carefully avoided both extremes. The true doctrine is set forth by means of a broad statement, accompanied by necessary explanations and qualifications. Too often opponents quote simply the broad statement, and so apply it as if no guarding and explanatory clause had ever been inserted. Now the Westminster doctrine can only be fairly represented when the Westminster expression of it is given complete. It is open to objectors to say that these qualifications militate against the substance of the statement they are meant to qualify. But if such a statement be made, we demand that proof for it be advanced. The general statement is :—That God from eternity chose a definite number out of the fallen race of Adam to everlasting life, rendering in time the means of grace effectual to their salvation, and that this choice is on the part of God an act of sovereign grace. The qualifying terms which are added, have reference to the case both of those who are not elected and of those who are elected to life. Every statement regarding the doctrine is so to be understood that these three propositions may be maintained : 1. God is not the author of sin ; 2. No violence is offered to the will of the creature ; 3. The liberty or contingency of second causes is not taken away. The special characteristic of Calvinism is the maintaining of the consistency of the doctrine of an eternal sovereign divine decree with the full assertion of these three propositions. The divine sovereignty and human responsibility,—Calvinism is interested in the one as well as in the other,—each is maintained in its full integrity. Whoever thinks that of these two statements the one is inconsistent with the other is Anti-Calvinist. The Westminster divines could not have put less into the third chapter of their Confession without abandoning the Calvinistic and Augustinian platform. While, then, one who holds by less than this is no Calvinist, and therefore cannot accept the Confession, there is nothing to prevent one who is inclined to determine points left here indeterminate accepting this formulary. The distinction of Supralapsarianism and Infralapsarianism may seem of little importance ; but if either of these theories had express and exclusive sanction given it in the Confession, those attached to the other theory would be harassed and hampered. If the statement of our Confession, ' They who are elected, being fallen in Adam, are redeemed by Christ,' naturally suggests sympathy with the Infralapsarian doctrine, it does not at least condemn the other ; and so Supralapsarians, accepting the Confession, may hold their own favourite theory as a private view. Another illustration of the liberal tone which characterizes the Westminster exposition of the doctrine of Predestination is seen in the statement, often ignorantly objected to, regarding the salvation of elect infants. All who honestly and intelligently hold a doctrine of election, of necessity maintain that only the elect are saved. Salvation is the palpable proof of election. When the term elect is applied to those dying in infancy or having their intellect undeveloped, it does not necessarily imply any restriction. Those who believe that all who die in infancy and all who have been denied the gift of reason are saved, thereby declare that they regard all such as elected to life ; and so they find their position covered by the statement in the Confession. Yet this absolute assertion is not made an article of faith, so that if any one should have a scruple or difficulty about this, he will not be disturbed by any dogmatic deliverance of the formulary.

It might at first seem as if the very express repudiation of the notion of a conditional decree rendered the doctrinal position of the divines unnecessarily narrow and severe. Such limitation, however, is absolutely necessary if a self-consistent scriptural type of doctrine is to be maintained. To found election on foreknowledge is as essentially Arminian as to repudiate a special election altogether. Predestination, as Calvinists understand the doctrine, is an absolute, irrespective decree. In the order of nature it precedes, and those gifts of grace necessary to the realization of the salvation decreed come after. The term 'conditional decree' is a mere sham and make-believe. It would be no better than a prophecy after the event. The conception of it is a denial of the divine prerogative. The repudiation of such a notion is no Ultraism, but an essential condition of Calvinism.

2. Original Sin. The doctrine of the imputation of Adam's sin to his posterity, in so far as it is the statement of a fact, is an accepted belief of all professing Christians. Differences arise when the attempt is made to define more exactly the idea of imputation. How precisely the first man is related to the race, and what the amount of injury the fall of Adam has wrought to individuals of that race in consequence of this relation,—these are questions that have occasioned keen debates even between those who claim alike the name of Calvinist. The doctrine of man's complete inability and utter moral depravity is a characteristic doctrine of Calvinism. On this point our Confession gives no uncertain sound. But the question of the precise nature of the relation in which individuals of the fallen race stand to him who first fell, is nowhere in the Confession expressly determined. Our first parents are described as the root of all mankind. Dr. Cunningham acknowledges that these terms are not so definite and precise as those generally employed by the divines of the seventeenth century. The words sound more like a statement such as Calvin would have used, than like one such as Turretine would have fully approved. Even Placæus, who advocated the doctrine of mediate imputation, might have unhesitatingly subscribed it. Though almost two years elapsed from the discussion of Placæus' doctrine in the Synod of Charenton to the issuing of our Confession, Dr. Cunningham rather gratuitously assumes that the Westminster divines 'were not yet much acquainted with the discussions which had been going on in France, and were in consequence not impressed with the necessity of being minute and precise in their

deliverance upon this subject.' (*Reformers and Theol. of Ref.* p. 383.)
He even thinks it necessary to refer to the more detailed utterances
of the Catechism, as if these might be taken to supplement and
determine the doctrine of the Confession. May we not rather
suppose that the more definite form of the doctrine proposed for
catechetical instruction was purposely omitted from the formulary
that was to be so particularly and solemnly accepted by its signa-
tories? When thus understood, the Confession is relieved of a
doctrinal theory which has occasioned scruples in some, who are
inclined to regard it as an extreme development of Calvinism, to
which they could not conscientiously subscribe. As it is, all who
maintain the fact of universal sinfulness, and believe that in some
way this springs originally from the connection which individuals of
the human race bear to Adam, will readily accept the moderate
statement of the Confession. The express doctrine of the Catechisms
(compare *Larger Catechism*, Qu. 22 and 25; *Shorter Catechism*,
Qu. 16 and 18) shows how definite were the opinions of the
divines in regard to all the points involved in the presentation of
this great Scripture truth; their reference to it in the Confession
shows how wisely they had discriminated between the statement of
doctrinal facts and the elaboration of explanatory theories.

3. The Extent of Redemption. In the Westminster Assembly
there were several distinguished members who were avowed
disciples of Davenant, and held views regarding the extent of
Redemption which the stricter Calvinists opposed, as inclining to
Arminianism. In the *Minutes of Assembly* we find the record of
a long-continued debate on this question, in which Calamy, Arrowsmith, Seaman, and other moderate Calvinists were opposed by the
Scottish divines, Reynolds, and others, who were more pronounced,
and more decidedly attached to those views usually regarded as
Calvinistic. Mr. Calamy said: ' I am far from universal redemption
in the Arminian sense; but that that I hold is in the sense of our
divines in the Synod of Dort, that Christ did pay a price for all,—
absolute intention for the elect, conditional intention for the reprobate in case they do believe,—that all men should be *salvabiles, non
obstante lapsu Adami.*' Mr. Seaman explains: ' He doth not say a
salvability *quoad homines,* but *quoad Deum* .... so far reconciled
himself to the world that He would have mercy on whom He would
have mercy. All in the first Adam were made liable to damnation,
so all are liable to salvation in the second Adam.' These views were
not recognised, and certainly they got no place in the Confession;
yet that formulary was so framed that Calamy and his party found
no difficulty in accepting it. The opinion of the great majority of
members was undoubtedly in favour of what we call, in the strictest
sense of the term, the doctrine of a limited atonement, that Christ
died for the elect only; yet even the express statement (iii. 6), that
the elect alone are saved by Christ, is not so put as necessarily to
offend evangelical men, who demand an unchallengeable ground for

the unrestricted offer of salvation. 'Those who in modern times have pronounced most confidently that the more restricted view is exclusively intended, seem to me,' says Dr. Mitchell, 'to have unconsciously construed or interpreted the words, "neither are any other redeemed by Christ, effectually called, justified, adopted, sanctified, and saved, but the elect only," as if they had run, "neither are any other redeemed by Christ, or effectually called, or justified, adopted, sanctified, and saved, but the elect only." But these two statements do not necessarily bear the same meaning. Calamy, Arrowsmith, and the others who agreed with them, may have felt justified in accepting the former, though they might have scrupled to accept the latter' (Introd. to *Minutes*, p. lvii.). We have adduced the positions maintained by our Confession on these three important and characteristic heads of doctrine as a specimen of the tone and spirit which pervade the entire formulary. The Calvinistic principle is consistently maintained throughout, but the extremes which many respected theologians advocated under one or more of those heads were most carefully avoided by the Westminster divines. We therefore feel quite warranted in styling the doctrine of our Standards, not modified, but moderate Calvinism. The system of doctrine developed in our Confession is thoroughly self-consistent. There is no indecision; no attempt to combine contrary tendencies. We find no concession to Arminianism, nor any departure from what is essential to the Calvinistic system. The Westminster Confession, in short, presents a pure and simple Calvinism, unencumbered by the private opinions and pet notions of individual Calvinists.

Views entertained by the Westminster Divines in regard to Christian Liberty.—Under the chapters where this subject is specially treated, the expressions of the Confession are examined in detail. It is only proposed in the conclusion of this introduction to indicate the characteristic position maintained in our Standards, as conceived by those who framed them, and by those who subscribe them. To determine exactly the Westminster doctrine of Christian Liberty, or, as it is often styled, the doctrine of Toleration, is no easy task. Extreme estimates have been formed as to the teaching of the Confession on this subject. On the one hand, we find certain enthusiastic vindicators of our church Standards speaking as if it were both necessary and possible to show that the divines entertained, and intended to express, a thoroughly-developed doctrine of toleration in the modern sense of the term. Such critics generally determine first of all what is to be regarded as the true notion of toleration, and then proceed to manipulate the statements of the Confession so as to make it appear that this modern attainment had been fully anticipated by those precocious liberals of the seventeenth century. On the other hand, we find not a few who, while sympathizing with the doctrinal substance of the Confession, yet maintain that certain of its statements are not only deficient, but essentially antagonistic to the principles now adopted and approved in those churches which accept the Westminster formulary as their doctrinal standard. [Read the able, though extreme, controversial treatise by Dr. Marshall, of Coupar - Angus, *Principles of the Westminster Standards Persecuting.*] A fair estimate of the matter in question can be formed only by considering the statements of the divines in relation to the opinions regarding toleration generally prevalent during their era. The doctrine which we now understand by the term toleration was not then formulated. Toleration, as we conceive it, is essentially a recent attainment. Contributions, however, were being made by individual members of different religious communities, among whom both Independents and Presbyterians in the Westminster Assembly were conspicuous ; and these have now been tabulated and wrought out into something like a consistent system. If we compare the Westminster divines with other religious parties of their time, we shall find that their views of Christian liberty, imperfect and inadequate as they may sometimes seem to us, indicated a very decided advance. Legislative measures which were passed under their influence, harsh as they now appear, are still to be reckoned essentially liberal movements, inasmuch as they mitigate and relax the severity of earlier enactments. It was no easy task, in passing from a system of the most stringent restrictions, to determine the mean between the repression of the bigot and the licence of the indifferent. It is not easy even now to express, without danger of misunderstanding, at once our respect for individual freedom, and our earnest devotion to the interests of pure and undefiled religious truth. The Westminster divines, as we understand their writings, more fully and more successfully than any other considerable body of men in their own or immediately subsequent times, enunciated the fundamental principle out of which our own doctrine of toleration has been constructed. So much it was necessary to say in vindication of the Westminster divines, to show that, judged by any standard that can fairly be applied, they deserve to be held in honour as, up to their time and beyond their time, the true-hearted supporters of the principles of civil and religious liberty. But having said this, we have still to face the question whether the expression which they give to this principle, however noble comparatively, however advanced and creditable for the seventeenth century, is adequate and suitable for a formulary to which subscription is still required. In order to answer this question we must recur to the central and general expression which they have given to their principle. That principle, just as affirmed in the Confession, will suffice for all ages. That no statements are to be found in the Confession irreconcilable with their central utterance on this subject, we are far from supposing. We are not, however, pledged to accept all the detailed utterances of the Confession. The true principle of Christian liberty clearly laid down in the oft-repeated phrase, ' God alone is Lord of the conscience,' is binding upon us, not according to the interpretation of the divines, which from their circumstances may have been restricted and imperfect, but according to the light which has been shed upon it in our own days. We have here a valid argument against Dr. Marshall. He objects to the quotation of this statement, unless we append to it other clauses, that show how the Westminster divines would have applied it. He instances such phrases as these, 'For their publishing of such opinions, etc., they may lawfully be called to account and proceeded against,' 'It is the civil magistrate's duty to take order that the truth of God be kept pure and entire,' and declares that all who accept the Confession pledge themselves to the acceptance of these express opinions. Our position, on the contrary, is this. We accept the general statement laid down without qualification. Our notion of Christian liberty is that laid down in the phrase, 'God alone is Lord of the conscience.' If any particular applications, elsewhere made in the Confession, are shown in modern light to be inconsistent with a proper understanding of this, we are not bound to these, but may so qualify our acceptance of them as to make our statement of the doctrine clear and self-consistent. So the Assembly of 1647 limits the statement of the magistrate's power to convene Synods more expressly than the divines had done to unsettled times ; and the Free Church Assembly of 1846 declares that 'while the Church firmly maintained the same scriptural principles as to the duties of nations and their rulers in reference to true religion and the Church of Christ, for which she has hitherto contended, she disclaims intolerant or persecuting principles, and does not regard her Confession of Faith, or any portion thereof, when fairly interpreted, as favouring intolerance or persecution, or consider that her office-bearers, by subscribing it, profess any principles inconsistent with liberty of conscience and the right of private judgment.' Of course the question may be raised, whether it were not better to alter or omit any phrase in the Confession which may be liable to construction in favour of persecution. This the American churches have done. But so long as we maintain the principle that acceptance of the Confession as a church symbol binds us to principles, and not to deductions or to details, we may rather express our satisfaction with the noble statement of the principle, and, by a declaratory deliverance like that of the Act of our Assembly above quoted, indicate in what spirit and to what extent we are prepared to make its application.

THE CONFESSION OF FAITH.

—◆—

CHAPTER I.

OF THE HOLY SCRIPTURE.

I.—*Although the light of nature, and the works of creation and providence, do so far manifest the goodness, wisdom, and power of God, as to leave men inexcusable; yet they are not sufficient to give that knowledge of God, and of his will, which is necessary unto salvation: therefore it pleased the Lord, at sundry times, and in divers manners, to reveal himself, and to declare that his will unto his Church; and afterwards, for the better preserving and propagating of the truth, and for the more sure establishment and comfort of the Church against the corruption of the flesh, and the malice of Satan and of the world, to commit the same wholly unto writing; which maketh the holy scripture to be most necessary; those former ways of God's revealing his will unto his people being now ceased.*

THIS chapter seems to have received from the Westminster divines more than ordinary consideration. They made it the subject of long deliberation and debate, and the deliverance to which they came regarding Holy Scripture was evidently viewed by them as very much like the issuing of a programme. Their whole system may be estimated by an examination of their first article. The Confession is characteristically Biblical, and consistently with this character it opens with the article 'Of the Holy Scripture,'—while most other Confessions, as for example the Thirty-nine Articles, open with chapters on God and the Trinity.

The first section of this chapter deals with the general question of Revelation,—the communication of God's will to man. It treats of three important points regarding revelation. 1. Natural religion, what it is and what it teaches. 2. Divine revelation, for what it is needed and in what it consists. 3. Revelation in the form of Scripture.

1. Full acknowledgment is made of the importance of natural religion within its own province. Apart from a divine revelation as an oral communication of God's will, man may arrive at a knowledge of God's being, and at least a partial perception of His character. The statement of our Confession sufficiently guards against errors in two extreme directions. On the one hand, some pious men were

38

led to deny altogether the reality of natural religion. Hutchinson (A.D. 1724) and his followers, including the well-known Bishop Horne, maintained that all true knowledge in science and philosophy, as well as in religion, is to be derived immediately from the Bible. On the other hand, the English Deists started with the assertion that all true knowledge, that of religion as well as of science and philosophy, is derived from the same revelation,—understanding by revelation simply the discoveries of man in the exercise of his natural powers. Thus Matthew Tindal used in the title of his well-known book the phrase that was then current in his school, *Christianity as old as the Creation, or the Gospel a Re-publication of the Religion of Nature* (A.D. 1730). These contrary errors sprung from a confusion of the natural and supernatural, the one ultimately ignoring the natural, the other ultimately ignoring the supernatural. [Illustrate by reference to the divergent courses of individual histories in the Oxford movement; also to the careers of Edward Irving and Macleod Campbell.] The results of that natural theology, which is recognised in our Confession, are reached by a twofold process of intuition and observation. There are certain mental aptitudes and moral convictions which belong to human nature, and together constitute an internal instinct. Of this, Bacon says that by means of it 'the soul receives some light for beholding and discerning the perfection of the moral law, though the light be not perfectly clear, but of such a nature as rather to reprehend vice than give a full information of duty' (*Advancement of Learning*, Book ix.). Then there are indica- tions of God from outward nature. Young has said, 'An undevout astronomer is mad.'

2. Revelation is the discovery which God makes of Himself and of His will for our salvation. The necessity for such a revelation becomes evident so soon as we come to deal with the problem of sin. This problem cannot be properly understood until we get the idea of grace, and this becomes first possible in an immediate revela- tion of God. Those revelations of saving truth which He gives, have a history and a development. They were repeated as often as necessary for retaining a correct knowledge of them, and new discoveries were made as fresh needs arose. The form, too, of those revelations varied according to the circumstances of the age and the recipients. Though in this place our Confession seems to speak expressly only of oral revelation, yet elsewhere (see chap. vii. 5) other modes for the saving revelation of God's will by divine institu- tions and ritual ordinances are fully recognised. But while thus the revelations were made at sundry times and in divers manners, it was still one revelation as to substance and purpose. In all ages the need to be satisfied was the same. And so, under all its varying forms, divine revelation made known to man God and His gracious will.

3. The Westminster divines with their usual caution do not seek to affirm at what time revelation first assumed the form of Scripture. [Read Hooker, *Eccles. Polity*, Bk. 1. c. xiii.] They had no interest

in doing so, for revelation, though not yet written, being fully inspired, had for them all the authority of Scripture. It was to the revelation rather than to the writing of it that the inspiration belonged. That the written word should take the place of oral revelations handed down, or frequently renewed by direct divine utterances, is not viewed as in itself necessary. Hence the position of those who follow the light afforded by remnants of those primitive revelations, is left here quite undetermined. On their condition the Confession does not dogmatize. Its declaration has reference only to the circumstances of those to whom the word of salvation in the form of Scripture has been sent. That divine revelation should assume the form of Scripture is declared to be necessary, though not for salvation, yet for the maintenance of a sound type of doctrine, for the successful propagation of the truth, and for the proper equipment of the believer in his warfare against the world, the Devil, and the flesh. It is necessary, in short, that the Word should be written, for the higher interests of the individual believer, the Church, and the world. What then would otherwise have been merely something desirable, must be regarded as a necessity, at least for Christendom, when we consider that no longer does God reveal Himself as in former days, but that, under the ministry of His Spirit, He uses the Word of Scripture as the only revelation of His will. This statement is given here in only a general form, and is repeated more particularly in section vi., where the completeness of the Scripture revelation is affirmed.

II. —*Under the name of Holy Scripture, or the Word of God written, are now contained all the Books of the Old and New Testament, which are these:—*

OF THE OLD TESTAMENT.

Genesis.	I. Kings.	Ecclesiastes.	Obadiah.
Exodus.	II. Kings.	The Song of Songs.	Jonah.
Leviticus.	I. Chronicles.	Isaiah.	Micah.
Numbers.	II. Chronicles.	Jeremiah.	Nahum.
Deuteronomy.	Ezra.	Lamentations.	Habakkuk.
Joshua.	Nehemiah.	Ezekiel.	Zephaniah.
Judges.	Esther.	Daniel.	Haggai.
Ruth.	Job.	Hosea.	Zechariah.
I. Samuel.	Psalms.	Joel.	Malachi.
II. Samuel.	Proverbs.	Amos	

OF THE NEW TESTAMENT.

The Gospels according to	Paul's Epistles to the Romans.	Thessalonians I.	The Epistle of James.
Matthew.	Corinthians I.	Thessalonians II.	The first and second Epistles of Peter.
Mark.	Corinthians II.	To Timothy I.	The first, second, and third Epistles of John.
Luke.	Galatians.	To Timothy II.	
John.	Ephesians.	To Titus.	
The Acts of the Apostles.	Philippians.	To Philemon.	The Epistle of Jude.
	Colossians.	The Epistle to the Hebrews.	The Revelation.

All which are given by inspiration of God, to be the rule of faith and life.

The Rule of Faith (κανὼν τῆς πίστεως, *regula fidei*) was the term used to indicate the sum of saving knowledge. Then as the subject-matter of this canon or rule was wholly derived from Holy Scripture, the inspired writings were distinguished from all others as canonical. The Canon, therefore, does not mean merely a catalogue of Scriptures received in the church, but the accepted rule or measure of Christian doctrine. [Comp. Westcott's *Bible in the Church*, p. 110.]

The enumeration of books in our Confession is given according to the distribution of these in our ordinary English Bibles. The Hebrew Bible followed another arrangement, grouping the books of the Old Testament according to subject, style, and date, under a threefold division. 1. Torah : the Law, comprising the five books, Genesis, Exodus, Leviticus, Numbers, Deuteronomy. 2. The Prophets, comprising—(1) Earlier Prophets: Joshua, Judges, Samuel, and Kings; (2) Later Prophets : Isaiah, Jeremiah, Ezekiel, and the twelve Minor Prophets. 3. Hagiographa (the sacred writings), comprising Psalms, Proverbs, Job, Song of Songs, Ruth, Lamentations, Ecclesiastes, Esther, Daniel, Ezra, Nehemiah, and Chronicles. It was to this early distribution of the Old Testament books that our Lord alluded when He claimed that things concerning Him had been written in the law of Moses, in the Prophets, and in the Psalms (Luke xxiv. 44). According to our present arrangement, the historical books of the last division of the Hebrew Bible are classed with the earlier Prophets Daniel gets the fourth place among the more directly prophetic writings, and Lamentations is placed beside Jeremiah. This distribution originated with the Septuagint, was thence adopted in the Vulgate, was followed by Luther, and has thus come to be regarded with general favour. It is supposed to correspond well with the distribution of the books of the New Testament. Thus in our Old Testament we have—(1) Historical Books : Genesis to Esther ; (2) Didactic Books : Job to Ecclesiastes ; (3) Prophetic Books : Isaiah to Malachi. In the New Testament we have—(1) Histories : Gospels and Acts ; (2) Didactic Treatises or Epistles : Romans to Jude ; (3) A Prophetic Book : The Apocalypse.

The caution shown by the Westminster divines in their choice of designations for the several books of the Canon of Scripture is very admirable. Wherever they found no author's name prefixed to a particular book, they have been careful to insert none ; and in this they have been scrupulously consistent. They showed their wisdom in refusing to imperil the position of any single book in the Canon by fixing for it an authorship which it did not itself claim—an authorship which, having been maintained by tradition in one age, might probably be repudiated by criticism in another.

Although no test of canonicity is here explicitly enounced, yet when the clause ' all which are given by inspiration of God, to be,' etc., is compared with the opening words of sec. 3, ' The Books commonly called Apocrypha, *not being of Divine inspiration*, are no part of the canon of the Scripture,' it appears that the framers of the Confession understood inspiration to be the test of canonicity. Writings which are inspired are canonical, writings which are not inspired are not canonical. This leaves us confronted by the further and formidable question, How are we to ascertain what writings are inspired?

There are two processes by which we can arrive at the conclusion that a writing is inspired. The internal evidence afforded by the marks appealed to in sec. 5 may be sufficient to warrant the conclusion. Or we may believe in the inspiration of a writing, because we first of all believe in Christ, and find that He authorized certain persons to speak in His name, and with His Spirit. But there are books in our Canon whose claims are justified by neither of these tests ; of such books as Chronicles and Esther we neither know the authorship nor can we unhesitatingly say that they carry in themselves indubitable marks of Divine origin. We are driven, therefore, to some test, such as Luther's, ' conformity to the main end of revelation.' If by ' canonical writings ' we mean the writings through which God conveys to us the knowledge of the revelation He has made,—if this be the prominent idea, and if their being the rule of faith and life be an inference from this,—then we find a broader basis for the Canon, and can admit into it all writings which have an immediate connection with God's revelation of Himself in Christ. If the book in question gives us a link in the history of that revelation, or if it represents a stage of God's dealings, and of the growth His people made under these dealings, and if it contains nothing which is quite inconsistent with the idea of its being inspired, then its claim to be admitted seems valid.

The Jewish teachers did not consider the Old Testament Canon fixed until after the fall of the Temple. The New Testament Canon was not finally adjusted till the end of the fourth century ; and even then the canonicity of certain books was disputed by one and another leader of the church. Those books that were universally accepted were entitled Homologoumena, and those that for a time had their place questioned, Antilegomena. The Reformers, notably Luther, were surprisingly free in their use of this distinction. In the latter division were placed James, 2 Peter, 2 and 3 John, Jude, and Revelation. The claims of these books to bear apostolic names are now almost universally admitted by evangelical scholars ; and with this the ground for the distinction has disappeared. Hence in our Confession all the books enumerated are regarded as having equal canonical rank. In order to determine the question of canonicity, we have to trace the history of the reception of the several books in the ancient church, and then the list thus arranged according to the authority of tradition must be subjected to criticism, to determine whether the writings contained in it really reflect apostolic doctrine. Apostolic origin, either as to writing or as to spirit, is indispensable to the securing for any book a place in the Canon. This was so early recognised as a mark of canonicity, that heretical works seeking canonical authority were put forth under the names of apostles.

The Westminster Confession, in common with most of the doctrinal

c

symbols of the Reformed or Calvinistic Churches, while not going into argument, accepts the definite results of tradition and criticism in the church, and so gives the list arrived at by those means. Luther stood free in regard to the Canon ; and Lutheran standards, in order to preserve this freedom, even from the earliest Reformation times, forbear to give an enumeration of the books of Scripture lest they should fetter critical inquiry. Dorner brings it as a reproach against the Reformed Confessions that they have inserted such lists.

The relation between Inspiration and Canonicity is very much like that between Creation and Providence. Each writing is the product of divine inspiration,—a creation of God's Spirit ; and the preservation and grouping together of these writings must be regarded as the result of a divine providence employing as instruments the spiritual and critical discernment of man. In regard to Inspiration the Confession gives its imprimatur to no particular theory, but clearly and strongly affirms the fact. All the books enumerated form one Canon, one rule of faith and life. 'The perfect and canonical authority of Holy Scripture does not depend upon any one writing, but upon the whole collection of writings, which supplement one another, and must therefore be taken together ; and in this dogma regarding Scripture is involved the truth, that we have in the New Testament, not merely fragments of the Apostolic Age, which have by chance been preserved to us, but a harmonious whole, complete within itself, wherein no principle of apostolic consciousness is wanting.'[1] The 'all' of our section involves exclusion of whatever is extra-canonical, and the doctrinal completeness of that circle of writings which forms the Canon.

III.—*The Books commonly called Apocrypha, not being of divine inspiration, are no part of the canon of the scripture; and therefore are of no authority in the Church of God, nor to be any otherwise approved, or made use of, than other human writings.*

The books called Apocrypha here referred to are those writings for which a place has been sought in or alongside of the Old Testament Canon. Their subjects are in the same line with those of the canonical Scriptures. Hence we have apocryphal histories—Ezra, Esther, Daniel, giving romantic additions to the books bearing these names, and the Books of the Maccabees, giving historical records of the period from 175 B.C. to 135 B.C. ; apocryphal prophecies—Baruch and Epistle of Jeremiah ; apocryphal books of wisdom—Ecclesiasticus and Wisdom of Solomon ; and finally, pure romances in historical form, with a purpose either directly religious (Tobit) or directly patriotic (Judith). These are not found in the Hebrew Canon, but only in the Greek. Yet through the use of the LXX. they were printed side by side with canonical books, which was never done with the so-called New Testament Apocrypha—pseudo-gospels, acts, epistles, and apocalypses [although the Apostolic Fathers are some-

[1] Martensen, *Christian Dogmatics*, page 402. Edinburgh, 1866.

times found in one MS. with the canonical writings of the New Testament]. In many of the apocryphal books there is an air of extravagance, and in even the best, the simple majesty and profound religious power of Scripture are absent. The Protestant Standards generally indicate a clear distinction between Canonical Scripture as inspired, and the Apocrypha as uninspired; and though in some churches, as the Anglican, portions from the Apocrypha are still read, they are not allowed to have independent authority in matters of faith. When this is admitted, the position of our own Standards is the only consistent one. Like other writings, useful and instructive, they should be relegated to private use and have no ecclesiastical sanction conferred upon them. Adopting this principle, the directors of the British Bible Societies, after long discussion, decided in 1825, that no copies of Scripture should be circulated by them in which the Apocrypha was bound up with the canonical books.

IV. —*The authority of the holy scripture, for which it ought to be believed and obeyed, dependeth not upon the testimony of any man or church, but wholly upon God (who is truth itself), the author thereof; and therefore it is to be received, because it is the word of God.*

The ultimate authority of Holy Scripture is declared to rest upon God Himself, from whom it comes. His Spirit inspires it, and this renders it infallible. Romanists, however, and Romanising Anglicans attribute to human testimony—either that of the church or that of patristic tradition—what our Confession, in consistency with the whole Protestant type of doctrine, attributes only to the testimony of God Himself. 'Men sometimes talk as if they had a vague notion of the early Fathers having had some inferior species of inspiration,— some peculiar divine guidance differing from that of the Apostles and Evangelists in degree rather than in kind,—and somehow entitling their views and statements to more deference and respect than those of ordinary men. All notions of this sort are utterly baseless, and should be carefully rejected. Authority, properly so called, can be rightly based only upon inspiration; and inspiration is the guidance of the Spirit of God, infallibly securing against all error. . . . The Fathers, individually or collectively, were not inspired; they therefore possess no authority whatever; and their statements must be estimated and treated just as those of any other ordinary men. . . . Most of them have given interpretations of important scriptural statements which no man now receives; many of them have erred and have contradicted themselves and each other in stating the doctrines of the Bible.'[1] The attribute, therefore, which specially characterises authentic Scripture is its inspiration; and as this is a divine operation—the energy of the Holy Spirit—it cannot be dependent for its authority upon human testimony. The Holy Spirit just as well as

[1] Cunningham, *Historical Theology*, vol. i. pp. 174, 175.

Christ receives not testimony from man. Hence the Scripture as the product of the Spirit's inspiration gives testimony to the believer and lends authority to the church, instead of receiving from the church its authority. Protestantism rightly understands the words of our Lord to Peter—upon this rock I will build my church—as referring not to the individual addressed, but to the truth which that individual, through the Spirit's influence, had recognised. According, therefore, to this fair interpretation of the *locus classicus*, the establishment of the authority of the church is made to depend upon the Word. The written Word, when understood in the spirit of Peter's highly commended confession, must be regarded as the reflex of the living Word. [Read Pressensé, *The Martyrs and Apologists*, reporting and criticising Clement's view of Scripture, pp. 557-561.] Christ, who said, 'I am the truth,' is the centre of all Scripture ; and so the authority of Scripture is properly made to rest wholly upon God, who is truth.

V.—*We may be moved and induced by the testimony of the Church to an high and reverend esteem of the holy scripture, and the heavenliness of the matter, the efficacy of the doctrine, the majesty of the style, the consent of all the parts, the scope of the whole (which is to give all glory to God), the full discovery it makes of the only way of man's salvation, the many other incomparable excellencies, and the entire perfection thereof, are arguments whereby it doth abundantly evidence itself to be the word of God; yet, notwithstanding, our full persuasion and assurance of the infallible truth, and divine authority thereof, is from the inward work of the Holy Spirit, bearing witness by and with the word in our hearts.*

This revelation specially commends itself to us by means of its adequacy for that which it professes to accomplish. It comes as a revelation of God, and the only satisfactory evidence of its worth is the result which it effects in us. Our Confession, therefore, gives only a subordinate place to external evidences in support of the authority of Scripture, such as the testimony of the church ; it gives a higher place to arguments from the manifest characteristics of Scripture itself, which declare its perfection ; and the highest place of all to the inward witness of the Holy Spirit. According to the teaching of this section, therefore, we may say that, while we do not overlook the aids to faith in Scripture which we obtain from external sources, while we lay emphasis upon the importance and truth of that which Scripture records, we are mainly influenced in our acceptance of Scripture as the ultimate and absolute rule of faith by the experience which we and other believers in the Christian church have had of the spiritual power of its doctrines. And here we might find a vindication of the wisdom of the compilers of the article on the

Canon in not laying any stress upon the question of the human authorship of the several books. The internal evidence, which, on the one hand, brings into view the special characteristics of Scripture, and on the other, insists upon reverent attention to the voice of the Spirit in the believing heart, is of primary importance in establishing for us, as believers, the supreme authority of the canonical Scriptures. [See Halyburton's *Reason of Faith.*]

VI.—*The whole counsel of God, concerning all things necessary for his own glory, man's salvation, faith, and life, is either expressly set down in scripture, or by good and necessary consequence may be deduced from scripture: unto which nothing at any time is to be added, whether by new revelations of the Spirit, or traditions of men. Nevertheless, we acknowledge the inward illumination of the Spirit of God to be necessary for the saving understanding of such things as are revealed in the word; and that there are some circumstances concerning the worship of God, and government of the Church, common to human actions and societies, which are to be ordered by the light of nature and Christian prudence, according to the general rules of the word, which are always to be observed.*

This article states very clearly the Protestant doctrine of the perfection and completeness of Scripture as the rule of faith. There are two theories that very evidently conflict with this doctrine—the theory of fanatical and pietistic sects regarding new revelations, and the theory of Rome regarding the value of ecclesiastical traditions. Luther showed that these were really two sides of the same theory. The history of Irvingism shows how the one passes into the other. Both are repudiated here, yet in a moderate manner. The Quakers maintain that though revelations to the pious individual can never contradict the true sense of Scripture, yet these revelations are not to be subjected to the Scripture as though they were in any way subordinate. These subjective spiritual experiences are viewed as co-ordinate in authority with the written Word; the subject-matter of these may be something outside of Scripture, and so they may render one wise beyond what is written. This extravagance the Westminster divines refused to countenance; yet they show how indispensable the illumination of the Holy Spirit is if we are to know the Scripture savingly. The Romanists again hold that in Scripture alone we have not a sufficient rule of faith and life, and that consequently the written Word must be supplemented by what they call divine, apostolical, and ecclesiastical traditions; meaning by these respectively, as explained by Bellarmine—those given by Christ Himself to the apostles, yet not recorded; those given by apostles under the Spirit's guidance, yet not in their epistles; and ancient customs or views which, by general consent, have received in the church the force and importance of laws. According to Quakers, the individual believer,—according to Romanists, the church,—possesses an inspiration like that of the apostles, which has an equal authority in matters of faith and life. Our Confession, in the true spirit of Protestantism, regards Scripture as the complete rule for us, in the examination of which we must use indeed the Spirit's guidance and all available helps from human thought and history, but with which we may co-ordinate nothing. In religious matters, and manifestly in these alone, we maintain the sufficiency of the written Word, which contains all that is necessary to salvation, all that is necessary to constitute a perfect rule of faith and morals.

VII.—*All things in scripture are not alike plain in themselves, nor alike clear unto all; yet those things which are necessary to be known, believed, and observed, for salvation, are so clearly propounded and opened in some place of scripture or other, that not only the learned, but the unlearned, in a due use of the ordinary means, may attain unto a sufficient understanding of them.*

Not all alike plain.—Mysteries in doctrine and varying natural capacities in readers are admitted. The perspicuity attributed to Scripture is relative, on the one hand, to the matter treated of—*e g.*, large portions of Ezekiel, Daniel, and Revelation are obscure—and on the other, to the condition of the person who reads the Word.

Necessary to be known for salvation.—Perspicuity is affirmed absolutely in regard to those truths that constitute the Rule of Faith —the leading doctrines of the Gospel. The knowledge of these being indispensable to all classes of men, each is found expressed in some particular part of Scripture with unmistakable clearness. The Romish Church maintains that Scripture is not in itself intelligible to the people in matters of faith, and insists that only the church tradition can give the true interpretation. What Rome thus affirms of the church and her tradition, Protestantism attributes to the individual reader of the Word who uses the ordained means.

The ordinary means.—What these means are depends on our idea of the understanding of Scripture,—whether we regard it as a merely literal or as a spiritual understanding. To understand the letter of Scripture we must know the language in which we read it, our natural powers must have reached some degree of maturity, and our minds must be unbiassed by prejudices and erroneous views. To understand the spirit of Scripture, and so to receive spiritual profit from our reading, we must have spiritual discernment through the indwelling of the Spirit, and even by the spiritual man prayer must be used as a means to secure enlightenment.

VIII.—*The Old Testament in Hebrew (which was the native language of the people of God of old), and the New Testament in Greek (which at the time of the writing of it was most generally known to the nations), being immediately inspired by God, and by his singular care and providence kept pure in all ages, are therefore authentical; so as in all controversies of religion, the church is finally to appeal unto them. But because these original tongues are not known to all the people of God, who have right unto and interest in the scriptures, and are commanded, in the fear of God, to read and search them, therefore they are to be translated into the vulgar language of every nation unto which they come, that the word of God dwelling plentifully in all, they may worship him in an acceptable manner, and, through patience and comfort of the scriptures, may have hope.*

Authenticity of original texts.—The principle here affirmed commends itself to every fair mind. Our final appeal in all controversies must be to the original sources. The Romish Church has given preference to the Latin translation called the Vulgate, and discourages, if it does not absolutely prohibit, all appeals to the Hebrew and Greek texts. The object of this was to gain some advantage over the Protestants by the use of a text that had been manipulated by Romish authorities and so reflected a Romish type of doctrine. Bellarmine holds that, as few and sometimes none in the general councils of the church knew Hebrew, it was necessary for the church that full confidence should be claimed in all important questions for the Latin Version. In opposition to his further assertion of the absolute correctness of the Vulgate, errors have been pointed out and divergences noted between the Clementine and Sixtine editions. The translators of our English Version used the originals as then accessible. 'These,' say they in their preface of 1611, 'these are the two golden pipes or rather conduits, wherethrough the olive branches empty themselves into the gold. St. Augustine calleth them precedent or original tongues, St. Hierome, fountains.' Augustine, it may be mentioned, knew Greek but not Hebrew, so he used the LXX. and praised it ; Jerome, knowing Hebrew, used and valued the Hebrew text,—each using the oldest form of Scripture within his reach. It is also to be remembered that Hebrew and Greek being almost unknown during the greater part of the Middle Ages, when Latin was familiarly known, the original texts were not so liable to intentional and doctrinal corruption as the Latin texts were, and slips of copyists, being often the result of sheer ignorance, are therefore the more easily corrected.

Right and use of translations. — Protestantism commends and enjoins the reading of the Bible by the people, and, in consequence, approves of the diffusion of translations of Scripture in all languages. In the early centuries no restriction was placed on the use of Scripture, but, as ignorance prevailed, it was first neglected by the people themselves, and then prohibited by their rulers. For popular instruction translations are indispensable; and our own version, viewed as the result of the combined labour of most competent men, and as having stood most searching criticism, may be guaranteed as correct on all important points of doctrine.

IX.—*The infallible rule of interpretation of scripture is the scripture itself; and therefore, when there is a question about the true and full sense of any scripture (which is not manifold, but one), it must be searched and known by other places that speak more clearly.*

In this section we have it clearly asserted that we do not require to go beyond Scripture itself, either to decisions of councils or to current views in the church, in order to determine the sense of Scripture : comparing Scripture with Scripture, the clearer parts will explain the more difficult; and in order to this, we must avoid all obscuring of Scripture by imagining in it a variety of senses.

Scripture its own interpreter.—This position does not overlook but really implies the careful use of all means of enlightenment and illustration. 'This statement seems to be founded on that of the *Confessio Helvetica Posterior*, where the rule of explaining Scripture by itself is stated to include the consideration of the genius of the language, and the circumstances in which it was written, as well as the comparison of similar passages, to throw light on each other. This rule, therefore, is virtually the sound principle of grammatico-historical exegesis.'[1] This is a necessary consequence of the Protestant doctrine of the perspicuity of Scripture. Only if itself essentially obscure, and hence calculated to mislead simple readers, would it be necessary that it should be authoritatively interpreted as to meaning and doctrine by any outward authority. The Old Scottish Confession has well said that, in order to gain the right sense of a passage, it concerns us to see not so much 'what men before us may have said or done, as what the Holy Spirit uniformly says in the body of the sacred Scripture.' The principle maintained here is that generally known as the Analogy of Faith.

Dark places to be explained by the clearer.—This is merely the carrying out of the principle referred to. We may, for example, have revelations of a truth, in a certain passage, in which some subordinate aspects of that truth are brought out, and yet that passage may be less clear than some others regarding the same general truth, in which, however, those particular aspects are not considered. The special teaching, then, of such a passage must be understood in a

[1] Professor Candlish, 'The Westminster Confession on Scripture,' in *British and Foreign Evangelical Review* for 1877, p. 177.

way that will harmonize with the general type of doctrine contained in the clearer passage.

The sense of Scripture one.—Some of our older divines so treated Scripture that they could take out of it anything they pleased. Many assumed a fourfold sense, and some even went further,—distinguishing the literal, analogical, allegorical, and tropological. By this sort of treatment the perspicuity of Scripture was utterly destroyed. If we are not to bring complete confusion into the contents of divine revelation, we must maintain only one sense for Scripture, and that the literal sense, reached by careful examination of the text itself. The spiritual truth is contained in the proper sense of Scripture language, and is lost instead of being rendered more conspicuous by the introduction of a mystical sense into our interpretation. A prophetic utterance may have an immediate reference and also the suggestion of some other thing, but this we may hold without tampering with the language of the prophet.

X.—*The supreme Judge, by which all controversies of religion are to be determined, and all decrees of councils, opinions of ancient writers, doctrines of men, and private spirits, are to be examined, and in whose sentence we are to rest, can be no other but the Holy Spirit speaking in the scripture.*

The last three sections of this chapter of our Confession are occupied in determining how we should use Scripture. We have seen in section viii. how Scripture should be used in dealing with the letter of the Word, whether original or translated. We have seen in section ix. how we must use Scripture in order to reach an understanding of its meaning or real contents. And now in section x. we have a statement in regard to the application of principles and views gained from Scripture to particular cases as they occur. When controversies arise, materials for a decision must be sought in that rule of faith which, according to the second section of this chapter, has been identified with the inspired Scriptures; but for the application of the contents of this rule in detail, we want something more than a mere impersonal written standard. Romanists, insisting upon the need of a living personal arbiter, find this in the person of the Pope speaking authoritatively for the church. Protestants find it in the presence of the Holy Spirit accompanying the Word, but not becoming identified with it. We have here, then, the illumination of the Spirit which was spoken of in section vi. as necessary for the saving understanding of Scripture. Controversies therefore must be decided, and the conclusions of church councils as well as all individual opinions must be tested by an appeal to the tribunal of Scripture, from which we shall hear the living Spirit speak; and in all ages, believing hearts, while reading the Word, will listen to what the Spirit saith unto the churches. [Comp. Prof. Robertson Smith's *The Old Testament in the Jewish Church*, Lect. i. pp. 11-16.]

CHAPTER II.

OF GOD, AND OF THE HOLY TRINITY.

I.—*There is but one only living and true God, who is infinite in being and perfection, a most pure spirit, invisible, without body, parts, or passions, immutable, immense, eternal, incomprehensible, almighty, most wise, most holy, most free, most absolute, working all things according to the counsel of his own immutable and most righteous will, for his own glory; most loving, gracious, merciful, long-suffering, abundant in goodness and truth, forgiving iniquity, transgression, and sin; the rewarder of them that diligently seek him; and withal most just and terrible in his judgments; hating all sin, and who will by no means clear the guilty.*

II.—*God hath all life, glory, goodness, blessedness, in and of himself; and is alone in and unto himself all-sufficient, not standing in need of any creatures which he hath made, not deriving any glory from them, but only manifesting his own glory in, by, unto, and upon them: he is the alone fountain of all being, of whom, through whom, and to whom, are all things; and hath most sovereign dominion over them, to do by them, for them, or upon them, whatsoever himself pleaseth. In his sight all things are open and manifest; his knowledge is infinite, infallible, and independent upon the creature, so as nothing is to him contingent or uncertain. He is most holy in all his counsels, in all his works, and in all his commands. To him is due from angels and men, and every other creature, whatsoever worship, service, or obedience he is pleased to require of them.*

The fact of God's existence had been assumed as the basis of the Confession. That God has spoken,—this is the first proposition, and all subsequent propositions claim to be simply an unfolding of what He has spoken. This chapter professes to bring together what He has said directly regarding Himself.

The first two sections are inseparable. They treat of God,—His unity and His attributes.

(1.) In the writings of the purer and more spiritual of the classical writers, both poets and philosophers, we find an eager groping after the notion of the divine unity. They could not rest in the thought that a power which divides itself among several beings is the last and highest of all. That God is one, was the most profound conviction of their souls, as the discovery of this one God was the deepest longing of their hearts. If only the idea of God as absolute and personal were reached, or even approached, the necessary consequence would be the affirmation of the unity of God. Indeed, the assertion of the divine personality — the acceptance, that is to say, of theism — leads necessarily to the recognition of deity as absolute being, and this, again, if intelligently entertained, to the adoption of a strict monotheism. From a purely speculative point of view, therefore, the doctrine that there is but one God may be placed beyond dispute among all who reject naturalism, whether in the form of materialism or in the form of pantheism. It is to be noted, however, that our Confession states this doctrine in immediate connection with the claims which God makes upon His creatures for their undivided homage. We are taught to regard Him as the fountain of our being, as the Lord who has dominion over us, the Searcher of our hearts, and the God to whom our worship, service, and obedience are due. Thus the doctrine of His unity is emphasized chiefly in order that we may recognise in Him the God with whom alone we have to do.

(2.) The enumeration of the divine perfections, given in these sections, is singularly lengthy; but there is no discoverable method or principle of arrangement. The attributes of God have been variously classified by different dogmatists; but as no attempt at classification is made in our Confession, we need take no notice of such schemes. In looking over the list of the divine perfections given here, we are at once impressed with its decidedly biblical aspect. Some of the terms indeed are not immediately biblical in form, but seem rather to have been derived from the Scholastic theology,—for example, Immense, Fountain of all being,—yet the ideas indicated by such phrases are very easily translated into well-known expressions of Scripture. On the other hand, we find that, repeatedly, complete clauses are introduced in their full and precise scriptural form. Without seeking formally to classify that which was not originally the subject of classification, we may notice the careful balancing of seemingly contrasted elements in the divine character, most free and most absolute, most loving, etc., and withal most just, etc.; and also the singular accuracy with which God's self-sufficiency is maintained consistently with a living and evangelical view of His relations to His creatures. To say of God that He does not derive any glory from His creatures, is at first sight somewhat startling, till we observe that the term 'derive' is used in its most exact and proper sense of obtaining from an original source. Thus understood, it is evident that from the creature no glory of God can take its origin, for that glory had its origin earlier in the very creative act itself. This is further explained in the phrase which follows : ' manifesting His own glory in them.' Whatever in the creature contributes to the glory of God, is really an exhibition of God's own glory by means of His own creation. Thus we have a sober and moderate view of man's place and dignity. It is man's high honour and privilege to show forth God's glory, yet he is prevented from boasting, as if he himself, God's creature, were regarded as of himself and independently contributing to the glory of God. Man has dignity, but it is creaturely dignity ; he can make no claim of being profitable to God. It was the grave error of mysticism to insist in an unguarded manner upon the importance of the creature for the Creator. One of the mystics of the Middle Ages ventured plainly to say, what is generally implied in those systems of mysticism that tend to Pantheism, 'God has as much need of me as I of Him.' As intended by its author, this saying is not impious ; but it is over-bold, and liable to be understood in accordance with the ordinary meaning of its terms in a sense that is nothing short of blasphemy. Our Confession, on the other hand, goes carefully upon scriptural lines. It is only the ignorant idolater that can suppose that God needs anything, and yet, when His creature turns away from Him, He cries out, 'How shall I give thee up?' Martensen has indicated a fair solution of the difficulty of reconciling God's independence of and interest in His creatures, by assuming that God has a twofold life, 'a life in Himself of unclouded peace and self-satis-faction, and a life in and with His creation.' To the one, we refer all those scriptural expressions that imply limitation, or the appearance of human passions in God ; and to the other, which is the fundamental and ultimately triumphant form of the divine life, we ascribe that complete independence of His creation in which the attribute of unchangeableness is fully realised.

In the closing part of these sections, we have the three doctrinally most important of the divine attributes—Sovereignty, Omniscience, and Holiness—expressed in almost the very words of Scripture, and their meaning explained with immediate reference to man. We find here a fit prelude to the chapter on the Divine Decrees. There is here a forecast of the same pure type of doctrine, and the exhibition thus made of God's sovereignty, absolute knowledge, and all-pervading holiness, yields all the essential elements of the doctrine of Predesti-nation which characterizes the whole of the Calvinistic symbols. In the declaration regarding God's sovereignty, the charge of arbitrari-ness is guarded against by the declaration as to the holiness of all His counsels. The perfection of His knowledge is explained, on the one hand, by His access to the most secret springs of human action, and on the other, by His independence of all creaturely conditions which introduce elements of contingency.

III.—*In the unity of the Godhead there be three persons, of one sub-stance, power, and eternity; God the Father, God the Son, and God the Holy Ghost. The Father is of none, neither begotten nor proceeding; the Son is eternally begotten of the Father; the Holy Ghost eternally proceeding from the Father and the Son.*

1. The unity of God is maintained in this section from quite another point of view from that of the former section. It was there made with an immediately practical, here it is made with an immediately doctrinal, intention. The unity of the Godhead is affirmed in full view of the personal distinctions which are recognised in it. In this unity, without disturbing it, those distinctions exist. We are not, however, to separate between Godhead and God. This had been attempted by the mystics when they distinguished the incomprehensible, abstract unity of God that cannot be revealed, and the manifestation of God under personal acts. It reappears in Delitzsch, who speaks of a divine *doxa* as the undivided centre of trinitarian distinctions. The same tendencies are found in Gregory of Nyssa and others, who viewed the relations of the divine unity to the divine personal distinctions as similar to the relation of the general notion of humanity to individual men. But just as the fulness of humanity is never realised in any individual, if we follow out such analogies, the fulness of divinity could not be found in each of the three persons. According to the indications of Scripture we may simply speak of one God, the unity of the Godhead, not bringing into view the distinctions of Father, Son, and Spirit, nor yet assuming any abstract ground separate from these distinctions. The God of Israel, who certainly related Himself to His people in a trinitarian manner, says, ' Hear, O Israel, the Lord our God is one Lord.'

2. Equality in substance, power, and eternity is ascribed to each of the divine persons. We must guard against a false subordinationism in regard to the second and third persons of the Trinity. We distinguish between the essential Godhead in which each person equally shares, and the economic manifestation of personal distinctions in which a relative subordination is ascribed to the Son and Spirit. The true doctrine is expressed by Jesus Himself when He explains His relation to the Father—in respect of being and dignity, I and the Father are one ; in respect of economic manifestation in the work of redemption, my Father is greater than I. More generally the equality of the persons is shown in this, that for each of them are claimed the same names, attributes, actions, and worship. In Scripture we have indications both of the essential and of the economic Trinity. We have the essential Trinity when the Word is shown to be God from the beginning and with God, and when the Spirit that searches the deep things of God is also acknowledged to be God. We have the economic Trinity in the whole scheme and work of redemption, and specifically in the terms of the Baptismal Formula and the Apostolic Benediction.

Various attempts were made by the Fathers to represent by means of some familiar figure what seemed to them expressible in the grand mystery of the Trinity. Gregory of Nyssa (331-394) regarded the name God as applicable to the Godhead, just as the name man is applicable to mankind as including individual men : the three persons are **one** Godhead, as individual men constitute the human race. Such a representation evidently endangers the doctrine of the Divine Unity, and tends towards Tritheism.   Augustine (354–430) thought to discover in man created in the image of God an analogue of this divine mystery.   In the union of being, knowledge and love, or of memory, intelligence, and will, in man, he seemed to find an analogy to the trinity of persons in the Godhead.   Here evidently there is a danger of falling into a monarchian conception of God, and through a doctrine of abstract unity of losing the thought of personal distinctions.   Similar analogies were attempted by most of the Schoolmen with no better success.   It may be interesting to refer to two attempts made by poets of the Middle Age to elucidate this doctrine.   Dante's (1265–1321) figure of the rainbow, its reflection, and a radiance proceeding from both, is well known (*Parad.* xxxiii. 107–112).   Less known, but interesting as illustrating old English thought and also for its own quaint ingeniousness, is that of Langland in *Piers Plowman's Vision* (written about 1362), where he represents the trinity of persons by the parts of the human hand—fist, palm, and fingers :—'Thus are thei alle but oon, As it an hand weere, And thre sondry sightes In oon shewynge, The pawme for it putteth forth fyngres, And the fust bothe.'   [The whole section is instructive and highly suggestive. Read especially ll. 11,644–11,865]   Hooker (*Eccles. Polity,* v. 51) expresses the doctrine thus . 'The substance of God with this property *to be of none* doth make the Person of the Father ; the very self-same substance in number with this property *to be of the Father* maketh the Person of the Son ; the same substance having added unto it the property of *proceeding from the other two* maketh the Person of the Holy Ghost.   So that in every Person there is implied both the substance of God which is one, and also that property which causeth the same person really and truly to differ from the other two.'

CHAPTER III.

OF GOD'S ETERNAL DECREE.

I.—*God from all eternity did, by the most wise and holy counsel of his own will, freely and unchangeably ordain whatsoever comes to pass : yet so, as thereby neither is God the author of sin, nor is violence offered to the will of the creatures, nor is the liberty or contingency of second causes taken away, but rather established.*

We have here, in the first place, a clear statement of the doctrine of the divine decrees, and in the second place, this doctrine guarded against misapprehension and abuse.

(1.) The divine decree (which being divine must have the divine characteristics—most wise, most holy, most free, most absolute) has reference to all that occurs, whether good or bad.   It is the divine plan of the world comprising not only the holy counsels of the divine will, but also whatever evil designs might arise threatening to thwart the divine will. The earliest expression given to this decree, with which we have to do, is the divine utterance in the creation of man: 'Let us make man.' The creature so called into being has given him the power of originating, if he will, that which opposes the will of the Creator. In thus ordaining the existence of man, God ordains the possibility of a contradiction to His own will; and in this statement, we have all that we can say of the mystery in regard to the divine permission of evil (See note on following section.)

(2.) The principle which characterises the saving clause of the section is this:—God cannot contradict Himself. He cannot ordain sin, for that is the contradiction of Himself, and though He has ordained the being who has originated sin, yet He is in no sense the author of it. He cannot override human freedom, for He is the author of this freedom, and if He ignored it, He would contradict and nullify His own creative act. 'Violence is done to the will of a creature,' says John Knox, 'when it willeth one thing, and yet by force, by tyranny, or by a greater power, it is compelled to do the things which it would not.' God cannot infringe upon the freedom of action in second causes, for this would militate against the good faith of the appointment of means, both natural and spiritual, which men are commanded to use. The divine decree has no determining power over us. As Milton says of our first parents, 'Foreknowledge had no influence on their fault, Which had no less proved certain, unforeseen.' In all this we find the conclusions of last chapter reproduced. What God is, determines what God's counsels are.

II.—*Although God knows whatsoever may or can come to pass upon all supposed conditions; yet hath he not decreed anything because he foresaw it as future, or as that which would come to pass upon such conditions.*

This statement seems to have been introduced in order to guard against a theory of conditional decrees, put forth by the Jesuits, and adopted by Arminians and others, under the name of *scientia media*. In history a certain event happens, and the result is important for all subsequent ages. If that event had happened not then, but at another time, and in different circumstances, the future course of history would have been quite different. There are various instances of important events, far-reaching in their consequences, being made dependent upon certain conditions. If David would remain at Keilah, he would be delivered up to Saul. If the sailors remained not in the ship, Paul and his fellow-travellers could not be saved. [See this subject admirably treated by Dr. Chalmers, *Sermons preached in St. John's, Glasgow*, Sermon on Acts xxvii. 31.] According to the theory of *scientia media*, these conditions depend wholly upon the human will, and, as possibilities, are outside of the divine purpose. What God foreknows is the result which will follow the fulfilment or non-fulfilment of these conditions. A certain freedom is thus vindicated for man at the expense of the perfection and the reality of the divine knowledge. The doctrine of the Confession is the doctrine of the Reformed Churches, and maintains that nothing in the future is undetermined before God. David and Paul were told what the conditions of their safety were ; but the fulfilment of these conditions was already part of the divine plan, and had a place unconditionally in the divine decree.

III.—*By the decree of God, for the manifestation of his glory, some men and angels are predestinated unto everlasting life, and others foreordained to everlasting death.*

IV.—*These angels and men, thus predestinated and foreordained, are particularly and unchangeably designed; and their number is so certain and definite, that it cannot be either increased or diminished.*

The decree of God is here set forth, (1) As to its end,—the manifestation of God's glory ; (2) As to its issue in regard to mankind,—the distinguishing between the saved and the unsaved ; (3) As to its finality,—it is in itself unchangeable, and in regard to its objects perfectly definite. That everything is designed to contribute to God's glory is regarded as an accepted and undisputed position ; and because God Himself is unchangeable, His decree with all that is really included in it must also be unchangeable. The one point requiring special attention here is the distinction made in the use of the terms predestination and foreordination. It is to be noticed that nowhere throughout this chapter is the term predestination used in reference to the evil, while foreordination is used of good and evil alike. Now there is nothing in the words to vindicate such a distinction in their use ; but evidently the Westminster divines wished to make it clear that they regarded God's proceedings in regard to the elect, and in regard to the reprobate respectively, as resting upon entirely different grounds. In the one instance, we have an act of grace, determined purely by God's good will ; in the other, an act of judgment, determined by the sin of the individual.

V.—*Those of mankind that are predestinated unto life, God, before the foundation of the world was laid, according to his eternal and immutable purpose, and the secret counsel and good pleasure of his will, hath chosen in Christ unto everlasting glory, out of his mere free grace and love, without any foresight of faith or good works, or perseverance in either of them, or any other thing in the creature, as conditions, or causes moving him thereunto ; and all to the praise of his glorious grace.*

This section speaks of election unto life ; and in it we have brought together those characteristic points which really distinguish our Standards as at once Evangelical and Calvinistic. The section that follows only develops the principle already contained in this. The two special points in it are these : The election is in Christ, and this election takes place without reference to any merit on the part of those elected, whether of faith or of works.

(1.) 'Chosen in Christ' is an expression used by the Apostle Paul, when he insists upon the eternity of the choice, the pure grace that characterises it, and its destination to everlasting glory (Eph. i. 4). The whole section in our Confession is thoroughly Pauline in language as well as in doctrine. While the cause of the election is God's free grace, the condition which had to be fulfilled, and which had necessarily a place in the eternal decree, is the substitutionary merit of Christ.

(2.) When we have repudiated the notion of a conditional decree, we have guarded against the error of supposing that election, which is an eternal act, is grounded on any foreseen faith. Besides, this would render our deliverance no more of grace but of works,—faith being in that case regarded as the meritorious cause of our election and subsequent salvation. The evangelical doctrine as expressed in this sentence of our Confession, and as similarly stated in a later chapter (see chap xi. 1), views faith not as the cause of election, but as one of its most blessed fruits, sovereignly ordained as the condition of our justification.

VI.—*As God hath appointed the elect unto glory, so hath he, by the eternal and most free purpose of his will, foreordained all the means thereunto. Wherefore they who are elected being fallen in Adam, are redeemed by Christ; are effectually called unto faith in Christ by his Spirit working in due season; are justified, adopted, sanctified, and kept by his power through faith unto salvation. Neither are any other redeemed by Christ, effectually called, justified, adopted, sanctified, and saved, but the elect only.*

There is here a careful definition of the relation which God, who disposes all things according to His own good pleasure, bears to established conditions and appointed means. He has chosen some to life everlasting, but for the attaining of this end He has appointed certain means ; and the reality of the election to glory rests in this, that He effectually applies to the elect the means that He requires to be employed. The redemption of the elect is complete, inasmuch as all the means are efficiently used ; and this redemption is only of the elect.

The statement that they who are elected being fallen in Adam are redeemed by Christ, is interesting as having given occasion to a keen debate in the Assembly. It had been proposed to say at this

D

place, 'To bring this to pass God ordained to permit man to fall.'
From the *Minutes of Assembly* we learn that Calamy very reasonably
objected to these words, that they made man's fall the means of the
divine decree.   God allowed man to fall in order to show man his
neediness, and so magnify the riches of His own grace in redemption.
This was the theory of Supralapsarianism.   It has appeared under
varying forms of expression in all ages of the church.   The fall is
sometimes spoken of even as a happy occurrence (*felix culpa*), inasmuch as it led to the manifestation of redeeming grace.   This notion
is contrary to the whole tenor of Scripture, where sin is consistently
regarded as the cause of misery, and God's holy love, which could
never work by sin, the alone cause of man's redemption through Christ.
This Supralapsarian view was held by Twisse, the president of the
Assembly, and by other members, but their opinions were not pressed.
The theory of Infralapsarianism, which the language of our Confession here naturally suggests, seems to have most countenance from
Scripture, which speaks of the subjects of the divine decrees as
already sinners.

VII.—*The rest of mankind, God was pleased, according to the unsearchable counsel of his own will, whereby he extendeth or withholdeth mercy as he pleaseth, for the glory of his sovereign power
over his creatures, to pass by, and to ordain them to dishonour
and wrath for their sin, to the praise of his glorious justice.*

The subject of this paragraph is a peculiarly solemn one, and the
Westminster divines have expressed themselves in regard to it with
admirable caution and moderation.   The doctrine here enunciated
has provoked much opposition, and the representations given of it
by objectors are generally little better than gross caricatures.   In
his *History of European Morals* (vol. i. p. 96), Lecky has absurdly
coupled together, in his condemnation, the Romish doctrine of the
Damnation of Unbaptized Infants and the Calvinistic doctrine of
Reprobation.   In very pleasing contrast to the passionate and irrational tirades of rejectors of the doctrine stands the calm and
measured statement of our Confession.   It is an utter misrepresenta-
tion of the doctrine of our Standards when election and reprobation
are described as respectively the cause of faith and the cause of
unbelief.   Calamy, one of the members of the Assembly, preaching
before the House of Commons, said that it was most certain that
God was not the cause of any sinner's damnation ; and others of the
divines called attention to the way in which the vessels of wrath are
only said to be fitted for destruction without naming by whom,—God,
Satan, or themselves ; whereas God Himself is expressly said to have
prepared His chosen vessels of mercy unto glory.   (Compare Mitchell,
Introduction to *Minutes of Assembly*, p. lxi.)   It is well to distinguish carefully between election and reprobation, according to the

distinctions indicated in the statement now before us. The points of difference have been very clearly stated by Amesius. Under three heads he has summed up (*Medulla*, l. xxv. 31–40) the particulars in which reprobation is not to be co-ordinated with election. (1.) In reprobation the end in view is not properly the perdition of the creature, but the manifestation of God's justice ; while in election the immediate end is not so much the glory of God's grace as the salvation of men. (2) In reprobation certain men are ordained to show forth God's justice, there being no communication of anything, but only privation ; while in election God communicates good in His grace. (3.) In reprobation there are simply granted the means whereby God's justice may be exhibited, the permission of sin and hardening in sin, so that reprobation is not the cause of condemnation nor of the sin that merits condemnation ; while in election as the electing love of God, we have the cause not only of salvation, but also of all that leads to it.

VIII.—*The doctrine of this high mystery of predestination is to be handled with special prudence and care, that men attending the will of God revealed in his word, and yielding obedience thereunto, may, from the certainty of their effectual vocation, be assured of their eternal election. So shall this doctrine afford matter of praise, reverence, and admiration of God, and of humility, diligence, and abundant consolation, to all that sincerely obey the Gospel.*

The use of this doctrine, which is here called a high mystery, is limited to those who savingly avail themselves of the Gospel. What we are required to do is to observe and obey God's revealed will. This produces in us a certainty of our effectual calling, and this certainty again assures us of our election (comp. John vii. 17). Let us love in deed and in truth (1 John iii. 18, 19) ; and hereby we know that we are of the truth, and shall assure our hearts before Him. It is after declaring his remembrance of the works of faith and labours of love of the Thessalonians, that Paul (1 Thess. i. 4) affirms his knowledge of their election. In treating of such matters as those treated of in this chapter of our Confession, we should carefully observe the limitations and the sage counsel of this last section. 'In these matters,' said the martyr Ridley (as quoted by Eadie *On Ephesians*), 'I am so fearful that I dare not speak further ; yea almost none otherwise than the text does, as it were, lead me by the hand.' [Read a beautiful argument and earnest appeal in behalf of caution and reverence in dealing with divine mysteries in Hooker, *Ecclesiastical Polity*, Bk. i. chap. ii.] If this manner of using the doctrine be observed, it will prevent the possibility of any fatalistic tendency, whether in the form of indolent indifference or hardening despair.

CHAPTER IV.

OF CREATION.

I.—*It pleased God the Father, Son, and Holy Ghost, for the mani-*
festation of the glory of his eternal power, wisdom, and goodness,
in the beginning, to create, or make of nothing, the world, and
all things therein, whether visible or invisible, in the space of six
days, and all very good.

The Confession here speaks of the plan of the world and the creation
which accomplished that plan as the work of the Godhead. Some
have too hastily sought to determine which of the divine persons
ought to be regarded as officially concerned in the creation. Calvin
is too intent upon the fanciful parallel suggested by the reference in
the original narrative to the Word of God as instrumental in the
creative act, and the use of the same name as applied to the Son of
God in the prologue to the Gospel of John. In recent times this
view has been frequently re-asserted. It, however, undoubtedly tends
toward a Sabellian theory of the Godhead. A parallel is also
sometimes maintained between the natural creation and the divine
revelation in Christ, on the ground that the world was created by the
Word of God. But while refusing to regard creation as in any
exclusive manner the work of the Son, we must not view its accomplishment as effected apart from the Son. If we say we believe in
God the Father, Almighty, Creator of heaven and earth, just because
we view the Creator as Father, we cannot conceive the work as
wrought apart from the co-operation of the Son and the Spirit.

To make of nothing is used simply to explain the word create.
The presupposition of all created things is found in the unbounded
sources of the divine omnipotence. In idea there originally exists
nothing but God. The statement of our Confession is nothing more
than a denial of the eternity of all that is not God. Let it be noted
that 'nothing' is not represented as the source of the creation,—*ex*
nihilo nihil fit. The idea or notion of thing is necessarily a temporal
idea, and out of time, before the beginning of time, it cannot be
conceived.

Much unreasonable opposition has been shown against the
retention in our Confession of the statement, 'in the space of six
days.' It might be answer enough to those who thus complain, to
remark that their complaint must tell equally against the Scriptures,
and also that whatever fair explanation can be given of the scriptural
account is equally available for that of the Confession. This has
been from earliest times a much debated point from the side of
science and from the side of theology. Philo regards the scriptural
expression as indicating merely the succession and order of events.
This notion gained general acceptance in the Christian church, and

with sundry modifications is the view now generally entertained. The early Protestant theologians are commendably cautious here, and while generally not denying, do not affirm the view that the world was created in six successive days. Some (as Amesius, *Medulla*, l. viii. 28) suggest that the active creative periods were six natural days, with indefinite intervals between them. So also Martensen says (*Christian Dogmatics*, p. 117) : 'Each new day dawned when the time was full, when all the conditions and presuppositions of its dawn had been developed.' This theory is not in Scripture nor in the Confession, but it is not inconsistent with either ; and this ought to show how little such a statement as that complained against in our Confession excludes fairly-attempted schemes of reconciliation with discovered facts of science. However, it should be observed that the notion of the six days as indicating the order of succession is still as obnoxious as ever to men of science. One period seems to overlap the other ; and it appears utterly inconceivable, as well as unscientific, that the works represented as belonging to one creative day should be declared finished, and then an immense period intervene before the work of the next day should be finished ;—that creations should remain for ages in themselves perfect, yet absolutely without the conditions of their efficient operation. The student of God's Word need not pledge himself to any theory. The statement of the Confession is purely biblical. 'According to the more obvious interpretation of the first chapter of Genesis, this work was accomplished in six days. This therefore has been the common belief of Christians. It is a belief founded on a given interpretation of the Mosaic record, which interpretation, however, must be controlled not only by the laws of language but by facts. This is at present an open question. The facts necessary for its decision have not yet been duly authenticated. The believer may calmly await the result.' (Hodge, *Systematic Theology*, vol. i. p. 557.)

II.—*After God had made all other creatures, he created man, male and female, with reasonable and immortal souls, endued with knowledge, righteousness, and true holiness, after his own image, having the law of God written in their hearts, and power to fulfil it; and yet under a possibility of transgressing, being left to the liberty of their own will, which was subject unto change. Beside this law written in their hearts, they received a command not to eat of the tree of the knowledge of good and evil; which while they kept, they were happy in their communion with God, and had dominion over the creatures.*

The image of God, according to the statement of this section, is evidently intended to include moral endowments (knowledge, righteousness, and holiness), and the capacity for receiving divine

impressions,—all, in short, that affords a ground for human responsibility. These characteristics, it will be observed, are taken from the
description of the new man. This is quite legitimate, for the new
man is represented as a renewal after the image of Him that created
him. Our Confession further indicates that communion with God
and dominion over the creatures are those consequences of the
possession of the divine image that are immediately lost in the fall.
We may therefore identify full human consciousness with the divine
image in man, if we are prepared to maintain that this consciousness, when possessed in its completeness, includes intellectual, moral,
and religious elements. We shall then find the ground of man's
dominion over creation in his possession of these endowments. His
superiority is the condition of his supremacy. [Consider wherein man's
true dignity consists. See Pascal's *Thoughts on the Greatness of Man.*]

When, therefore, Romanists make the divine image to consist in
free-will, they simply seize upon that in the original constitution of
man which renders change of condition possible. The law in the
heart, and power to fulfil it, together constitute man's original
righteousness; which we regard as an essential element in man's
being, and not as a merely superadded gift. It was only to a
creature possessing in his very nature this moral character that God
could address the commands of a moral law—commands which
might be obeyed or disobeyed on ethical principles. This possession
of an alternative choice distinguishes the subject of moral from the
subject of mere natural law. Man's true dignity is thus seen to
consist in his personal moral power. Positive law in the form of an
express command may bring into view man's relation to that law
written in the heart, just as a well-chosen question may test one's
proficiency in a whole department of science.

The original condition is described as one of happiness. There
are two extremes which ought to be guarded against. [Consult
Martensen, *Dogmatics,* § 78.] An exaggerated Augustinianism tends
to regard the primitive innocence as perfected holiness; while
thoroughgoing Pelagianism confounds this original innocence with
the absence of all spiritual manifestations. Our Confession does not
indicate the degree of this original happiness. It is, however, a
mutable state, and could therefore be enhanced by being rendered
permanent as the reward of obedience. [On the image of God in
man, see the third chapter of Dr. Laidlaw's *Bible Doctrine of Man,*
especially p. 134.]

CHAPTER V.

OF PROVIDENCE.

I.—*God, the great Creator of all things, doth uphold, direct, dispose,
and govern all creatures, actions, and things, from the greatest*

even to the least, by his most wise and holy providence, according to his infallible foreknowledge, and the free and immutable counsel of his own will, to the praise of the glory of his wisdom, power, justice, goodness, and mercy.

The subject of this chapter is really the problem of the present day. God's relation to the world is the most absorbing question under discussion in popular theology. It is here that the relations of science and religion present themselves for examination.

Providence is coextensive with creation. The constant and consistent recognition of God's care as extending to all persons and things both great and small is characteristic of Christian theology. The popular doctrine of Pagan antiquity acknowledged a divine oversight only of the more important persons and events. 'Great things,' says Cicero, 'the gods care for, small things they neglect.' In the doctrine of Providence the distinction is generally observed between preservation and government—the continued existence and the regular development of creation.

(1.) God in providence upholds His creation. The personal act of God in His preservation of the world is distinguished from those impersonal agencies in nature (influences, powers, tendencies) which Pantheistic modes of thought represent as supporting and continuing the life and properties of created beings; and also from the action of mere natural energies originally set in motion by the first cause, according to the theory of the Deists.

(2.) God in providence directs, disposes, and governs His creatures. The personal God is here represented as exercising His attributes of wisdom and power on behalf of His creation. He directs to a given end, disposes separate acts and individuals so as to produce certain determinate results, and so controls all actions, separate or complicated, that, in ways that are holy and wise, His own counsels are accomplished.

II.—*Although, in relation to the foreknowledge and decree of God, the first cause, all things come to pass immutably and infallibly; yet, by the same providence, he ordereth them to fall out according to the nature of second causes, either necessarily, freely, or contingently.*

Here we have stated the relations of divine providence and human freedom. It is the simple statement of a mystery that cannot be explained : the consistency of a belief in the supreme all-determining first cause, and a belief in the reign of law in nature, and the freedom of action among intelligent creatures. We know, from revelation and also from partial and fragmentary intimations of experience, that these two positions are true ; how perfectly to reconcile them, we do not know. [Show from practical instances that our knowledge of fact is not dependent on our knowledge of a theory to account for the fact.] When we consider the laws of nature we find in these a wondrous flexibility, so that the results may be modified by the rearrangement and new combination of these laws. All such combinations are not fully known to us, nor can we estimate exactly the results of certain arrangements of established laws. Hence to us the results obtained must often be contingent and uncertain. What is variable to us, however, is certain and determinate before Him from whom these several laws and their combinations take origin as the expression of His will.

III.—*God in his ordinary providence maketh use of means, yet is free to work without, above, and against them, at his pleasure.*

This section maintains the possibility of miracles. In His providence God is pleased usually to employ means which either by association or by inherent quality are recognised as immediately fitted to secure the result aimed at. Yet such employment of means is wholly dependent upon the divine pleasure. In describing the divine freedom in regard to the accomplishment of God's work, our Confession determines the essential idea of a miracle. It consists in God's working without, above, and against ordinary means. This exactly corresponds with the scholastic description of a miracle as something *præter naturam, supra naturam, contra naturam.* In the seventeenth and eighteenth centuries the *contra* was frequently omitted. Properly understood, however, no miracle can be conceived as so against nature as to be unnatural. Yet in a sense the *contra* is indispensable. 'If an effect occurs,' says Steinmeyer, 'which certainly would not have happened if the laws of nature had been left to their own organic processes, we must then agree that it has resulted *contra leges naturæ*' (Steinmeyer, *Miracles*, p. 14). In this 'against,' therefore, there is no conflict of powers, but the suspension of the operation of ordinary laws. We should distinguish between the definition of a miracle as something against nature,—meaning thereby the actings of the ordinary laws of nature,—and the contention of those who deny the miraculous, that the idea of the miracle is a notion of something contrary to reason. Our phrase 'law of nature' expresses our expectation of the uniformity of nature. Mozley, however, argues that as the expectation of general uniformity is no dictum of reason, a miracle cannot be regarded as an offence against reason. 'And now,' he concludes, 'the belief in the order of nature being thus, however powerful and useful, an unintelligent impulse, of which we can give no rational account, in what way does this discovery affect the question of miracles? In this way : that this belief not having itself its foundations in reason, the ground is gone on which it might have been maintained that miracles as opposed to the order of nature were opposed to reason.' (*Miracles*, p. 38.)

IV.—*The almighty power, unsearchable wisdom, and infinite goodness of God, so far manifest themselves in his providence, that it extendeth itself even to the first fall, and all other sins of angels and men, and that not by a bare permission, but such as hath joined with it a most wise and powerful bounding, and otherwise ordering and governing of them, in a manifold dispensation, to his own holy ends; yet so as the sinfulness thereof proceedeth only from the creature, and not from God; who, being most holy and righteous, neither is nor can be the author or approver of sin.*

This section treats of the relation which God's holy providence bears to the appearance of evil in the world. The Westminster divines take advantage of every opportunity to renew the assertion first made in chapter iii. 1, that God is not the author of sin. It is often brought as a charge against the doctrine of Divine Providence, that it makes God the immediate cause of evil. Here note a distinction between God as Creator and God as Providence. In creating, His action is causal; in providence, His action necessarily has respect to the characteristics and rights of His own creatures. Evidently, if there were anything bad in creation, the responsibility would rest upon the creator; but in the domain of providence something bad may result from the presence of an element not belonging to the divine creation. [Consult Calderwood, *Handbook of Moral Philosophy*, pp. 256–259.] God's relation to evil is only permissive, and not causal; yet not merely permissive in the sense that He in no wise interferes in the course of a sinful development. When, from other causes than divine, evil has originated, God is pleased to show His power over sinners and their sins, and so orders these, whether by limiting their scope or directing their course, that the end is not the overthrow, but the establishment of His holy rule. All things take place according to the will of God in providence. He wills the trials which test men and under which many fall. The assertion that God permits those falls which indicate failure under trial, is not inconsistent with the declaration that God would have all men repent and come to a knowledge of the truth.

V.—*The most wise, righteous, and gracious God, doth oftentimes leave for a season his own children to manifold temptations, and the corruption of their own hearts, to chastise them for their former sins, or to discover unto them the hidden strength of corruption, and deceitfulness of their hearts, that they may be humbled; and to raise them to a more close and constant dependence for their support upon himself, and to make them more watchful against all future occasions of sin, and for sundry other just and holy ends.*

God's dealings in providence with His own children often seem dark and severe. In these, however, when they are understood, He shows Himself wise, righteous, and gracious. The full contents of this section may be distributed under two heads.

(1.) Instruments in the hand of providence. According to the doctrine of the preceding section, God maintains His authority over all the powers of evil so that He can use their energies and overrule their actions for His own ends. Those evil powers which are permitted to assail God's own children are distinguished in the present section as manifold temptations and the corruptions of their own hearts; that is, temptations from without and from within. This distinction is not thoroughgoing. No temptation is wholly from without, and none wholly from within. There are Satanic and fleshly elements in all temptations. Under one form or another, and by the predominant use of one instrument or another, the great tempter, as the determined opponent of God, is found working. But just as material things are morally indifferent, and can form an element in temptation only when brought into relation to the heart and desires of man, so the endeavours of Satan can be regarded as temptations only when they come into contact with something within man to which they make appeal. In order to extinguish the very possibility of temptation in the regenerate, not the destruction of Satan, but rather the utter destruction of the corruption of the heart, is necessary.

(2) The purpose of God in permitting such trials is to remind His people of His hatred of sin, their own weakness, and the unfailing source of strength. (a) He shows His hatred of sin by chastising them so often as He finds it in them. It is the punishment of sin, but the spirit of the child recognises in it the action of the loving Father chastising that He may remove that which, if it remain, must call down eternal judgment. (b) He shows them their own weakness in their falls, especially when they fall at that very point at which they were regarded as particularly strong. (Illustrate from histories of Moses, Elijah, Peter.) 'Those who did eat the bread of angels,' says A'Kempis, 'I have seen delighting themselves with the husks of swine. There is, therefore, no holiness, if Thou, O Lord, withdraw Thine hand. No wisdom availeth, if Thou cease to guide. No courage helpeth, if Thou leave off to defend. No chastity is secure, if Thou do not protect it. No vigilance of our own availeth, if Thy sacred watchfulness be not present with us.' (c) The ultimate end which God intends by all His trials of His people is the firm establishment of their trust in Him. They are driven out of sin and self, that they may find rest and strength in God. The believer's fall brings into view the horrors of perdition; his restoration brings into view the glories of heaven.

VI.—*As for those wicked and ungodly men, whom God as a righteous judge, for former sins, doth blind and harden, from them he not only withholdeth his grace, whereby they might have been enlightened in their understandings, and wrought upon in their hearts; but sometimes also withdraweth the gifts which they had, and exposeth them to such objects as their corruption makes occasion of sin; and withal, gives them over to their own lusts, the temptations of the world, and the power of Satan: whereby it comes to pass, that they harden themselves, even under those means which God useth for the softening of others.*

This section shows how judicial hardening in sin is embraced in the divine providence. Such hardening is judicial, inasmuch as it is the act of the righteous God upon men on account of their former sins. This dispensation of providence might be fully described as the withholding of divine influences. This, however, must be understood as implying not only that further gifts of grace have ceased, but also that what was given before has been withdrawn. Reproofs and warnings have been addressed in vain, and now in judgment God causes these to cease. 'When He sees,' says Calvin, 'that it is altogether lost labour to reason any longer with us, and that His admonitions have no effect, He holds His peace, and by this teaches us that He has ceased to make our salvation the object of His care.' Just as in nature organs not exercised lose their power, so that even when the outward conditions of their exercise recur they can no longer be taken advantage of; so in the moral and religious sphere spiritual capacities unused are removed, or become so inoperative that the means of grace prove altogether ineffectual. And while by guilty and determined resistance of grace men may deprive themselves of opportunities of grace, so by guilty fostering of their corruptions they may render themselves incapable of resisting temptations through the presentation of certain objects. God in judgment allows the presentation of those objects before which the Spirit-forsaken and self-weakened soul will assuredly fall. The outward means of grace may be continued, but to those from whom the Spirit has been judicially withdrawn they are no longer means of grace, nor yet merely things indifferent. The gospel message that does not prove a savour of life must prove a savour of death. The prayer of faith would bring deliverance; but they cannot believe, and they cannot pray. The hardened soul may be thoroughly convinced of the truth of revelation, and may feel himself lost; but the divine influences needed to soften the heart, and to form in it sincere desires, have been withdrawn. The day of grace may be shorter than the term of the earthly life. Rollock describes in his own vigorous way the influence which Satan gains over such a one: 'The first turne that ever he dois he bindis him. Quhat bindis he, his handis or his feit? Na, he lets them louse, and lets him work on with them his awin ruine, and run on to his awin perditioun. Bot he bindis his eies, or rather pullis them out, that the miserabill bodie may not see the gracious face of Christ. Quhairfour is he send to him? The cause is nocht onlie in the ordinance of God, bot in the cative himself that malitiouslie repynis to the licht, and will not receive the gospell, thairfoir the God of hevin sends the Divil, to put out his eies that he suld not see' (*Works*, vol. i. p. 394). ' Self-will brings on itself the curse of blindness' (Sophocles, *Antigone*, 1028). This miserable state shows itself in the form either of hardened indifference, or of violent and inconsolable despair. [Illustrate from the case of the man in the iron cage, in the *Pilgrim's Progress;* or by an instance from real life in the case of the apostate Spira in the Italian Reformation. Show, on the other hand, how far the state-ment may be received, that while there is life there is hope (Eccles. ix. 4); and what practical application of it is legitimate.]

VII.—*As the providence of God doth, in general, reach to all creatures; so, after a most special manner, it taketh care of his church, and disposeth all things to the good thereof.*

The distinction has generally been made between a general and a special providence. It is, however, really improper to distinguish between the care God has for His universe and the care He has for individual creatures. The whole is conserved only in so far as each individual is maintained in the place and for the time assigned to him in the general plan. But this distinction is valid when employed to indicate a difference between God's care for the world, and God's care for those whom He has chosen out of the world. The exercise of divine providence upon those without is made to tell directly upon the development of His own elect. All things work together for good to those who love God. What falls upon the hardened for judgment, secures the advancement and further development of the saved. While, therefore, in regard to the world at large, we have in provi-dence a mingled display of mercy and judgment, we have in regard to the elect unmingled mercy,—what seems judgment being fatherly chastisement. The course of providence in the world is not regular and progressive; but the course of providence among the redeemed is steadily directed to their establishment and growth in grace. The course of the world is, according to the divine plan, always sub-ordinate to that of the church.

CHAPTER VI.

OF THE FALL OF MAN, OF SIN, AND OF THE PUNISHMENT THEREOF

I.—*Our first parents being seduced by the subtilty and temptation of Satan, sinned in eating the forbidden fruit. This their sin God was pleased, according to his wise and holy counsel, to permit, having purposed to order it to his own glory.*

We have here an extremely condensed statement regarding the nature and the origin of sin.

(1.) Sin consists in disobedience. As to the ultimate essence of this disobedience and the spirit out of which it springs, our Confession gives no indication. Two theories have been proposed. According to the one, sin is sensuousness—giving an undue place to the lower elements of our nature. For this we might find some apparent ground in the material nature of the original test. According to the other theory, sin is selfishness—giving prominence to the spiritual forms of evil desire. For this we might find support in the spiritual element introduced into the first temptation in the promise of equality with God. This latter theory has been ably maintained by Muller (see *Christian Doctrine of Sin*, Part I. c. iii. secs. 2-4). The statement of our Confession embraces the principles of the sensuous and of the selfish theories, which, viewed separately, do not render a complete account of the nature of sin. The biblical declaration that this first sin consisted in eating the forbidden fruit, gives a broad basis for our doctrine of the nature of sin as at once sensuous and selfish—transgression of the law and disobedience against God. [As against the charge that the particular act of disobedience is trifling, compare remarks on Shibboleth in Dods' *Israel's Iron Age*, pp. 111-115.]

(2.) The origin of sin. No complete answer can be given to the question, How was it possible for the holy creatures of God to fall? The Confession therefore does not attempt this, but confines itself to repeating the statements of Scripture referring to this. The fall was brought about by the seduction of Satan, which could take place only under the divine permission; but Satan's seduction and God's permission secured only the possibility of a fall—the realising of it is man's own act [see chap. ix. 2]. Our first parents sinned : it was their sin. God's relation to human sin, therefore, has to do with the possibility of it only, and not with its reality. This must be our doctrine if we hold by the personality of God. It is only when, drifting into Pantheism, we confound God and the universe, that we are forced to regard God as necessarily involved in the realising of the evil. And when thus evil is viewed as not only permitted but created by God, it in consequence loses for us its guiltiness. Much of our popular literature is pervaded by pantheistic tendencies, and sin is viewed in an unscriptural way as a limitation consequent upon our finite existence, a weakness inhering in our nature, unfortunate but inevitable.

II.—*By this sin they fell from their original righteousness, and communion with God, and so became dead in sin, and wholly defiled in all the faculties and parts of soul and body.*

The very terms employed in this section connect it closely with chapter iv. 2. The original condition is described as one of communion with God ; the present condition, as a fallen state of utter corruption. This doctrine of Total Depravity has been the subject of attacks in every age. In modern times, opposition to this doctrine has been manifested under the most contradictory. views of the original state of mankind. Rousseau in his own extreme and violent style denies anything like original sin. According to him, the state of nature is a state of innocence ; we have only to lay aside the results of a false culture and return to nature in order to have all imperfections and guilt removed. This notion had its day among the sentimentalists of the eighteenth century, but now it is seriously maintained by none. The other extreme is somewhat popular in our own day. Lubbock and his school regard the primitive condition as a state of general savagery. Whatever ill is yet present in man, and in human society, is the remains of this primitive state, and whatever good has been attained is the result of culture and civilisation. When this culture has become complete and universal, evil will have disappeared. The assumption of an original universal savage state has not been proved by Lubbock; and the array of professed discoveries of utterly savage peoples has been shown in detail to be unwarranted. This school of investigators has failed to bring forward a single undisputed instance of an utterly atheistic people—a race exhibiting none of the higher longings and beliefs of the human spirit. The biblical doctrine. as reflected in our Confession, maintains, in opposition to such a view, that man's original state was pure and noble—a condition, however, very different from that state of nature of which Rousseau had dreamed.

We find here, too, the distinctively Protestant doctrine in opposition to that of Rome. The loss suffered in the fall, according to Romish theologians, was simply that of a superadded gift, involving a certain general enfeebling of the nature. Protestant theology, on the other hand, regarding original righteousness, with the right and privilege of divine communion, as an endowment of man's nature, viewed the consequence of the fall as affecting the whole being of man. Original sin with the Romanists is the deprivation of a supernatural gift, and so is merely negative ; the Protestant doctrine regards it as the positive removal of what had been natural to man, the loss of which involves spiritual death and utter corruption.

III.—*They being the root of all mankind, the guilt of this sin was imputed, and the same death in sin and corrupted nature conveyed to all their posterity, descending from them by ordinary generation.*

The transmission of original sin. This section speaks of the consequences to the race of that original sin defined in the previous section. This consequence is twofold ; the imputation of the guilt of Adam's sin, and the derivation of a corrupted nature. The doctrine of the Confession is here most pronouncedly Augustinian and Anti-

Pelagian.   The controversy known as the Pelagian controversy was concerned with the question of the imputation of Adam's sin to his posterity.   This Pelagius denied, while Augustine affirmed it.   The Romish theologians have advocated a more or less modified Pelagianism; the Reformed Churches have generally maintained the Augustinian doctrine.   In regard to the utterance of our Confession here, it is to be noted that the imputation of guilt, because of the sin of Adam, is first mentioned and made prominent, and that the statement regarding the inheriting a corrupted nature comes after, and is made to rest upon the doctrine of Immediate Imputation.   What Müller (*Chr. Doctr. of Sin*, vol. ii. p. 334) claims for Lutheranism,—that it finds a real basis for mediate imputation in the positive depravity of individuals, and explains hereditary guilt on the principle of immediate imputation,— may be applied to this statement of our Confession.   Placæus is not supported, nor is he condemned. (See Introd. p 24.   Read also Dorner, *Hist. of Prot. Theol.*, ii. pp. 26–28.)   But Adam is viewed by the Westminster divines as not only natural but also moral head of mankind. He is natural head, and consequently from him as fallen we inherit a corrupted nature; he is moral head, and consequently the guilt of his sin is imputed to us.   To indicate in what sense Adam is regarded as the moral head and representative of his race, theologians have employed various figurative expressions.   Here our first parents are spoken of as the root of all mankind.   This figure corresponds well with the use of the symbol of the vine-stock by our Saviour.   [Compare John xv. 5 with Rom. v. 19: all in Adam=all men; all in Christ =all believers.]

IV.—*From this original corruption, whereby we are utterly indisposed, disabled, and made opposite to all good, and wholly inclined to all evil, do proceed all actual transgressions.*

This is a characteristic and summary statement of man's inability. [See a somewhat more emphatic statement in chapter xvi. 7.]   The doctrine here maintained is the necessary consequence of that already expressed in regard to original sin.   Where a Pelagian theory of sin is accepted, this doctrine of Human Inability is denied.   An Arminian view of sin leads to what has been called Synergism in a more or less developed form : man has not ability, for his nature has been weakened by the fall, but he can co-operate with the Spirit in doing good. The Westminster doctrine of sin as Total Depravity leads necessarily to the doctrine of Total Inability.   This inability, which, while the characteristic of our fallen nature, is essentially moral, involves the commission of actual sin.   Out of the heart, which has lost its original righteousness and is thoroughly corrupted, proceed evil thoughts and their consequences, which are here described as actual transgressions.   We cannot have original sin without actual sins following ; nor could we account for the beginning of actual sin apart from original corruption.

V.—*This corruption of nature, during this life, doth remain in those that are regenerated: and although it be through Christ pardoned and mortified, yet both itself, and all the motions thereof, are truly and properly sin.*

It is here affirmed that a particular element in original sin—the corruption of the nature—adheres to man even after regeneration; and that this remaining corruption in the believer is properly regarded as sin. The corruption of original sin is not in this life wholly removed by grace, but only its imputation. That imperfections remain in believers is surely beyond reasonable dispute. Scripture gives no countenance to Perfectionism. Paul represents perfection as the goal striven after in the earthly life, but only attained at the resurrection and in the heavenly existence (Phil. iii. 11, 12). The justification of the sinner, indeed, is complete, and this constitutes evangelical perfection. The believer's holiness is developing from stage to stage, and is complete at no point on this side the grave— when completed, it constitutes sinless perfection. [Read a very valuable paper—Rae, 'Christian Doctrine of Perfection,' in *British and Foreign Evangelical Review* for January 1876.] In the regenerate, says our Confession, the corruption of nature remains, denying legal or sinless perfection; through Christ it is pardoned and modified, affirming evangelical perfection. (For a most admirable application of this doctrine to devotional uses, see *Imitation of Christ*, chap. lv., 'Of the Corruption of Nature and the Efficacy of Divine Grace.') Sin is always exceeding sinful, and must be spoken of and treated as sin under whatsoever form it may appear. Paul does not suggest any new name for his indwelling corruption after his conversion to distinguish it from what had appeared in him before.

VI.—*Every sin, both original and actual, being a transgression of the righteous law of God, and contrary thereunto, doth, in its own nature, bring guilt upon the sinner, whereby he is bound over to the wrath of God, and curse of the law, and so made subject to death, with all miseries, spiritual, temporal, and eternal.*

The description of sin as involving the consequences here mentioned is very definite and comprehensive: original sin involving guilt as well as actual sin; and sin being viewed as comprising sins of omission and of commission,—transgression, that is, evasion of the law, and also being contrary, that is, actively committed offences against the law.

Sin thus comprehensively understood involves the sinner in guilt. Properly the guilt of sin does not mean its pollution, but its rendering us amenable to penalty. So here the sinner's guilt is his subjection to God's wrath, expressed in the curse and the doom of the law. It is misleading to speak of death as the natural lot of man; it is the ιot only of fallen man. It has been well said, ' Death is not from God as ordering nature, but is from God as avenging sin.' (Amesius, *Medulla*, l. xii. § 31.) Death, at least as man knows it, can only be regarded as the wages of sin. The miseries involved in this sin-wrought death are described as threefold—spiritual, temporal, and eternal. It is evident that the first includes the other two. Just as sin beginning in the spirit soon manifests itself in the flesh, so spiritual decay, which is the immediate consequence of sin, soon manifests itself in the debilitation of the body Death spiritual thus manifests itself outwardly, first of all, in temporal enfeeblement and death; and eternal death can be nothing else than the permanence of this spiritual death.

CHAPTER VII.

OF GOD'S COVENANT WITH MAN.

I.—*The distance between God and the creature is so great, that although reasonable creatures do owe obedience unto him as their Creator, yet they could never have any fruition of him as their blessedness and reward, but by some voluntary condescension on God's part, which he hath been pleased to express by way of covenant.*

In this statement the Westminster divines have distinctly connected their theological system with that known as the covenant scheme. The Fœderal theology (so called from *fœdus*, a covenant) was first thoroughly elaborated by Cocceius in the middle of the seventeenth century, who made the twofold covenant of works and of grace the middle point of his system. This principle, however, was generally recognised in Reformation theology, and is in reality, though not always in phraseology, reproduced in modern systems reflecting the spirit of the Reformation.

The propriety of making the notion of a covenant the central point in theology has been disputed by many who are thoroughly in sympathy with the doctrinal substance of the covenant theology. The conclusion really depends upon the proved adequacy or inadequacy of the notion as a category to comprehend all the essential points of theology. In our Confession no one principle has been adopted according to which the distribution of the whole matter should be made. It follows, as is appropriate in a Confession, and almost inevitable, the local method,—treating severally the main heads of doctrine without closely articulating them. But the importance of the covenant relation is acknowledged as affording a convenient principle of arrangement for the doctrines of grace. (Compare with this, chapter xix.) The representation of the relation between God and man by means of the notion of a covenant is undoubtedly scriptural. It has biblical warrant both from express statements, and still more convincingly from a fair induction of scripture facts. [Give illustrations from Scripture of these two statements.]

In this opening section the origin of the covenant relation between God and man is very clearly set forth. It is not implied that man was under no obligation until this covenant agreement had been made, but it is rather affirmed that man, simply as creature, owed obedience, and that the entering into a covenant was on God's part a voluntary act of condescension. Man's obligation was not thereby originated, nor rendered more strict, but, for man's sake, through God's grace, it was rendered more evident. The law written on the heart (see chap. iv. 2), when viewed by itself, represents the state of man before any covenant was entered into; the receiving of the command not to eat of the fruit of the tree represents the position under the covenant. Absolute obedience is required in either case. God, therefore, does not bind man under any new obligation, but by some voluntary condescension he places Himself under covenant obligations and promises. The difference between the position of God and the position of man in the making of the covenant is well stated by Patrick Gillespie in his work, *Ark of the Testament Opened:* 'It is condescension on God's part that He will enter in covenant with man, and make promises to him for anything performed by man, which He might require of him by His sovereignty over him; yet there is not such a freedom upon the other part, whereby man may indifferently engage with God or not, as pleaseth him; for he is otherwise engaged to God than by covenant, yea, he is so far engaged to his Maker that he is bound to the same things by God's giving him a law, which are required of him by covenant, and when it pleaseth the Lord to propound to him a covenant upon whatsoever terms and conditions it be, he is bound to accept the terms and to obey the same.' (Page 100.)

II.—*The first covenant made with man was a covenant of works, wherein life was promised to Adam, and in him to his posterity, upon condition of perfect and personal obedience.*

The statements of this section have been for the most part anticipated by the previous chapter. What is special is the exact expression given to the condition of the covenant of works. The obedience rendered must be perfect; so far as this covenant goes, if only it be broken, there can be no recognition of degrees in the breach. The obedience must be personal; no special aids are promised or allowed, but by the creature's own natural strength is the covenant to be fulfilled. Grace may have been shown in the condescension that entered into a covenant, but the covenant in its terms is not of grace but of works.

Many who do not deny that we have scriptural ground for treating the doctrine of Redemption under the category of a covenant of grace, object to the statement that a covenant was made with Adam. They regard this as going beyond Scripture. It should be noticed, however, that the idea of a covenant is necessarily present to the mind when we conceive the probationary state of our first parents as described to us in Scripture. The very same doctrine as is stated here is expressed before (chap. vi. 1–3) in more strictly biblical terms; it is here simply reproduced in another connection. The arrangement with Adam possesses all the characteristics of a covenant. At the same time, as Dr. Hugh Martin has very properly remarked, the covenant of works comes into view from the analogy and antithesis to the covenant of grace, rather than from any very express or direct evidence of its own. Our perception of the principle of the covenant of works depends upon our perception of the principle of the covenant of grace. 'It will uniformly be found,' says Dr. Martin, 'that the theology which is meagre in reference to the covenant of grace, is still more so as to the covenant of works. The first Adam was but the type of Him that was to come, the shadow of the last Adam. And where the last Adam is little recognised as a Covenant Head, there can be little reason or inducement to recognise the first in that light either.' (*Atonement*, p. 35.)

For the race, the covenant of works, regarded as a dispensation, ended with the address of the evangelical promise to fallen Adam; for the individual sinner, it only ends when, by union with Christ, he enters into the covenant of grace.

III.—*Man by his fall having made himself incapable of life by that covenant, the Lord was pleased to make a second, commonly called the Covenant of Grace: whereby he freely offereth to sinners life and salvation by Jesus Christ, requiring of them faith in him, that they may be saved; and promising to give unto all those that are ordained unto life his Holy Spirit, to make them willing and able to believe.*

The covenant of works being set aside on account of the breach of its imperative condition, God was pleased in its place to make a new covenant, a covenant of grace. This covenant of grace was made with Christ as the second Adam; and therefore the condition of this covenant, properly speaking, is the satisfaction rendered by the obedience of Christ. He is the representative head of His church, and on His fulfilment of the condition of the covenant all those who are in Him as members share in the purchased blessing. In regard to man, however, the condition of this covenant is not their perfect obedience to the law, but faith in their covenant head; and the promise to those who fulfil this condition is the same as that given under the covenant of works on condition of obedience, that is, salvation. When the truth is thus carefully stated, the need is removed for distinguishing the covenant of redemption, as between God the Father and Christ, and the covenant of grace, as between God and the elect. This new covenant then, as related to us, is distinguished from the old, not only by the change in the condition from works to faith, but also in this, that a special promise of effective spiritual help is made to those who are ordained to life, so that this saving faith — the condition for them of this covenant — may be wrought in them.

The question may here be fairly raised, as to whether the idea of a covenant is really helpful in solving any difficulty regarding the substitution for us of Christ and His righteousness. To this it may be safely answered, that while it does not remove the difficulty, it affords a convenient scheme for the representation and collocation of well-established facts of scripture revelation. There seems good ground for maintaining with Dr. Martin, that many of the objections brought against the doctrine of the Atonement in recent times would lose their plausibility if, in presenting the doctrine of the Atonement, care was taken to make prominent those characteristics which belong to it when viewed under the category of the covenant.

It ought to be noticed, that while the covenant is said to be a covenant of grace, and its benefits said to be offered freely, this is not regarded as inconsistent with the appointment of certain conditions. This grace and this freeness are attributed to a covenant into which only those ordained to life enter, and that through the exercise of faith. The nature of this condition as pertaining to a covenant of grace is very clearly apprehended by Rollock as comprising faith with Christ and Christ with faith. ‘These three,’ says he, ‘are one in substance, the ground of the covenant of grace, the condition of it, and the cause wherefore God performeth the condition. Yet in reason they differ something. For Jesus Christ is the ground, being absolutely considered, without any respect of application unto us. But Christ is the condition of the covenant, as He is to be applied unto us, and must be embraced by faith, for every condition is of a future thing to be done. And the cause also of the performance of the covenant is Jesus Christ already embraced and applied unto us by faith.’ (*Treatise on Effectual Calling*, pp. 40, 41.)

IV.—*This covenant of grace is frequently set forth in the scripture by the name of a Testament, in reference to the death of Jesus Christ the testator, and to the everlasting inheritance, with all things belonging to it, therein bequeathed.*

It is here affirmed that the name Testament as given to the covenant of grace is appropriate on the twofold ground that there is a Testator, and that there are benefits bequeathed. This has been clearly and briefly expressed by Patrick Gillespie : ‘ So is the covenant of grace a testament, because the same things which the covenant requireth from us as conditions to be performed on our part, the same things are bequeathed to us among Christ's goods, which by His testament and latter will He disponed and left to His people absolutely.' (*The Ark of the Testament Opened*, p. 302.) What our Confession maintains is not the synonymity of two scripture words,— for the same word is rendered sometimes covenant, sometimes testament,—but the sameness of the idea conveyed.

V.—*This covenant was differently administered in the time of the law, and in the time of the gospel; under the law it was administered by promises, prophecies, sacrifices, circumcision, the paschal lamb, and other types and ordinances delivered to the people of the Jews, all fore-signifying Christ to come, which were for that time sufficient and efficacious, through the operation of the Spirit, to instruct and build up the elect in faith in the promised Messiah, by whom they had full remission of sins, and eternal salvation; and is called the Old Testament.*

VI.—*Under the gospel, when Christ the substance was exhibited, the ordinances in which this covenant is dispensed are the preaching of the word, and the administration of the sacraments of Baptism and the Lord's Supper; which, though fewer in number, and administered with more simplicity and less outward glory, yet in them it is held forth in more fulness, evidence, and spiritual efficacy, to all nations, both Jews and Gentiles; and is called the New Testament. There are not therefore two covenants of grace differing in substance, but one and the same under various dispensations.*

We have seen that the reign of the covenant of grace begins as soon as the condition of the covenant of works had been broken. The covenant of works can exist as an effective arrangement only for unfallen man. Adam being representative head of the race, his failure under the covenant of works is the failure of mankind. Fallen man, therefore, though formally under the covenant of works, stands not under the promise of this covenant, but only under the penalty of its breach. According to the doctrine of our Confession (xix. 1, 2), the law requiring strict obedience was a covenant of works for Adam. As such it continues to fallen man still unregenerate, promising life for works of perfect righteousness done by nature, and pronouncing doom on sin. To regenerate man under the dispensation of the covenant of grace the law presents itself as a perfect rule of righteousness.

In distinguishing the position of God's people living before the time of our Lord's appearing in the flesh, and that of those living after it, we ought, in order to avoid confusion, to employ the terms old and new dispensations, rather than old and new covenants. Some speak as if the covenant of works had been made not with

Adam, but with Abraham or Moses, thus identifying it with the dispensation of law in Israel. The law, however, is a dispensation of the covenant of grace, under which the same conditions appear, though differently administered. The Old Testament saints were not justified by the observance of a covenant of works, but in accordance with the conditions of the covenant of grace, which according to the eternal decree took historical origin when the promise of redemption was made to the fallen creatures. It was indeed necessary that in these different dispensations there should be differences of administration. Its earliest form was that of the promise referred to ; then its provisions were shown in fuller detail, and, in immediate application to the rise of particular needs, in prophecy, sacrificial ceremonies, sacramental ordinances, and other Messianic types. Yet the condition of salvation was essentially the same as that required under the later dispensation. It is said that Abraham was justified by faith, and that under the dispensation of the law only by shedding of blood was there remission of sins. The administration of this covenant of grace under the new or gospel dispensation, though still essentially the same, is fuller and clearer than that under the old dispensation. The ordinances are simpler just because the substance to which they refer is no longer hidden under a veil.

In chap. viii. 6 and in chap. xi. 6 the doctrines of this section are consistently carried out.

CHAPTER VIII.

OF CHRIST THE MEDIATOR.

I.—*It pleased God, in his eternal purpose, to choose and ordain the Lord Jesus, his only begotten Son, to be the Mediator between God and man; the Prophet, Priest, and King; the Head and Saviour of his Church; the Heir of all things; and Judge of the world; unto whom he did from all eternity give a people to be his seed, and to be by him in time redeemed, called, justified, sanctified, and glorified.*

The work which Christ has to do is described as that of a Mediator, and in the discharge of this office He acts in the threefold capacity of Prophet, Priest, and King, and has all power committed to Him. This latter characteristic may be reduced under the head of His kingly authority. We have then here to do simply with the threefold representation of Christ as to person and work. The distinction of the prophetic, priestly, and kingly elements in Christ's mediatorial work in so many offices is one with which we have become very familiar. It was hinted at by some of the Fathers, partially developed by the Schoolmen, and very generally adopted and carried out by theologians since the Reformation. Yet we must ever remember that in every official act of the Mediator there is something prophetic, something priestly, something kingly. It is the one person, the one Mediator between God and man, who is Prophet, Priest, and King; and in every mediatorial act His whole person is concerned. It is important, too, to notice that the idea of priesthood does not fully correspond to that of Christ's sacrificial work, inasmuch as that sacrifice, viewed as a supreme act of obedience, affords the most glorious revelation of God's will, and, viewed as a purely voluntary act on the part of Him who gave Himself, gives a most vivid representation of Christ's kingly power. Thus even in His death Christ must be regarded not only as Priest, but also as Prophet and King. The distinction, thus understood, is convenient and useful. When the unity of the person, who exercises these three offices, is clearly and vigorously maintained, we shall be able under the usual threefold division to present a most comprehensive view of the saving work of Christ.

II.—*The Son of God, the second person in the Trinity, being very and eternal God, of one substance, and equal with the Father, did, when the fulness of time was come, take upon him man's nature, with all the essential properties and common infirmities thereof, yet without sin; being conceived by the power of the Holy Ghost, in the womb of the Virgin Mary, of her substance. So that two whole, perfect, and distinct natures, the Godhead and the manhood, were inseparably joined together in one person, without conversion, composition, or confusion. Which person is very God and very man, yet one Christ, the only Mediator between God and man.*

We have here very clearly stated the doctrine of the distinctness of the natures and the unity of the person in Jesus Christ the Mediator. The careful and well-balanced statement of our Confession may be considered as guarding against two extreme views that troubled the early church. The heresy known under the name of Nestorianism sacrificed the unity of the person of Christ in order to maintain the completeness of His humanity, so that the supporters of it were charged with making two persons as well as two natures. This view was condemned at the Council of Ephesus in A.D. 431. There was now a recoil from this error, and the opponents of Nestorius, in their zeal for orthodoxy, sought to get as far as possible from the condemned heresy. As the result of this, Eutyches, exaggerating the position of Cyril the great opponent of Nestorianism, rushed to the other extreme of Monophysitism. The heresy known under the name of Eutychianism laid emphasis so extravagantly on the unity of the person, that the truth of the duality of natures was lost to view. This error was condemned finally at the Council of Chalcedon in A.D. 451. The Chalcedonian symbol gives a very complete expression to the orthodox doctrine in opposition both to Eutychianism and to Nestorianism ;

and in the statement of our Confession in the section before us it has been almost verbally reproduced. This doctrine rests wholly on revelation, and cannot be rationally explained. But as to the biblical doctrine there can be no doubt. The Son of man is perfect man; there is no defect in His humanity; for in all points He is made like unto His brethren. The Son of God is perfect God, and as such claims full equality with God. There is no such intermingling of these natures that the one is modified or impaired by the other. Nevertheless we have but the one person—the man Christ Jesus.

' Four principal heresies there are which have in those things withstood the truth : Arians, by bending themselves against the Deity of Christ; Apollinarians, by maiming and misinterpreting that which belongeth to His human nature; Nestorians, by rending Christ asunder, and dividing Him into two persons; the followers of Eutychyes, by confounding in His person those natures which they should distinguish. Against these there have been four most famous general councils : the council of Nice to define against Arians; against Apollinarians, the council of Constantinople; the council of Ephesus, against Nestorians; against Eutychians, the Chalcedon council. In four words, ἀληθῶς, τελέως, ἀδιαιρέτως, ἀσυγχύτως, *truly, perfectly, indivisibly, distinctly;* the first applied to His being God, and the second to His being man; the third to His being of both One, and the fourth to His still continuing in that one Both : we may fully by way of abridgment comprise whatsoever antiquity hath at large handled either in declaration of Christian belief, or in refutation of the foresaid heresies.' (Hooker, *Eccles. Polity,* v. 54.)

III.—*The Lord Jesus, in his human nature thus united to the divine, was sanctified ana anointed with the Holy Spirit above measure; having in him all the treasures of wisdom and knowledge; in whom it pleased the Father that all fulness should dwell: to the end, that being holy, harmless, undefiled, and full of grace and truth, he might be thoroughly furnished to execute the office of a Mediator and Surety. Which office he took not unto himself, but was thereunto called by his Father; who put all power and judgment into his hand, and gave him commandment to execute the same.*

In this section we have enumerated the qualifications found in the God-man for His mediatorial office, and his appointment of God to this work.

(1.) His equipment for the office of Mediator. To say that He had the Spirit bestowed on Him above measure, really comprises all that has to be said on this point. This Spirit is the Spirit of wisdom and knowledge. He is also the Spirit of holiness; and the unlimited outpouring of the Spirit upon the Saviour secures the sinless perfection of our Lord's humanity. The gift of the Spirit above measure to the Son is the result of the Father's love, and involves His thorough equipment for His work (John iii. 34, 35).

(2.) His designation to this work. His appointment is from the Father, and in His official position He receives authority and power from the Father. This is the true biblical doctrine of Subordinationism. In essential being, the Son is the equal of the Father; in relation to His official work, the Son takes on Him the form of a servant. And just as truly as the form of God in Him was a reality, so also was the servant's form. He receives from God what He will exercise for men. Throughout Scripture, and especially in the writings of Paul, the name of God is used not to designate the Godhead generally, but rather the Father. In a specially noticeable manner, in Trinitarian passages, the Father is called God (1 Pet. i. 2); in the benediction and other such expressions. So Paul says Christ is God's, the head of Christ is God. Our Lord Himself, under varying phrases, repeatedly declares, 'Of myself I can do nothing;' 'My Father is greater than I.' All these expressions of Christ regarding Himself, and of the apostles about him, refer not to His eternal existence, and in no way militate against it. It is as Mediator, as manifested to us in the incarnation, that He subordinates Himself to His Father's will, in order that the Father, by the execution of that will, may secure our salvation.

IV.—*This office the Lord Jesus did most willingly undertake; which that he may discharge, he was made under the law, and did perfectly fulfil it; endured most grievous torments immediately in his soul, and most painful sufferings in his body; was crucified, and died; was buried, and remained under the power of death, yet saw no corruption. On the third day he rose from the dead, with the same body in which he suffered; with which also he ascended into heaven, and there sitteth at the right hand of his Father, making intercession; and shall return to judge men and angels at the end of the world.*

His discharge of the office of Mediator is described as—(1.) Voluntary; (2) Embracing both doing and suffering; (3.) Extending to both states of humiliation and exaltation.

(1.) The voluntariness of Christ's service is everywhere throughout the Scriptures made most clear. He willingly undertook the office of Mediator, assuming a nature which was subject to weakness and pain, and a position that necessarily involved suffering unto death. This voluntariness of the Redeemer does not mean that He allowed Himself to show occasional signs of weakness and fatigue, and permitted temptation to approach Him. It applies rather to His willing entrance into and continuance upon that path in which all these real trials had of necessity to be encountered.

(2.) A distinction has been made between the active and the passive obedience of Christ. It is here clearly shown that Christ as Mediator yielded a perfect obedience to God throughout a life in which He was called both to do and to suffer. Those two forms of obedience are so blended in the life of Christ that they cannot really be separated. In every official act of the incarnate Son there is something of suffering, and in every instance of suffering there is some work done. To His active obedience belongs His sinlessness, but His perfect fulfilment of the law is to be regarded not as rendered for Himself in order to deliver Him from death, but for man ; and thus His active obedience is coupled with His sufferings to constitute His work of satisfaction. Only Socinians maintain that He required as a man to obey the law for Himself in order to secure personal merit.

(3.) The work of the Mediator is described as carried out in both states of humiliation and exaltation. And just as in the case of the distinction between active and passive obedience, so also here, we should be careful not to think of the two states as completely separable. In what we regard as the state of humiliation there is peculiar exaltation and glory. In the Epistle to the Hebrews, our Lord's tasting of death for men is described as His coronation in glory and honour (chap. ii. 9). This passage has been applied by several able exegetes immediately to the state of exaltation, but it is much more in accordance with the whole scope of the passage to interpret it of the exaltation inherent in the outward lowliness of the Mediator. Humiliations are experienced at every stage of the work of the Mediator, but the office itself is unspeakably dignified, and the appointment to such an office is the most conspicuous favour. ' It is the honour and glory of being appointed to the high office of apostle and high priest of the Christian profession, the Moses and the Aaron of the new dispensation. That office doubtless involves humiliation, inasmuch as it imposes on Him who holds it the necessity of tasting death ; but even in that respect His experience is not exclusively humiliating. For while it is a humiliation to die, it is glorious to taste death for others ; and by dying to abolish death, and bring life and immortality to light.' (Bruce, *Humiliation of Christ*, p. 39.) In this section of our Confession, this truth of the glory that is visible amid, and even because of, humiliation in the historical development of our Lord the Mediator, is implied by the continuous history of the two states, the one gradually passing without hiatus into the other. In the grave—yet seeing no corruption : here is glory amid humiliation.

V.—*The Lord Jesus, by his perfect obedience and sacrifice of himself, which he through the eternal Spirit once offered up unto God, hath fully satisfied the justice of his Father; and purchased not only reconciliation, but an everlasting inheritance in the kingdom of heaven, for all those whom the Father hath given unto him.*

This section opens with the reassertion of the combination of the active and passive forms of obedience in the atoning work of Christ. This atonement is declared to be a perfect satisfaction to God's justice, and the securing of a sufficient title to an everlasting inheritance for those who believe. Our Confession does not say (although Hodge strangely affirms that it does) that by His sufferings Christ purchased for us reconciliation, and that by His fulfilling of the precepts of the law He purchased for us an everlasting inheritance in the kingdom of heaven. The precision with which this section is worded seems intended to guard against this partition of Christ's atoning work. It is most distinctly affirmed that by means of His whole work,—comprising His active and His passive obedience, —He satisfies justice, and purchases for us an inheritance. All the work was needed in order to render satisfaction, and when this satisfaction was rendered, it was seen to carry with it the eternal reward. According to strictly scriptural phraseology, the purchased inheritance is the company of the Redeemed. In the midst of them in the kingdom of heaven, Christ shall say, ' Behold I and the children whom God has given me.'

VI.—*Although the work of redemption was not actually wrought by Christ till after his incarnation, yet the virtue, efficacy, and benefits thereof, were communicated unto the elect in all ages successively from the beginning of the world, in and by those promises, types, and sacrifices, wherein he was revealed and signified to be the Seed of the woman, which should bruise the serpent's head, and the Lamb slain from the beginning of the world, being yesterday and to-day the same, and for ever.*

We have here a statement regarding the effects of the work of Christ on those who lived before His incarnation, the Old Testament believers. It has been already affirmed (chap. vii. 5), that by faith in the promised Messiah, the Old Testament saints had full remission of sins [compare what is said in regard to the implied limitation in the notes on Justification, chap. xi. 6]. The promise made immediately after the fall is regarded as the basis of all further revelations under the covenant of grace. The doctrinal utterances of the Old Testament believers as they are recorded in Scripture show that they exercised faith, were deeply conscious of sin, and understood the need and the reality of forgiveness. The doctrinal expressions in their devotions were just the same as those of believers in the present day — so thoroughly the same that believers now find that they can give most suitable utterance to the feelings of their devoutest moments by using the sweet and hallowed words of Psalmists and Prophets.

VII.—*Christ, in the work of mediation, acteth according to both natures; by each nature doing that which is proper to itself: yet, by reason of the unity of the person, that which is proper to one nature is sometimes in scripture attributed to the person denominated by the other nature.*

Lutherans maintain that, as a consequence of the intimate union between the two natures in the person of Christ, there is what they call *communicatio idiomatum,*—an interchange of properties between the two natures. They apply this principle only to the imparting of divine properties to the human nature, and so they claim for our Lord's humanity certain attributes of deity. This section of our Confession asserts the true Reformed doctrine, that each nature in the one person of Christ retains its own properties, and does its own peculiar work. If this doctrine be not asserted, we lose the idea of the perfection of those natures. Our view of Christ's humanity becomes purely Doketic; He is man only in appearance. For if properties of deities, such as omnipotence, omniscience, and omnipresence, are to be attributed to the human nature of Jesus, then it is evidently something very different from ours, and His experiences of human weakness in body and spirit cannot prove helpful to us. We hold, therefore, that the human nature of Christ is true human nature with no intermixture of divinity;—that literally He has become one with us, that He was made like unto His brethren. At the same time, we must constantly affirm the reality of the union of those two natures in the one person. Hence we find in Scripture that where a property belonging strictly to one nature is attributed to the *person,* the name used may be one taken from the other nature. The person is the God-man; now what is wrought by the God-man according to His human nature is sometimes attributed to the Son of God (Rom. v. 10), and what is wrought according to His divine nature is attributed to the Son of man (John iii. 13, vi. 62). Yet these interchanges are comparatively rare in Scripture, and generally the designation most characteristic of the circumstance or act is used. And the reason for the occasional departure from the usual phraseology lies in this, that when we regard the Saviour in His person as Mediator, we rise above distinctions of the natures, and seeing that the one nature as well as the other is a necessary and constituent element in His personality, the names derived from the several natures may be applied indifferently to the person. This evidently is very different from a confusion in regard to the actions proper to the different natures.

VIII.—*To all those for whom Christ hath purchased redemption, he doth certainly and effectually apply and communicate the same; making intercession for them; and revealing unto them, in and by the word, the mysteries of salvation; effectually persuading*

them by his Spirit to believe and obey; and governing their hearts
by his word and Spirit; overcoming all their enemies by his
almighty power and wisdom, in such manner and ways as are
most consonant to his wonderful and unsearchable dispensation.

In the Westminster Assembly there was a long-continued debate
regarding the redemption of the elect only by Christ. Calamy and
several distinguished members inclined to a modified form of the
doctrine sometimes called Universal Redemption,—holding that
' Christ did pay a price for all, with absolute intention for the elect,
with conditional intention for the reprobate in case they do believe,
that all men should be *salvabiles non obstante lapsu Adami;* that
Jesus Christ did not only die sufficiently for all, but God did intend
in giving of Christ, and Christ in giving Himself did intend, to put
all men in a state of salvation in case they do believe.' In view of
such a statement, however, it is important to guard against the
notion, which seems in some quarters to gain favour, that the work
of Christ merely renders God reconcileable, ready to be reconciled
to men generally, and that in this sense the sufferings of Christ
secured the redemption of the whole world. This is unscriptural;
and the immediate result of such a notion is the false doctrine
repudiated by the apostle, that by works of righteousness that we
have done God has saved us. The statement in our Confession
is cautiously expressed. It is simply an anticipation of the doctrine
of Effectual Calling. It really leaves untouched the question of the
worth of Christ's work, which is surely in itself infinite, and thus,
viewed in its essential worth, abundantly sufficient to satisfy the
justice of God for the sins of the whole world. Arminians hold a
theory that has been called Acceptilatio, according to which the
death of Christ had no expiatory power in itself, but God was pleased
to reckon it satisfactory. The Westminster divines heartily repudiated such a notion, and maintained the doctrine of a full satisfaction rendered by Christ's death. Passing from the question of
the intrinsic value of Christ's life and sacrifice, this section of our
Confession determines the extent of its actual application, limiting
this to the elect, who are the effectually called. The merit of Christ
which is without measure is sufficient for the reconciliation unto
God of all those whom the Father has given unto Him. It is worthy
of notice that in the wisdom of our fathers attention is directed,
both in this section and also in the fifth section, to the sufficiency of
Christ's work for all His own, yielding to them a precious ground
of comfort; not to its limitation, which might foster in them an
undue self-gratulation, and an offensive and hurtful spirit of self-
righteous exclusiveness.

CHAPTER IX.

OF FREE-WILL.

I.—*God hath endued the will of man with that natural liberty, thai it is neither forced, nor by any absolute necessity of nature determined, to good or evil.*

There are two rival philosophical theories of the will, the Libertarian and the Necessitarian, either of which may be held quite consistently with the statement of this section of our Confession. According to the former, the will has a self-determining power; according to the latter, self-determination of the will is denied. Among theologians who accept this Confession and at the same time maintain the doctrine of Philosophical Necessity, are Chalmers and Edwards. They maintain that self-determination of the will is utterly untenable as a philosophical theory, and that upon such a hypothesis we lose all grounds of certainty, and endanger the doctrines of Divine Providence and Foreknowledge. They reject therefore at once the notion of self-determination of the will, the liberty of indifference, and the contingency of volitions (see Edwards, *Freedom of the Will*, Part II.). Cunningham has admirably shown that it is unwise to hamper our theological system by absolutely binding up with it any purely philosophical theory, and that the Westminster divines avoided this error (*Reformers and Theol. of Reform.* pp. 511, 512). The doctrines actually maintained in this section of our Confession are these :—(1) That the general constitution of man's nature has not been so changed that the power of choice, which forms an essential element in the very idea of a moral agent, has been taken away; and (2) That no outward force has been exercised to deprive man of this endowment. There is no necessity from the nature of the human will to choose evil. Man is free from any compulsion; and so the determination to evil is his own act of will. It is held that such a statement as this lays a sufficient basis for the doctrine of Human Responsibility. The conservation of this important truth forms the practical reason for a properly-conceived doctrine of the Freedom of the Will. One of the characters met by Dante in Purgatory, having defended the doctrine of Free-Will, concludes, 'If, then, the present race of mankind err, seek in yourself the cause and find it there.' (*Purgatorio*, xvi. 66–85.) The affirmation is made in the Confession that the will is a real and not a mere phantom power. It has its own legitimate place in the human constitution. 'Appetite,' says Hooker, 'is the Will's solicitor, and Will is Appetite's controller.' [The whole section may be read here with profit, *Eccles. Polity*, Book I. chap. vii., 'Of Man's Will, which is the thing that laws of action are made to guide.']

The four following sections, as most commentators seem to have

observed, describe the condition of the human will in choosing between good and evil, according to man's fourfold state—in innocence,
in sin, in grace, and in glory.

II.—*Man, in his state of innocency, had freedom and power to will
and to do that which is good and well-pleasing to God; but yet
mutably, so that he might fall from it.*

Man's will in its original purity was efficient for good, and yet
from its very nature arose the possibility of the loss of this efficiency.
When man was first called to exercise his power of will, he was
surrounded by good, and he himself was in sympathy with it. In
the good he lived and moved. Yet there was in this a certain
bondage of the will to good. Man must have his freedom
vindicated, and this he could have only when an opportunity had
been afforded him of independently attaching himself to good or to
evil. In the exercise of this liberty he chose to free himself from
righteousness, and to attach himself dependently to evil. There was
a need be for the presentation of a choice; there was no need be
for the particular choice actually made. An opportunity for change
was given. Indeed, a change must be made; unfree goodness—a
mere childish innocence — must be changed for something free,
which may be either righteousness or sin. In the state of innocence,
therefore, there was, first of all, an increased fellowship with good,
which had straightway to be personally and freely ratified, or else to
be personally and freely repudiated.

III.—*Man, by his fall into a state of sin, hath wholly lost all
ability of will to any spiritual good accompanying salvation; so
as a natural man, being altogether averse from that good, and
dead in sin, is not able, by his own strength, to convert himself,
or to prepare himself thereunto.*

This section treats of the bondage of the human will in the fallen
state. Loss of power to will what is good is regarded as an immediate consequence of sin. The sinful state involves aversion to good,
and spiritual death; and in consequence, the loss of ability to do
anything toward his own conversion. Under the covenant of works
there is thus no hope for fallen man. By his own strength,—by the
unaided exercise of his own faculties implanted in him as a creature,
—man could in innocence will and do God's pleasure. This he has
lost by sin. Our Confession speaks of this loss as a loss of ability
to will what is good. Edwards warns us against the literal signifi-
cation of the term ability. 'The thing wanting,' he says, 'is not a
being able, but a being willing. There are faculties of mind and
capacity of nature, and everything else sufficient, but a disposition;

nothing is wanting but a will.' This statement well accords with
that given in the first section of this chapter.

The will of man under sin is weak, but this has been determined
by its own act. The blame, therefore, of all that happens on account
of our weakness of will falls upon ourselves because we voluntarily
resigned our strength. 'We finally fall into the abyss,' says
Rousseau (and his own miserable experience sadly illustrates the
truth of his words), 'saying to the Almighty, Why hast Thou made
me so weak? But notwithstanding our vain pretext, He addresses
our conscience, saying, I have made thee too weak to rise from the
pit, because I made thee strong enough not to fall therein.' Hence
it is that man may be described as in one sense free, and in
another, unfree. He is free, as we have seen, from all outward con-
straint, and also from all inner necessity of nature; but he is unfree
in regard to his evil inclination which is the product of his own will.
Yet he has freely come under obligation to this evil inclination, and
for the formation of this inclination by which he is now enslaved he
is himself responsible.

The special religious interest in the statement before us lies in
this, that it affords a ground for the doctrine that we owe our salvation wholly to divine grace. In so far as the accomplishment of
God's pleasure is concerned, it is necessary that God should work
in us, not only to do, but also to will.

IV.—*When God converts a sinner, and translates him into the state
of grace, he freeth him from his natural bondage under sin, and
by his grace alone enables him freely to will and to do that
which is spiritually good; yet so as that, by reason of his
remaining corruption, he doth not perfectly nor only will tha
which is good, but doth also will that which is evil.*

We have here the condition of the will described in the case of
a sinner saved by grace. Deliverance of the human will from the
bondage of sin is viewed as purely an act of divine grace. To
establish this doctrine, both Luther and Calvin, in the interest of
the cardinal doctrine of Protestantism, Justification by Faith only,
felt called on to discuss in special and elaborate treatises the doctrine of the Bondage of the Human Will. This natural bondage can
be undone only by supernatural grace. What grace does, however,
is not merely to restore to man the ability to will good which he
possessed before the fall. This would be merely to place the individual in that state of probation in which the head of the race had
failed. This would not be desirable. If Adam failed, there is no
reason to suppose that any individual among his descendants, if
again placed on trial, would succeed. What God actually does by
His grace in conversion, is to place the Redeemed under the covenant
of grace. No longer by his own strength is he required to will

what is good, but by God's grace he is enabled to will and to do God's pleasure. His condition is not now probationary, but confirmed.

But while it is maintained that the condition of the will in the regenerate is confirmed, this only applies to its general tendency or ultimate destination. There are fluctuations in the actual working of the will under grace. Indwelling sin prevents alike the perfection and the constancy of a good will. The most powerful expression ever given to this truth is found in Rom. vii. In that chapter we have set forth, not the essential and normal experience of a Christian, but rather the outlines of an occasional experience not inconsistent with a genuine Christian character and condition—an experience that can be understood only from the Christian standpoint. Sin which, though indwelling, is repudiated by the believer as not himself, nor anything that he would wish to tolerate, is yet recognised as working in a direction contrary to that of the renewed will. 'There is,' says Delitzsch, 'as our every-day experience teaches us, in our life referred to God, a region pervaded by grace, and a region only, so to speak, shone upon by grace. Certainly, in the regenerate person, an all-powerful might of good shows itself effectual; but, opposed to it, there is also a power of evil, which, although overcome, is still constantly needing to be restrained.' (*Biblical Psychology*, p. 455.) Even during such experiences, however, the believer realizes in that grace which he actually has in possession a power which will finally prevail over and completely remove every corrupting element from his nature.

V.—*The will of man is made perfectly and immutably free to do good alone in the state of glory only.*

There are in this section two statements. It is said that perfect freedom of will to do good is realized in heaven, and that this perfection is realized only there. This latter statement necessarily follows from what was said in the last section regarding the imperfection of saints during the earthly life.

To speak of the will as immutably free may seem at first sight a contradiction in terms. Reflection, however, will show that it is quite consistent with the scriptural view of freedom to predicate of it immutability in doing and willing good, and that only when this immutable condition of the will has been reached can its state be regarded as perfect. An act of freedom brings us into a condition of freedom. By a free act we choose between good and evil, and choosing good we thereby become free from evil. We therefore have no longer any reference to evil; we are free from it, no longer under its dominion. The alternative of choice has ceased. Having put away the one side of the alternative, there is nothing left to appeal to the renewed will but good only. This is the Christian ideal; not perfectly attained unto on earth, but realized in the state of glory. (How far would the distinction here apply to the condition of the saint on earth, and in heaven,—*posse non peccare*, and *non posse peccare ?*)   When we say that all evil is excluded from the heavenly state, which surely is our chief certainty as regards that state, we must consider the statement of this section self-evident.   We have through grace freely excluded evil.   On earth its dominion, but not its presence, is excluded ; in glory the exclusion is absolute.   This is simply one feature of the divine nature that is imparted to the glorified saint.   He is like God his Saviour in this ; he cannot, because he will not, sin.   He cannot look upon sin, for he looks only on Him in whom is no sin ; he cannot will to do evil, for he has willed that evil be shut out for ever.

CHAPTER X.

OF EFFECTUAL CALLING.

1.—*All those whom God has predestinated unto life, and those only, he is pleased, in his appointed and accepted time, effectually to call, by his word and Spirit, out of that state of sin and death in which they are by nature, to grace and salvation by Jesus Christ ; enlightening their minds spiritually and savingly to understand the things of God ; taking away their heart of stone, and giving unto them an heart of flesh ; renewing their wills, and by his almighty power determining them to that which is good ; and effectually drawing them to Jesus Christ ; yet so as they can come most freely, being made willing by his grace.*

This section does not speak of general, but only of efficacious grace.   The common operations of the Spirit are referred to in the fourth section.   Preparatory grace (*gratia præveniens*) is recognised, by means of which the soul is awakened, rendered susceptible to impressions, placed in circumstances advantageous, and brought under the influence of the means of grace.   This was what older practical divines called the law-work.   [Illustrate from the experience of Augustine prior to his conversion as described in his *Confessions ;* from that of Halyburton in his *Memoirs ;* or from that of Christian before he reached the Cross.]   All these preparatory movements are operations of the Spirit.   Yet they may be all opposed, and by the reprobate are actually rejected.   The awakened are not always led on to conversion ; not all the called are chosen.   The good presented by the Spirit may be received only to be perverted ; the means of grace used as a cloak to sin.   The condition of the awakened soul is therefore a critical one.   'Here he is placed in that critical and testing position in which he may resist grace.   He may be unwilling to surrender himself self-denyingly to the obedience of truth, although he was willing for a season to rejoice in its light ; or by indolence he may let slip and lose the acceptable time of grace ; or by self-will he may arrest the awakening in its progress, instead of letting it lead him on to regeneration.' (Martensen, *Dogmatics*, p. 385.) Those, however, who are predestinated unto life are enabled by the Spirit to use aright this prævenient grace. At the accepted time those preparations of grace take the form of efficient grace for those who are both called and chosen. From the scope of the present section it will be seen that the chapter on Effectual Calling forms an important and comprehensive division in theology. When its various contents are examined, we shall be able to appreciate the treatment given to it by such divines as Rollock, who under this head deals with such questions as the Word of God, Sin, Faith, Repentance, the Human Will, and Free Grace. All these subjects are referred to in the present section.

The effectual call is distinguished from the general call by this, that it is to salvation. It is simply the carrying out of the provisions of the eternal decree.

The effectual call is accomplished by means of the Word and Spirit. These two powers are here conjoined, not identified. It is the main error of the Arminians that they confound the agency of the Word and of the Spirit in conversion. They speak of the spiritual power of the Word, which by moral suasion effectually appeals to the heart and conscience; whereas Calvinists speak besides of the separate power of the Spirit, by which he works mightily on the human will.

What in effectual calling is wrought by Word and Spirit, according to our Confession, may be arranged under three heads.

1. Illumination. The call affects the intellect. Preparatory grace first passes into efficacious grace by producing spiritual enlightenment. This illumination involves the supplying of a new light, and not merely rendering clear and available something previously possessed. The effectually called sees sin in the light of God, and realizes his own position as a sinner. There is thus furnished, spiritual discernment of the truth. The light that shineth on all only lighteth upon some ; but, in the case of the effectually called, it enters into the man, and appeals to an organ or spiritual sense, by which it can be used.

2. Repentance. The call affects the heart. As the seat of the affections, the heart of the called is awakened to hate and to love— to hate what, by enlightenment of mind, he is enabled to discern as sin, and to love what, by the same influence, he recognises as holiness. The effectually called hates the darkness, and that which endures the darkness, and loves the light, and that which endures the light.

3. Renewal. The call affects the will. The Spirit in the effectual call not only overcomes the enmity and opposition of the will, but delivers from impotence, and imparts the power to will and to do

that which is good. This is the most completely determining act of the Spirit. 'Grace,' says Vinet, 'is a divine eloquence that persuades the free will.' By this power brought to it by the Spirit the will acquires a new tendency, and is enabled to make a free self-surrender to Christ.

These three operations of grace, which are only separable in idea, not in reality or in point of time, constitute together that effectual calling which finds its fullest expression in the union of the believer with Christ (*unio mystica*). The salvation that is by Christ is found at last to consist in rest in Christ.

II.—*This effectual call is of God's free and special grace alone, not from any thing at all foreseen in man; who is altogether passive therein, until, being quickened and renewed by the Holy Spirit, he is thereby enabled to answer this call, and to embrace the grace offered and conveyed in it.*

Care has been taken in this section to show that the doctrine maintained secures for man in regard to the will, the recognition of the active and the passive in its operations and condition. Man remains passive until quickened and renewed by the Holy Spirit. But the new man possesses the renewed will, and by the exercise of this new power he is able to give a hearty response to the call, and to embrace the offered grace. The theologians at Dort (1618) give in their canons a clear definition of this doctrine, avoiding the extremes that in the interests of grace deny freedom, or in the interests of freedom practically ignore divine grace. 'As man by the fall has not ceased to be man, so also this divine grace of regeneration acts not on man as on stocks and stones, nor takes away his will and properties, but makes him spiritually alive, heals, amends, and bends him in a way which is alike gracious and potent ; so that, where previously the violence and resistance of the flesh exercised an absolute sway, now a voluntary and sincere obedience of the Spirit begins to rule.' The doctrine of our Confession is highly reasonable. We acknowledge that the Spirit must be received before any act can be done by us well-pleasing to God. Then our receiving the Spirit in His first operation of grace cannot be regarded as an act on our part, otherwise we would have done something at the very outset toward our own salvation. In this sense the human spirit is described as altogether passive before experiencing the quickening and renewing influence of the Holy Spirit. Thus we hold that the Spirit, which is the free gift of God's grace, has been already received before any gracious act is performed by man. Amesius sententiously expresses this truth regarding the state of the will on the first receiving of grace : ' Voluntas neque libere agentis, neque naturaliter patientis rationem habet, sed obedientialis tantum subjectionis.'

Grace is rightly called irresistible in its action upon those pre-destinated unto life. This does not imply any overbearing force (*coactio*) that works outside of, or apart from, the human will, but it indicates an effectual working in and through the will, which in the end assuredly produces the aimed-at results. Resistance may be long continued, but at last the corruption of will is overcome, the rebellious spirit throws down his weapons, and yields himself in willing surrender.

III.—*Elect infants, dying in infancy, are regenerated and saved by Christ through the Spirit, who worketh when, and where, and how he pleaseth. So also are all other elect persons, who are incapable of being outwardly called by the ministry of the word.*

This statement has been the subject of much misunderstanding. It is often referred to as a denial of infant salvation. Because elect infants are specified, it is supposed that this necessarily implies that there are non-elect infants who perish. This does not follow. Election of some certainly involves the non-election of others. We refer election, however, to that choice made by God out of the human race. To this election, we may believe that all infants dying in infancy belong. In this case we would properly call them elect infants. Our Confession merely indicates that the case of such does not come under the ordinary rules. In ordinary cases, where the human will is in a condition sufficiently developed to render the individual a responsible being, God's call is addressed so that it becomes operative through the will of the creature. But in cases of immaturity and of imbecility, the personal will cannot be so acted upon ; and therefore God deals with such cases in special ways according to His righteousness and grace. Beyond this we cannot safely go. Only it is to be remembered that it is original sin, and not actual transgression, that lies upon such. The Romish church has dogmatized here, beyond what scripture has affirmed. According to Roman Catholic theology, this original sin is removed by baptism, and the unbaptized cannot be saved. Lecky, in his *History of European Morals*, has collected some most atrocious utterances of recent Romish theological writers describing the agonies of infants condemned to eternal misery (vol. ii. pp. 223–225) ; interesting as a warning against dogmatizing where Scripture gives no warrant; all the horrid blasphemies of these Romish diabolical romances springing from the doctrine of the absolute necessity of the sacraments for salvation. In Dante we find the same type of doctrine, though set forth in a form as little revolting as possible. All the unbaptized are necessarily found in the *Inferno*, as they have no hope of deliverance ; but infants share with the most virtuous of the heathen, a place where the suffering consists simply in privation of heavenly bliss. Of this company it is said that whether void of sin, or even deserving, 'it profits not, since baptism was not theirs.' (*Inferno,*

iv. 24-39.) [Consider the force of Christ's comparison of the salvable
condition to that of a little child, and His declaration that of such is
the kingdom of heaven — in relation to the question of infant
salvation.]

IV.—*Others not elected, although they may be called by the ministry
of the word, and may have some common operations of the Spirit,
yet they never truly come unto Christ, and therefore cannot be
saved: much less can men not professing the Christian religion
be saved in any other way whatsoever, be they ever so diligent to
frame their lives according to the light of nature, and the law of
that religion they do profess; and to assert and maintain that
they may, is very pernicious, and to be detested.*

Many are called who are not chosen. Salvation is only through
Christ. Beyond these undisputed statements, our Confession here
refers directly to the question of the salvability of those who have
never been favoured with gospel privileges. This is a matter on
which we should not dogmatize. The anathema of this section
(strange that it should just appear on such a question as this !)
against rash conclusions on the one side should apply equally to
rash conclusions on the other. 'These things are beyond the reach
of man, neither is it in the power of any reason or disputation to
search out the judgments of God. When, therefore, the enemy
suggesteth those things unto thee, or some curious people raise the
question, let thy answer be that of the prophet : Thou are just, O
Lord, and Thy judgment is right.' (A'Kempis, Bk. iii. chap. lviii.)
As to the statement regarding the condition of the heathen world,
it has been variously understood, either as a severely exclusive
utterance, or as a less determinate deliverance, almost equivalent
to a suspension of judgment. When, however, we place this section
side by side with the opening section of the Confession, we feel
disposed to adopt the latter interpretation. Professor Candlish, in
vindicating the judiciousness and moderation of the doctrinal
positions of our Standards, indicates his opinion that the statement
of the opening section would have been enough, as this later utterance has been so generally interpreted (wrongly, as he thinks) in
the narrowest and severest sense (*British and Foreign Evangelical
Review* for 1877, p. 169). Professor Bruce, again, considers that the
statement in the first chapter seems to make the balance incline in
favour of the severer interpretation, on the ground that there 'the
insufficiency of the light of nature to give that knowledge of God
which is necessary for salvation is affirmed, and the affirmation is
made the basis of the doctrine of Revelation.' (See *Training of the
Twelve*, pp. 386, 387.) In all ages, we believe, there have been rays
of light emanating from primitive revelations, generally so meagre
and distorted that only the slightest vestige appeared ; yet this would

be something more than the light of nature or mere natural religion, and in it there might be that element of truth according to which those who availed themselves of it should, for the sake of Christ, be saved. The main point to be insisted upon is that there is salvation in no other but in Christ only. Whoever are saved, are saved for His sake, and will celebrate His praise in their deliverance. Baxter's words (as quoted by Bruce) are sober and wise : ' I am not much inclined to pass a peremptory sentence of damnation upon all who never heard of Christ, having some more reasons than I knew of before to think that God's dealings with such is much unknown to us.' It is interesting to notice how Dante, when assigning to Ripheus the Trojan, and Trajan the Roman emperor, places in Paradise, is careful to affirm that both had on earth exercised Christian faith.

> ' They quitted not their bodies, as thou deem'st,
> Gentiles, but Christians ; in firm rooted faith,
> This, of the feet in future to be pierced,
> That, of feet nailed already to the cross.' (*Paradiso*, xx. 95–98.)

CHAPTER XI.

OF JUSTIFICATION.

I.—*Those whom God effectually calleth he also freely justifieth; not by infusing righteousness into them, but by pardoning their sins, and by accounting and accepting their persons as righteous : not for any thing wrought in them or done by them, but for Christ's sake alone : not by imputing faith itself, the act of believing, or any other evangelical obedience, to them as their righteousness; but by imputing the obedience and satisfaction of Christ unto them, they receiving and resting on him and his righteousness by faith : which faith they have not of themselves; it is the gift of God.*

The leading propositions maintained in this section are these : (1.) Justification is an imputed, not an infused, righteousness ; (2.) Not faith but only Christ's work is the meritorious ground of justification

(1.) Justification in the sense of our Standards has been called a forensic or judicial act. By such a designation it is distinguished from that which is called justification in the Romish theology. By Romanists justification and sanctification are confounded, but in Protestant theology they are clearly distinguished. According to the scripture doctrine, justification is simply acquittal, there is no condemnation, sins are forgiven, and the persons of the guilty are accepted. The doctrinal statement agreed upon in the Council of

Trent was that justification is not simply remission of sins, but also the sanctification and renewal of the inner man by the voluntary acceptance of grace and gifts. Reformed theology, however, nowhere regards justification as merely remission of sins, but adds to forgiveness the accounting and accepting the persons as righteous. Thus our definition is twofold : forgiveness of sins and imputation of righteousness. Justification from its very nature must be complete, otherwise it is of no use whatever. Now if justification be identified with sanctification, then it is clear we cannot have it complete in this life. We maintain the doctrine of Counter-imputations,—the imputation of Christ's righteousness to the sinner, and the imputation of the sinner's sin to Christ ; but if imputation meant infusion, we should be maintaining the blasphemous doctrine that our sins were infused into Christ. They are counted to Him, and just so, according to the Protestant doctrine of Justification, His righteousness is counted to us.

(2.) It is an immediate consequence of the Romish doctrine of Justification to regard faith as itself the ground of our acceptance, and not, as we maintain, simply the instrumental means. In Protestant theology, faith is not regarded as a work which may carry with it a ground of merit. [Distinguish the different meanings of the word work in John vi. 28, 29.] Faith is not imputed as a work of righteousness done by us : for even if faith saved, faith is the gift of God. Not faith, however, but only Christ saves. Justification can only result to us in consequence of the work of one who can of himself do the works of righteousness. By faith we do not mean mere assent to a truth, but trust in a person who is himself the centre of the truth. Justification therefore rests on a person. 'Is faith a person?' asked Dr. John Duncan ; 'was faith crucified for you?' That faith which is the gift of God, also rests in God. The Reformed theologians have always shown themselves as eager to maintain that all the merit as a ground for justification lay in the work of Christ, as they were to maintain that the means for appropriating this meritorious ground was the exercise of faith.

II.—*Faith, thus receiving and resting on Christ and his righteousness, is the alone instrument of justification; yet it is not alone in the person justified, but is ever accompanied with all other saving graces, and is no dead faith, but worketh by love.*

In this place it is shown how works are excluded from the ground of our justification, and how good works afterwards necessarily appear in the life of the justified. We may attend to these two main propositions : (1.) Faith is the only instrument in justification ; (2.) Faith manifests its genuineness by means of the good works which follow.

(1.) When we rightly understand what the function of faith is in reference to our justification, we shall find no difficulty in declaring that faith alone can justify. To say, in this sense, that faith justifies, is to say that Christ justifies. And all Protestants at least, and even Romanists in their express doctrinal treatises, admit that there is salvation in Jesus, and in no other. It is the error of Romish theology, however, to join works to faith, and thus to corrupt the simplicity that is in Christ, and open the way for the admission of other mediators besides the one appointed. Let us hold firmly that faith alone means Christ alone : and that the introduction of additions to faith means the introduction of additions to Christ as the Saviour. The Romish distinction between mere faith (*fides informis*), and faith developed by love (*fides formata*), as used in Romish theology, is utterly false. Only faith—without any additions, is saving faith.

(2.) Romanists have objected to this Protestant doctrine that it is dangerous, that it opens the door to licentiousness and moral indifference. But the Protestant theologian is just as careful to maintain the indissoluble association of justification and sanctification, as he is to resist any confusion of the two. The same Christ whose righteousness is imputed in justification is the fountain of all holy actions in the life of the justified. Good works are the effects of faith and the evidence of justification. [Illustrate this doctrine from the admirable representation of it in the *Pilgrim's Progress*,—the conversation of Christian and Ignorance regarding justification.]

III.—*Christ, by his obedience and death, did fully discharge the debt of all those that are thus justified, and did make a proper, real, and full satisfaction to his Father's justice in their behalf. Yet, in as much as he was given by the Father for them, and his obedience and satisfaction accepted in their stead, and both freely, not for any thing in them, their justification is only of free grace; that both the exact justice and rich grace of God might be glorified in the justification of sinners.*

This section maintains that the justification of sinners is wholly a work of God's free grace. The price is fully paid, but it is God Himself who paid it.

(1.) The debt of the justified has been fully paid. The Westminster divines wisely confine themselves to the statement of the actual efficiency of the atonement. As to the sufficiency of Christ's death, orthodox theologians generally admit that its worth was so great that, to use the words of Owen, 'it was every way able and perfectly sufficient to redeem, justify, reconcile, and save all the sinners in the world, to satisfy the justice of God for all the sins of all mankind, and to bring them every one to everlasting glory.' In perfect consistency with such views, reference is here made simply to those in whose case this all-sufficient atonement becomes actually efficient. This is really the practical point ; and here the special characteristic of Calvinism appears to advantage. The Arminian

says that the atonement renders salvation possible to all : the Cal
vinist asserts the same, as a position of comparatively subordinate
interest, because he goes beyond possibilities to certainties, and
affirms that the atonement actually and efficiently secures salvation
to all the elect.

(2.) And that is all of grace. The term grace has been used in two
senses. It means generally the free, unmerited favour or good-will
that God has for man, and in a restricted sense, the spiritual character
inwrought in man. There is justifying grace and sanctifying grace.
Romanists have for a purpose restricted the use of the term to the
latter. [Show that this restriction is unwarrantable ; and that
certain effects of grace are changes of relation to God and not infused
graces. Buchanan, *Justification*, page 342.] In this section of our
Confession, grace is used to mean justifying grace. Justification is
the fruit of it, and by means of it every prerequisite of complete
justification is provided.

IV.—*God did, from all eternity, decree to justify all the elect; and
Christ did, in the fulness of time, die for their sins, and rise again
for their justification: nevertheless they are not justified, until the
Holy Spirit doth in due time actually apply Christ unto them.*

It is here affirmed that while the eternal decree, and the death of
Christ in time, are the presuppositions of the salvation of the individual, the efficiency of this redemption is only experienced through
its personal application by the Holy Spirit. Among the older divines,
in their discussions regarding the operations of grace, it was usual
elaborately to distinguish between the order of nature and the order
in time. It was maintained generally, that in the order of nature
regeneration preceded justification, though in order of time they were
contemporary. The distinction may not seem very profitable or important, yet, if carefully made, it contributes to clearness of definition
in theology. Our Confession indicates that prior to justification
there must be the effectual and personal application of Christ, considered as the source and seat of all gracious influence. The justification of all the elect is provided for by the decree, and the ransom for
all such is fully paid and secured by the death and resurrection of
Christ, yet there is also a time determined by the decree for the actual
conferring of those purchased blessings, and till such time, even those
elected to be justified remain under the curse. And the reason of
this is, as Halyburton says, ' that all these privileges, being contrived
and provided by a concert betwixt the Father and Son, without the
sinner's knowledge, or any contribution of counsel, performance, or
consent, it did belong to them who had brought about all this, by the
best of rights, to give out, at what time or in what order they pleased,
the good things designed, which was accordingly fixed in the covenant of redemption, all being adjusted as to order and time.'
(*Works*, p. 550.)

V.—*God doth continue to forgive the sins of those that are justified: and although they can never fall from the state of justification, yet they may by their sins fall under God's fatherly displeasure, and not have the light of his countenance restored unto them, until they humble themselves, confess their sins, beg pardon, and renew their faith and repentance.*

This section shows particularly how God deals with the sins of believers. 1. It assumes as a fact of experience that sin does continue to exist in the justified. Its dominion is broken ; and ignorance of it, and insensible indifference toward it, are no longer possible. The experience it produces expresses itself first in wretchedness, and then in thanksgiving (Rom. vii. 24, 25). The need of forgiveness for all such acts of sin is keenly felt ; and believers are taught to pray for daily forgiveness of daily committed sin. 2. Sin in the justified has no power to destroy the reality of their justification. This, we have already seen, depends not on anything wrought in them or done by them ; so that it cannot be destroyed even by their falling into sin. Yet the sins of the justified, no less than the sins of others, must be punished. God, as a Father, shows His displeasure, so that the child may abhor and abandon that which displeases Him : He withdraws the light of His presence until the offending one realizes in its absence his need of it, and in penitence cries out for restoration. The experience of the Psalmist, as given in Psalm xxx. 6–11, has been traced with deep spiritual insight and sympathy by the author of the *Imitation of Christ* (see book ii. chap. ix. 5). 3. The gracious results of such fatherly dealings show themselves in the chastened believer's increased humbleness of mind, sense of sins, realized need of forgiveness, and in the general development of the graces of the soul.

VI.—*The justification of believers under the Old Testament was, in all these respects, one and the same with the justification of believers under the New Testament.*

We have here a more general and comprehensive statement regarding the justification of Old Testament saints than that given before in chapter vii 5.

' Not by works ' applies to them as well as to the saved under the new dispensation. The great number of outward rites and ceremonies, and the imposing and obtrusive form of these, might lead one to suppose that by works of righteousness, ritual or moral, which they had done, they secured acceptance with God. This, however, is an error resulting from a superficial view of their histories The animating principle which underlay those acts was faith ; the same as the New Testament grace, though under their peculiar circumstances it necessarily assumed peculiar forms of manifestation. In two Epistles (Rom. iv. and Gal. iii.) Paul insists upon Abraham's faith and not his works being the ground of his justification. The case of Abraham is thus singled out for the sake of his argument, because the Jews with one consent traced their spiritual privileges from him.

CHAPTER XII.

OF ADOPTION.

I.—*All those that are justified, God vouchsafeth, in and for his only Son Jesus Christ, to make partakers of the grace of adoption ; by which they are taken into the number, and enjoy the liberties ana privileges of the children of God; have his name put upon them, receive the spirit of adoption ; have access to the throne of grace with boldness; are enabled to cry, Abba, Father; are pitied, protected, provided for, and chastened by him as by a father; yet never cast off, but sealed to the day of redemption, and inherit the promises, as heirs of everlasting salvation.*

The complaint has been very often raised, that in the Confession no attempt has been made to define adoption, and that the present section is little more than the statement of an identical proposition. The subject has certainly been much more fully discussed and more frequently referred to in this century than in Reformation times. It could not, therefore, be expected that it should receive in the seventeenth century the same careful and elaborate examination that was given to the subject of justification. At the same time, it should be said that in a Confession of Faith adoption should not receive so detailed a treatment as justification. In general or practical theological works it may be desirable to give it a very large place, but here we have to do with it only as it concerns the general fabric of the church faith. But, though no formal definition of adoption is given here, we have a sufficiently detailed and exact description. Adoption is described as a grace, is conferred on all the justified, is received by them in and for the sake of Christ, and it secures to them at once the right to and the enjoyment of all the privileges of children of God. No better formal definition has been given than that of Amesius : Adoption is a gracious sentence of God, whereby for the sake of Christ He receives believers into the rank of sons. This definition gives no more than the Confession's description.

It is here stated that justification is presupposed. In the order of nature we have justification preceding and securing a ground for the act of adoption. In following the course of development in the regenerate, we have first of all justification as that change in the relations between God and man which is indispensable to all further experiences of grace ; and then, as rendered possible on the part of those who are in this state of justification, we have the exercise of the graces of faith and repentance ; and in return for the exercise of these respective graces, we have the rewards of grace conferred,—the grace of adoption and the forgiveness of sins.

Then, again, it is said that God vouchsafes this grace in and for His only Son Jesus Christ. When He who is expressly called the only Son of God took on Him the nature of man, and that of man under the curse, He rendered it possible that the members of that race, into which He came without foregoing His Sonship, might become sharers of His Sonship. The Incarnation, ideal in the eternal decree and realized in the earthly life of Jesus Christ, is at once the device according to which God will communicate to the justified participation in the divine nature, and the reason for which He will confer on them the grace of adoption. 'The only way by which a man receives that new life from God that has nothing to do with sin, and that consciousness of kindred with God which makes the name " Father " natural to his heart, is by simple faith in Christ, who gives power to become sons of God to as many as receive Him.' (Maclaren's *Sermons*, 3d series,—a striking sermon on John viii. 35.)

It is customary to draw a parallel between human and divine adoption. In human adoption there is ordinarily a defect supplied and a mere outward advantage conferred ; in divine adoption there is, on the one hand, no want in God to supply, but the movement is one of pure grace, and, on the part of man, there is received no mere outward advantage, but an inner spiritual gift of a new life. More important is this other distinction. In human adoption there is no right to the inheritance, anterior to the act of adoption, and so in this case the privilege and the spirit of adoption are separable ; in divine adoption the right to the inheritance, as embracing all the privileges of children, is founded on a previous spiritual birth, and consequently the spirit of adoption in this case is not separable from participation in and enjoyment of its privileges. This latter distinction leads us to notice that too much attention is usually paid to the relation between the act of adoption and the act of justification, and too little to the relation between the spirit of adoption and the operation of the new birth. When adoption is viewed as the act of receiving into the rank of the sons of God, it is evident that it should be described as formal ; like justification, it is a declaratory and forensic act. But just as the forensic act of justification presupposed the previous spiritual operation of regeneration, so this forensic act of declaring the sonship of the justified by which justification is immediately followed up, is grounded upon the previous conferring of the Spirit of the Son, which is but another way of expressing the great change of nature on which the change of relation is based.

The latter part of the section, which treats of the privileges of believers as children of God, is ill arranged, and not quite grammatical in its structure. The apostle's figure of the seal might have been made more prominent   The sealing involves the ideas of ownership and security,—has a side toward God, and a side toward man.   The privileges of adoption enumerated here may be grouped under two heads.   (1) God discharges for us the duties of a Father—gives us His name, pities, protects, provides for, and chastens.   (2) He enables us to fulfil the duties of children—gives the spirit of adoption, boldness to draw near, and grace to use the promises.

Adoption links together justification and sanctification.   The grace of adoption is the immediate result of justification, and the spirit of adoption is the real germ of sanctification.   The title to life eternal evidently rests upon justification alone, yet the presence of the spirit of adoption is an unfailing test of the reality of our justification, inasmuch as it is received by all the justified.

It is the special service rendered to theology by the late Dr. Candlish that he called attention to the great truth of the adoption of the justified.   In almost all his published works the practical aspects of this blessed truth are strikingly illustrated.   See especially *The Fatherhood of God;* and a more recent volume of sermons, *The Sonship and Brotherhood of Believers.*

CHAPTER XIII.

OF SANCTIFICATION.

I.—*They who are effectually called and regenerated, having a new heart and a new spirit created in them, are farther sanctified really and personally, through the virtue of Christ's death and resurrection, by his word and Spirit dwelling in them; the dominion of the whole body of sin is destroyed, and the several lusts thereof are more and more weakened and mortified, and they more and more quickened and strengthened in all saving graces, to the practice of true holiness, without which no man shall see the Lord.*

We have here two main points of doctrine : 1st. The idea of sanctification , and 2d. The means whereby sanctification is secured.

1. The idea of sanctification,—that in which sanctification consists, —is here described in reference to sin and in reference to holiness. The gradual destruction of remaining corruptions, and the growth of the saving graces, are evidently two sides of the same process.   It is the development of the saving graces that accomplishes the death of indwelling sin in the believer.   The proportion in which the one is present, determines the proportion in which the other is present.   Let the saving graces—the graces of the Christian life—be increased sevenfold, then just in that proportion is corruption in the heart of

the believer checked and destroyed. Here we come upon the main distinctions between justification and sanctification. In justification, we speak of saving grace; in sanctification, of saving graces: in justification, of grace immediately sufficient; in sanctification, of graces that are quickened and strengthened more and more. In justification, of the complete removal of condemnation; in sanctification, of the weakening more and more of the lusts of sin. In justification, of forgiveness and acceptance; in sanctification, of holiness in the life. These differences are admirably stated in the *Larger Catechism*, Question 77. The righteousness of justification and the righteousness of sanctification have been carefully distinguished by Hooker: 'The righteousness, wherewith we shall be clothed in the world to come, is both perfect and inherent. That whereby here we are justified is perfect, but not inherent. That whereby we are sanctified is inherent, but not perfect.' (*Discourse of Justification*, sect. iii.) The Romish Church, overlooking this distinction, has described justifying righteousness as an infused grace; and so justification is confounded with sanctification.

2. This sanctification of the believer is accomplished by means of the Holy Spirit. The gift of the Spirit is secured by the merits of Christ, and is the fruit of personal justification. Hence the Spirit is called the Spirit of Christ, because the Spirit dwells in Christ. By necessary consequence, then, this Spirit dwells in all who are in Christ. If we observe here the connection between justification and sanctification, as we have before considered their differences, we shall best understand how sanctification is said to be through the virtue of Christ's death and resurrection. The elect are viewed from eternity as one in the body of Christ, and the decree of justification has reference to this body of Christ as one whole. 'This is what Calvinists call justification in general; and the particular justification of each member is effected at the moment of his union with this justified body of Christ, since he therein comes to have communion in the merit and justification of Christ the head. The church stands in the state of union, yea, of unity with Christ; and as each member is added, he is admitted to communion in Christ's grace and glory.'[1] Now the Holy Spirit is the Spirit of Christ, and when the justified sinner becomes a member of Christ's body, the Spirit which belongs to the person of Christ must enter into and pervade this new member.

The gift of the Spirit is thus the condition of sanctification. He is also the efficient agent of the work of sanctification that proceeds in the soul of the believer. All that we have of Christ's must necessarily exert a sanctifying influence upon us. Hence His Word as well as His Spirit, though never apart from the Spirit (for the word that is separated from His Spirit is not His Word), works sanctification by its truth.

[1] *The Glory of the Holy Ghost* by Rev. P. M'Laren, late of Lossiemouth, page 109.

II.—*This sanctification is throughout in the whole man, yet imperfect in this life; there abideth still some remnants of corruption in every part: whence ariseth a continual and irreconcilable war; the flesh lusting against the spirit, and the spirit against the flesh.*

III.—*In which war, although the remaining corruption for a time may much prevail, yet, through the continual supply of strength from the sanctifying Spirit of Christ, the regenerate part doth overcome: and so the saints grow in grace, perfecting holiness in the fear of God.*

These two sections treat of the imperfection of the saints in this present life. What is here laid down may be arranged under three heads.

1. Imperfection, though all-pervading, does not exclude an all-pervading sanctification. Those complementary truths are clearly stated in the first two clauses of the second section. No faculty of the man remains unaffected by regeneration. This ought to show that religion cannot fairly be regarded as a matter merely of intellect, or merely of feeling, or even merely of will. The religious spirit shows itself under each of these powers, because each has been powerfully affected by the new birth. Yet in none of these faculties is holiness, as the product of this new life, perfected.

2. Imperfection occasions a continual struggle. The end striven after being perfection in every part, there is of necessity in the regenerate a continual war throughout the whole being. The presence of the Spirit in every part alongside of remaining sin involves a state of war. Whether we describe the Christian life as a pilgrimage or as a war, the idea of struggle forms an essential element. Compare Bunyan's *Holy War* and *Pilgrim's Progress*. This struggle is carried on within the man. It is a struggle for the mastery. Sin in the regenerate has not the dominion as it had in the unregenerate; but so long as it is present at all, it will be seeking to regain that dominion. If it did not so, it would no longer be sin,—it would no longer exist as a lust. Sin implies contrariety to holiness. The Spirit and the flesh war against each other; and so long as any element of the fleshly life continues,—that is, throughout the earthly existence,—this struggle will continue. The knowledge of this should lead to the exercise of patience. This time is for struggle, not for rest, for wrestling against evil especially within. 'Dispose not thyself,' says A'Kempis, 'for much rest, but for great patience.' The best illustration and description of this war carried on in the believer's heart, is found in Rom. vii. 14-25. [Read Fraser *On Sanctification;* especially the Dissertation on Rom. vii. and the admirably explanatory Paraphrase of vv. 14-25.] This, however, is not the normal experience of the Christian. Paul aspires to the experience of

chap. viii. ; to which indeed he passes in the thanksgiving with which he closes the previous chapter.

3. Imperfection in the believer is gradually overcome, and will be at last completely removed. The third section thus represents the true aim and goal of sanctification. Victory is in view, and this should encourage the struggling saint. He has within him the holy seed. He and sin will never be identified. It is indeed already true that he who is remaining in Christ cannot sin. Dwelling in Christ, who is without sin, and dwelling in sin are necessarily contradictory. The regenerate has a power within him which will yet render him free from sin ; and so he engages in a conflict, the end of which is not doubtful. The result of each act of wrestling is to weaken sin and strengthen the saving graces. The increase of grace is the earnest of the fulness of grace in bliss.

CHAPTER XIV.

OF SAVING FAITH.

I.—*The grace of faith, whereby the elect are enabled to believe to the saving of their souls, is the work of the Spirit of Christ in their hearts, and is ordinarily wrought by the ministry of the word· by which also, and by the administration of the sacraments, and prayer, it is increased and strengthened.*

This section treats of the origin, and the increase of faith.

(1.) As to its origin, faith is a grace, the gift of God, enabling the elect to exercise and accomplish the condition of salvation. The origin of faith is thus from God Himself working by the Spirit of Christ. The message is delivered to all, but the natural man cannot receive it, and his whole nature rises in rebellion against it. 'From this message,' says O'Brien, 'fallen man naturally recoils with an aversion just proportioned to the degree in which he understands it. And if this be the case,—if it be that when this message of mercy is best understood, it is naturally most distasteful,—there is plainly an obstacle to trust in the Redeemer, which no degree of knowledge and no strength of conviction can of themselves overcome ; which nothing but the power of God's Spirit can effectually subdue.' (*Nature and Effects of Faith*, p. 38.) As to the origin of faith, this section further shows, that the Spirit of God ordinarily works mediately on the heart of man, employing the ministry of the Word. The relation of faith and the Word is more fully brought out in the following paragraph. Justification by faith and the supreme authority of Scripture constitute the evangelical principle — the ultimate principle of Protestantism, and are distinguished as respectively the material and the formal principle.

G

(2.) The increase of faith is secured by the continued use of the Word under the Spirit's blessing, and by the use in addition of means of grace appropriated to believers — the sacraments and prayer. It was through prayer that the disciples sought increase of faith (Luke xvii. 5); and this prayer was offered just when the enumeration of moral requirements made evident the insufficiency of the faith which they possessed. The prayer was addressed to Christ for faith. [The relation of Christ, faith, and the ordinances has been illustrated by reference to the story of the woman of Samaria : Christ, the well ; the ordinance, the pitcher ; and faith, the muscular action which lifted the pitcher. See Goulburn, *Thoughts on Personal Religion*, Part I. chap. 3] It belongs to the very idea of ordinances, but very specially to the idea of the sacra- ments, to be viewed as means for securing increase and confirma- tion of grace. The strength of faith depends upon the measure in which we possess Christ. That faith is perfect which rests on Christ without exception. Now, just as divinely-appointed ordi- nances enable us to draw out of His fulness more than we had before, their rightful use secures the increase of faith.

II.—*By this faith, a Christian believeth to be true whatsoever is revealed in the word, for the authority of God himself speaking therein; and acteth differently upon that which each particular passage thereof containeth ; yielding obedience to the commands, trembling at the threatenings, and embracing the promises of God for this life and that which is to come. But the principal acts of saving faith are, accepting, receiving, and resting upon Christ alone for justification, sanctification, and eternal life, by virtue of the covenant of grace.*

We have here what has been called the formal reason or ground of faith. Why does the Christian believe the Scriptures? The ultimate ground of belief cannot be found in human testimony whether of a man or of the church, nor in rational conviction of their truth, nor in any private revelation, nor in any single text bearing witness to the rest, nor in the suitableness of the matter of Scripture to our circumstances. (See Halyburton, *Essay on Faith*, chap. iii.) On no one of these reasons does our faith in Scripture finally rest. But when we acknowledge with our Confession that the ultimate ground is the authority of God Himself speaking therein, we recognise as essential conditions to our believing accept- ance of Scripture, the spirit of faith in us, and the personal witness in us of the Holy Spirit, rendering us capable of beholding the divine light in the Word, which only then is known to us as self- revealing.

When our Confession says that the Christian by faith acteth differently upon that contained in each particular passage, Hodge strangely misses the meaning, and discourses of something entirely different. He proceeds as if he had read acteth indifferently, and goes on to affirm that the Word of God must in all its parts be accepted with equal faith. After having so precisely stated that the Christian's faith extends to whatsoever is revealed, it is not likely that the Westminster divines would bring in a new sentence to repeat in a feebler way the same thing. What this clause actually says, as is clearly explained by what follows, is that faith so accepts each particular passage as to understand and use it in accordance with its evident intention—if it be a command, obeying it ; if a threatening, taking warning by it ; if a promise, laying hold on it, and applying it either to this life or to the future life, as a fair interpretation requires. The principle is a most useful one, and most evidently true.

III.—*This faith is different in degrees, weak or strong; may be often and many ways assailed and weakened, but gets the victory; growing up in many to the attainment of a full assurance through Christ, who is both the author and finisher of our faith.*

Faith is here declared to vary in degree ; and this is true whether we regard different individuals in the Christian church, or the same individual at different stages of his history. The development of faith is not in appearance a regular advancement and steady growth. It is so in reality ; but often, not only the immediate movement of the Christian, but his whole tendency for a time may seem retrograde. When the entire life is viewed, however, the course of the development of faith will be seen to have been really progressive. Some Christians never make the same evident attainment in faith as others. Yet the weak may be no less genuine than the strong ; and real faith is saving faith. [Consider the experience of Mr. Little Faith ; also that of Feeble Mind and Ready to Halt, in *Pilgrim's Progress*.] Speaking of genuine believers in darkness, Hooker expresses this true and comfortable doctrine : ' Their faith, when it is at the strongest, is but weak ; yet even then, when it is at the weakest, so strong that utterly it never faileth.' If we have faith, it is God's gift, His work in us ; and He will take care that His work will not fail. The assurance of faith—to be afterwards fully treated of—is here set in its true relation to faith, as its final product. It comes from the repeated experience of His faithfulness in whom we have believed, and His sufficiency for upholding us in trial and giving us the victory over all that opposes.

CHAPTER XV

OF REPENTANCE UNTO LIFE.

I.—*Repentance unto life is an evangelical grace, the doctrine whereof is to be preached by every minister of the gospel, as well as that of faith in Christ.*

This section states the relation between repentance and faith. Like faith, repentance is an evangelical grace. ' Faith,' says Boston, ' is the spring and source of repentance, so that though the graces of faith and repentance are given together and at once in espect of time, yet in the order of nature, faith goes before repentance, and the acting of faith before the exercise of repentance, and he that would repent must first believe in Christ that he may repent.' We do not then co-ordinate repentance with faith as the instrumental grace in a sinner's justification; but as a sister grace we maintain that it is never wanting where true faith is found. But if we say that repentance cannot be without faith, we must also say that without repentance there can be no faith. Hence in Scripture the call to repentance, as necessarily implying faith, is sometimes put for the full sum of gospel preaching. The admonition of this section is strictly in accordance with Scripture practice.

The grace of repentance is the indispensable bridge between justification and sanctification. In the very moment of justification the grace of repentance takes origin, and the active development of this grace is sanctification. ' Repentance,' says Thomas Fuller, ' is the younger brother of innocence itself.'

II.—*By it a sinner, out of the sight and sense, not only of the danger, but also of the filthiness and odiousness of his sins, as contrary to the holy nature and righteous law of God, and upon the apprehension of his mercy in Christ to such as are penitent, so grieves for and hates his sins, as to turn from them all unto God, purposing and endeavouring to walk with him in all the ways of his commandments.*

This statement does full justice to both influences that are at work in moving to genuine evangelical repentance. These are—the terrors of the Lord, and the persuasions of grace. We find in the history of the church instances of a tendency to onesidedness in describing the origin of repentance. Agricola (1527), carrying out some rather unguarded utterances of Luther, maintained that evangelical repentance has no connection whatever with the law, that it is awakened simply by a view of the offence committed against God's grace and love in Christ, and that it is therefore of faith in the sense of not being produced by any representation of the divine justice and anger. This error both Luther and Calvin vigorously opposed, and they introduced special statements into their writings to guard against any such violent misapplication of the evangelical doctrine.   Repentance is an evangelical grace ; but the law is not to be regarded as anti - evangelical.   It forms an introductory discipline.   The spiritually awakened is rendered conscious of the danger, odiousness, and filthiness of his sins, by having these brought into contrast with the holy and righteous law of God.   In order of nature, these convictions of sin, as an element in repentance, have precedence of the apprehension of God's mercy in Christ ; but in actual occurrence these two are simultaneous.   The one is the emotion of penitence ; the other, the assurance that God will receive the penitent.   The full exercise of the grace of repentance is possible only when this emotion, having been awakened in the soul, is encouraged by a view of God's grace.   It consists in grief for, and forsaking of, sin— the turning to, and following after, God.   It has thus a reference to the past and a reference to the future.   The godly sorrow is an indispensable element in true repentance.   As Henry Taylor says in *Philip van Artevelde :—*

> 'He that lacks time to mourn, lacks time to mend.
> Eternity mourns that.   'Tis an ill cure
> For life's worst ills, to have no time to feel them,
> Where sorrow's held intrusive and turned out,
> There wisdom will not enter, nor true power,
> Nor aught that dignifies humanity.'

That genuine repentance involves the quitting not only of sinful practices, but also of those possessions that have been sinfully obtained, was clearly recognised by Shakespeare : ' May one be pardoned and retain the offence ? ' etc.   (Read *Hamlet*, Act iii. Scene iii. ll. 36–72.)

III.—*Although repentance be not to be rested in, as any satisfaction for sin, or any cause of the pardon thereof, which is the act of God's free grace in Christ ; yet is it of such necessity to all sinners, that none may expect pardon without it.*

Faith and repentance, though very frequently mentioned together in God's Word, are not, as we have seen from the first section, co-ordinated as means of salvation.   Christ saves, and faith as uniting to Christ, is saving faith.   We cannot in the same sense say that repentance saves.   Neither faith nor repentance, however, are to be viewed as meritorious means of salvation.   The Bible ' calls upon all to repent and to believe ; and brings to act upon all, forces fitted to move in all remorse and alarm.   But it treats our sorrow and fear not as means of propitiating an offended Deity, but as the course through which sinners are to be brought to confide in a reconciled

God.' (O'Brien, *Nature and Effects of Faith*, p 44.) The emotions in repentance separable from faith, when viewed apart, could only produce despair, which is first removed by the entrance of faith. 'All repentance,' says Harless, 'is the consciousness of not being righteous before God.' 'Justification is the silencing of our despair.' (*Chr. Ethics*, p. 218.)

Though not the ground of the sinner's justification, there can be no justifying faith that is not accompanied by repentance. It is a negative condition (*conditio sine qua non*), not the meritorious cause of pardon. 'Let no man,' says Hooker, 'look for pardon which doth smother and conceal sin where in duty it should be revealed.'

IV.—*As there is no sin so small but it deserves damnation; so there is no sin so great, that it can bring damnation upon those who truly repent.*

In the statement of this section we have a preservative against frivolity and hopelessness in view of our sins. What an old divine said of the story of the penitent thief, may be said of the twofold statement now before us. It is given so that no one may presume, and so that no one need despair. The doctrine of the aggravation of sin is indeed here recognised. Sins are relatively distinguished as great and small. Yet this difference is not such that the least any more than the greatest lies out of the range of God's condemnation. Every sin deserves God's wrath and curse. Nor is the difference such that the greatest any more than the least lies beyond the range of God's mercy promised to the penitent. The only apparent exception is that sin which is called unpardonable. When we resolve this into persistent unbelief, the exception is seen to be only apparent. One of the Westminster divines, speaking of the absoluteness of the proposition that whosoever believes not shall be damned, says : 'This is so positively set down as it implies not only to be a sin against a law, but a sin against a remedy.' (*Minutes of Assembly*, p. 159.) Hence, while it is true that in every act of sin, sinners sin against their own souls, this is in a special sense true regarding the rejection of the only hope of recovery. Where faith is necessary, repentance is necessary. In reference to our need of Christ, according to Paul's doctrine there is no difference between one and another, between the great sinner and the less. Where no distinction can be made as to the need of faith, none can be made as to the need of repentance. This evidently does not affect the question of varying forms and degrees of faith and repentance in different individuals. It may be held that a great sinner, who has realized the greatness of his sin, and trusted the all-sufficient Saviour, will manifest his faith and repentance in deeper form than he will who had not sinned so grievously. Varying temperaments and differences of spiritual constitution must be taken into account. [Illustrate this by con trasting the experiences of Augustine and Pelagius, Luther and

Erasmus—showing how different courses in life, both moral and social, combined with varying personal characteristics to produce different spiritual experiences ; and how these again were reflected in their diverse types of doctrine.] It must be remembered, too, that these differences depend on the quality of our sense of sin, rather than on the relatively less or more heinous character of our sins. Consider Paul's estimate of himself as a sinner.

V.—*Men ought not to content themselves with a general repentance, but it is every man's duty to endeavour to repent of his particular sins particularly.*

Such a particular enumeration and remembrance of our faults is necessary to produce in us a proper and becoming frame. ' A general persuasion that thou art a sinner,' says Hooker, ' will neither so humble nor bridle thy soul, as if the catalogue of thy sins examined severally be continually kept in mind.' Without this we cannot preserve sufficiently clear views of the heinousness of all sin as such, apart from all distinctions greater or less, few or more.

At the same time one may be thoroughly penitent, and yet be in certain circumstances unable to individualize particular acts of sin. He may be disturbed, profoundly moved by the thought of his general sinfulness. It was so with Luther, who, while groaning under the load of his sins, could not name any in the Confessional.

It is necessary, on the other hand, to guard against a view of repentance which would make it consist simply in isolated acts of penitence on account of separate acts of sin. ' Repentance,' says Luther, ' goes not to work piecemeal in regard to particular deeds which thou hast openly committed against the ten commandments, but deals with the whole person, with all its life and character, yea, with the entire nature, and shows to thee that thou liest under God's wrath and art condemned to hell.' (See Harless, p. 215.) True repentance is no mere external thing. It does not essentially consist in lopping off, but in rooting out ; not in reforming the sinful life, but in removing the sinful heart. Thoroughness in repentance, however, can only follow that hatred of the sinful principle which renders one jealous of every single manifestation thereof.

VI.—*As every man is bound to make private confession of his sins to God, praying for the pardon thereof; upon which, and the forsaking of them, he shall find mercy; so he that scandalizeth his brother, or the church of Christ, ought to be willing, by a private or publick confession and sorrow for his sin, to declare his repentance to those that are offended; who are thereupon to be reconciled to him, and in love to receive him.*

We have here first of all the general statement that all sins without exception ought to be confessed to God. This act of confession, properly understood, comprises prayer for pardon and penitent resolve ; real prayer and true repentance are invariably followed by the exercise of divine mercy. God refuses forgiveness to all who refuse to confess their sin. We are next told in what special cases confession should be made not only privately to God, but also publicly before men. The main errors of the Romish doctrine are the prescribing confession before the priest as a habitual practice, and the destroying the voluntary character of the act by systematic questioning, and ranging over all manner of conceivable offences. The Reformed Church makes such confessions exceptional, and their form less or more public according as an individual or a community has been offended by the sin committed. If a brother is offended, go to him ; if the church, go to the church. The term scandal was commonly employed by theologians in the Westminster Assembly period to indicate anything, especially in doctrine or ritual, that was calculated to give offence or encourage abuse. That which scandalized a brother or the church at large is here applied, not to things in themselves indifferent, but to sins. Such sins have special aggravation from this, that the evil effects have evidently spread to others, who have, to some extent, been compromised by them. If we have wronged a man, be it by personal violence, evil speaking, purloining of his goods, or any other injury, we are bound to make confession before him, with such reparation as is possible, to show the honesty of our confession. If our offence is such that it would, when brought to light, bring special reproach upon the church to which we belong, we are required to tell it to the church. Then, lastly, we have here laid down the duty of those to whom such confession is made. The penitent is to be received in the spirit of love. By such a reception his penitence will be deepened. Where there is a lack of love among Christians, there will be a lack of sinners repenting. Iniquity abounding is as much the effect as the cause of the waxing cold of the love of many.

There is, however, no contradiction between faithfulness and fervent love. Of the members of the early church it was said, ' See how those Christians love one another ;' yet their mode of dealing with delinquents was most rigorous, and their discipline prescribed a long and humiliating course. [See a vigorous sketch of the stern discipline of the first Christian centuries in Pressensé's *Life and Practice in the Early Church*, Bk. I. chap. iii.]

CHAPTER XVI.

OF GOOD WORKS.

I.—*Good works are only such as God hath commanded in his holy word, and not such as, without the warrant thereof, are devised*

*by men out of blind zeal, and upon any pretence of good in-
tention.*

The rule of obedience is God's own Word. That which is done
because required of God can alone be regarded by Him as a good
work. Thus in this section we have the first exclusion of things
irrelevant by way of fixing the definition of a truly good work in the
evangelical sense — all that is done according to merely human
impulse must be set aside. If one misinterpret the will of God, his
work, not being in accordance with the Divine will, cannot be called
good ; but his misinterpretation is rather charged against him inasmuch as some element of selfishness, or some sinful inclination, has
biassed him in his interpretation. So, for example, Saul of Tarsus,
and all the nobler and more conscientious spirits among persecutors
in every age.

Under humanly-devised works here condemned may be included
the *Counsels of Perfection*, as distinguished in the Romish Church
from commands of duty. In so far as they may be reducible under
commands, they are simply of ordinary obligation. In so far as they
are not commanded, they are no better than the burdens which the
Pharisees were condemned for laying upon men.

II.—*These good works, done in obedience to God's commandments, are
the fruits and evidences of a true and lively faith: and by them
believers manifest their thankfulness, strengthen their assurance,
edify their brethren, adorn the profession of the gospel, stop the
mouths of the adversaries, and glorify God, whose workmanship
they are, created in Christ Jesus thereunto; that, having their
fruit unto holiness, they may have in the end eternal life.*

This section treats of the place and uses of good works. The
statement here given is very decidedly opposed to a false legalist
doctrine, as well as to all Antinomian extremes. When Romanism
proclaimed salvation by works, and the Anabaptists proclaimed
salvation without works, the true Protestantism re-echoed the doctrine
of the New Testament—salvation by faith, not through, nor without,
but unto good works. Those works, then, which according to the
Gospel are reckoned good, are not meritorious, but result from our
fellowship with Him in whom is the sole ground of merit.

The uses of good works may be distinguished as partly personal
and partly social. They are viewed as affording an expression to
the grace of thankfulness, and as contributing to the comfort and
establishment of the graces of the believer. They are viewed also
as furnishing means for the encouragement, growth, and blessing of
brethren, and as commending the Gospel to those who are without.
For those necessary uses good works are enjoined.

The end is that, by means of them, God's glory is advanced, and
the believer's sanctification is carried on.

III.—*Their ability to do good works is not at all of themselves, but wholly from the Spirit of Christ. And that they may be enabled thereunto, besides the graces they have already received, there is required an actual influence of the same Holy Spirit to work in them to will and to do of his good pleasure: yet are they not hereupon to grow negligent, as if they were not bound to perform any duty unless upon a special motion of the Spirit; but they ought to be diligent in stirring up the grace of God that is in them.*

In this and in the following sections we are shown that whatever good results appear in the Christian life, the praise belongs to God, as they are the fruits of His Spirit; and inasmuch as all the best endeavours of the saints are marred by their own sinful imperfections, shame belongs to them.

Here we have the doctrine laid down that the good works of regenerate men are the immediate result of the Spirit's influence. The good work is not the result of the simple operation of our Christian graces. This doctrine in regard to the Spirit, would be like that which regards the Creator, after the manner of the Deists, as giving a movement to the world and then withdrawing. Just as God the Creator continues in providence to uphold and govern His creation, so does God the Spirit continue to strengthen and direct His new creation in its spiritual course. He who will daily accomplish good works before God, must have his inward man renewed day by day.

Dependence on the Spirit, however, must not be made an excuse for sloth. It is true of the regenerate especially, as it is in a general way of all men, that God helps those who help themselves. If His offers of help previously made have been cheerfully accepted, and powers hitherto bestowed by Him diligently used, He will more readily grant further help and qualify for greater occasions. He who is faithful in little, will have ampler opportunities given, and will be fitted for showing his faithfulness in much. Those who honestly address themselves to the discharge of any duty, not sparing themselves any more than if all had to be done by them, and yet humbly and heartily acknowledging before God that only His Spirit's power can secure success, will have that spiritual influence bestowed if the work is for God's glory and should be done by them. And it is only under such condition that the saint can desire to work.

IV.—*They who in their obedience attain to the greatest height which is possible in this life, are so far from being able to supererogate, and to do more than God requires, as that they fall short of much which in duty they are bound to do.*

Those good works done do not come up to God's demands. Notwithstanding the special influence of the Holy Spirit, the sinful element remaining in the regenerate (see chap. xi. 5) renders the work done imperfect according to the standard of God's law. Those who think otherwise must have very false views of the condition of their own hearts, or very low views of the holiness of the Divine law. Our Confession opposes the doctrine of Rome. According to Bellarmine, works of supererogation are the fulfilment of the Counsels of Perfection. Others use the term more generally for the superabundant graces of the saints. In either case, it is implied that the believer may possibly do more than the law of God absolutely requires. The Counsels of Perfection (*consilia evangelica*) are not commanded but commended by Christ. According to Bellarmine, they are more difficult than and superior to ordinary commandments : if done, they secure a great reward ; if left undone, they bring no punishment ;—while ordinary commands, if obeyed, bring a reward ; if not obeyed, call down punishment. He compares the counsels to heroic enterprises on which no one is obliged to enter, for which, however, special premiums are offered. Out of such notions sprang the commendation of monastic vows. Asceticism was the endeavour to supererogate. Despising bounden duties as common and mean, it left these undone ; and surely the observance of vows, which according to their definition were not duties, could not reasonably be expected to supply the defect. Hence by the omission which it occasioned, apart altogether from the question of its positive merits or demerits, monasticism must be pronounced a failure.

V.—*We cannot, by our best works, merit pardon of sin, or eternal life, at the hand of God, by reason of the great disproportion that is between them and the glory to come, and the infinite distance that is between us and God, whom by them we can neither profit nor satisfy for the debt of our former sins; but when we have done all we can, we have done but our duty, and are unprofitable servants ; and because, as they are good, they proceed from his Spirit; and as they are wrought by us, they are defiled and mixed with so much weakness and imperfection, that they cannot endure the severity of God's judgment.*

VI.—*Yet notwithstanding, the persons of believers being accepted through Christ, their good works also are accepted in him ; not as though they were in this life wholly unblameable and unreproveable in God's sight ; but that he, looking upon them in his Son, is pleased to accept and reward that which is sincere, although accompanied with many weaknesses and imperfections*

The fifth section re-states what has been already commented on under the third and fourth sections. The reasons are more par-

ticularly given why the good works of believers cannot be regarded
as affording a ground of merit.   Supposing they had a value, the
reward of eternal life is out of all proportion beyond their worth.
Besides, they cannot be regarded as profitable to God.   Only if all
commands were first obeyed, and counsels of perfection kept, could
we be called profitable servants.

These sections indicate very clearly what place must be resolutely
refused to good works, and what place must be assigned to them.
On the one hand, care must be taken that in no way is the pure
Scripture doctrine of Justification by Faith alone imperilled ; that no
countenance is given to the legalist doctrine, which appeared first of
all in a false Judaism, and then in the teaching of the Romish Church,
according to which we are not saved by faith only, but by faith and
works.   On the other hand, care must be taken to avoid the contrary extreme by which a healthy Christian morality is placed in
danger, — the onesided appreciation of the bare act of faith apart
from any understanding of its necessary contents ; which was seen
in the Antinomian licence of enthusiasts, especially in the early
church, and in Reformation times.   No better single example of the
careful avoidance of those contrary errors can be pointed to than
that of Luther.   His controversial activity may be represented under
a twofold division—his polemic against the unevangelical legalism
of Rome, and his polemic against the immoral rejection of the law
by the Anabaptist sects.   Without in the least modifying his doctrine
of Justification by Faith only, Luther maintained the necessity of
good works, inasmuch as the principle of faith carried in it both
the inclination and the power, and therefore, by consequence, the
obligation to perform good works.

To him that worketh not, but believeth (Rom. iv. 5) ;—this represents the one side of the truth.   The Reformers, however, called
attention to the connection in which it was uttered by Paul, and
showed that it had reference only to works of the law done in the
hope of securing and meriting salvation.   Nicholas Amsdorf (1559)
maintains the thesis that good works are injurious to salvation
(*perniciosa ad salutem*) as a good Christian proposition.   This, of
course, was intended to refer to works done in a legal spirit, but was
fitted to mislead and encourage error, and was therefore condemned
by all wiser Protestants.

It has been shown by Dorner (*History of Protestant Theology*,
vol. i. p. 352), that in the Lutheran Church, Antinomianism, when it
appeared, arose from an unwise fear of depreciating the all-sufficiency
of faith for salvation ; while in the Reformed or Calvinistic Church,
it arose from the unbalanced statement of an absolute doctrine of
Predestination, which lays stress upon the irrespective character of
God's choice.   Thus, different as the tendencies of those doctrines
might seem, the exaggeration of them leads to the same error.   A
warning this against all onesidedness in doctrine.

Our Confession speaks here of rewards ; yet these are not of debt but of grace. It is by grace that we are joined to Christ, and it is in Christ that the reward is enjoyed. He is rewarded for His righteousness ; and as those who are in Him share His righteousness, so also they share His rewards.

VII.—*Works done by unregenerate men, although, for the matter of them, they may be things which God commands, and of good use both to themselves and others ; yet, because they proceed not from an heart purified by faith ; nor are done in a right manner, according to the word ; nor to a right end, the glory of God ; they are therefore sinful, and cannot please God, or make a man meet to receive grace from God. And yet their neglect of them is more sinful, and displeasing unto God.*

This is no extreme doctrine, as some would represent it. That among unregenerate men there are great differences of natural character and temperament is admitted. While all the unregenerate are sinful before God, their sinfulness is greater or less. The unconverted man who reaches a high moral standard is more pleasing to God than one who is callously and carelessly making no effort. And yet the one no more than the other is to be called righteous, nor can his works be really pleasing to God. Even more the improvement of God's gifts of common grace before regeneration, and the diligent use of talents and opportunities given, are taken into account. In God's election we mark the recognition of certain useful characteristics in the subjects of His choice. 'Because,' says Luther, ' Paul did the work (the persecution of the Christians) so earnestly, our Lord Jesus had Him in His thoughts, and said thus to Himself, "This man may become good, for what he does he does in earnest." In the same manner,' he adds, ' our Lord and God makes use of me at this day against the Pope and his whole party.'[1] Yet in regard to claims upon God, there is among natural men no difference. If we admit the doctrine of Total Depravity and Inherited Corruption (see chap. vi 4), we must accept the doctrine of this section. Without faith it is impossible to please Him. Hence, though unregenerate men do acts which in themselves are good and beneficial,—relieve the distressed, support and advance by contributions a good cause,—yet for want of faith in the heart of the worker, and that love which characterizes faithful work, they cannot be pleasing or acceptable to God.

[1] See Martensen, *Dogmatics*, pp. 378, 379.

CHAPTER XVII.

OF THE PERSEVERANCE OF THE SAINTS.

I.—*They whom God hath accepted in his Beloved, effectually called and sanctified by his Spirit, can neither totally nor finally fall away from the state of grace; but shall certainly persevere therein to the end, and be eternally saved.*

The term perseverance, as here used, evidently suggests first of all the necessity of continuing to the end in the exercise of those graces which characterize the state of the regenerate. To begin well is not enough; he that endures to the end shall be saved. This doctrine is both scriptural and reasonable. But then immediately the question arises, 'Is it possible that one should begin well,—not in appearance merely, but in reality,—and nevertheless so fall away as to come short of eternal life?' This is a fundamental question as to the character of that grace received by the regenerate and justified. Is this grace defectible or indefectible? Calvin maintains that, however small and weak faith may be in the elect, still the Spirit of God is so to them an earnest and seal of their adoption, that His impress can never be removed from their hearts (see *Institutes*, Book iii. chap. ii. sec. 12). Our Confession here lays down the same doctrine, carefully guarding against any unwarrantable extreme by affirming the impossibility only of a total and final fall from grace. The certainty of salvation at last to all who have been recipients of justifying grace, is firmly maintained. In the third section it is shown in what ways there may be a partial and temporary fall from grace. God's Word abounds with warnings and encouragements to believers; and both are addressed for the purpose of rendering a complete apostasy impossible. Records of utter falling away are certainly given; but John explains these cases by saying that their going out showed that they never belonged to Christ (1 John ii. 19).

II.—*This perseverance of the saints depends not upon their own free will, but upon the immutability of the decree of election, flowing from the free and unchangeable love of God the Father; upon the efficacy of the merit and intercession of Jesus Christ; the abiding of the Spirit, and of the seed of God within them; and the nature of the covenant of grace: from all which ariseth also the certainty and infallibility thereof.*

It is only on the ground of the doctrine of Predestination that the doctrine of Perseverance can be consistently maintained. The election which we affirm as the biblical doctrine, is an election unto life. If this end be not determined by an immutable decree, it is evidently left undetermined.   If the endurance of the believer in his faith be made to depend on anything mutable, it is no longer indefectible,—it may be lost.   Had faith been created in us by an act of free will, then indeed another act of free will might undo it. When, however, we accept the doctrine of the Immutable Divine Decree, faith is recognised as bearing an indestructible character (*character indelebilis*).   'Free grace,' says Boston, 'will fix those whom free will shook down into a gulf of misery.'   Faith is not viewed as a magical influence, which has any inherent virtue of perseverance.   All depends on God's grace, whereby, according to the Divine decree, salvation in the end is secured to all the chosen. As we have seen, this decree takes the form of a covenant of grace, which involves the impetration of Christ's work, and the effectual calling of those predestinated to life.   [The doctrine that perseverance in faith unto the end is wholly from God's grace, is admirably illustrated by Bunyan, in the scene at the Interpreter's house, where Christ, by pouring in oil, checks the malicious efforts of the enemy to quench the fire.]

III.—*Nevertheless they may, through the temptations of Satan and of the world, the prevalency of corruption remaining in them, and the neglect of the means of their preservation, fall into grievous sins; and for a time continue therein: whereby they incur God's displeasure, and grieve his Holy Spirit; come to be deprived of some measure of their graces and comforts; have their hearts hardened, and their consciences wounded; hurt and scandalize others, and bring temporal judgments upon themselves.*

Here the possibility of believers falling into sin is fully recognised, and the causes and consequences of such falls are enumerated.

The possibility is admitted of believers falling into grievous sins. There has been a distinction made between mortal and venial sins. According to Romish theologians, venial sins are distinguished from mortal sins as to their nature, inasmuch as they do not affect the state of grace, and occasion not eternal, but only temporal punishment.   They are further generally described as those acts which, though wrong, do not offend against the love of God and our neighbour, but rather arise from some small imperfection.   This sort of distinction is utterly repudiated by Protestants.   The very use of the terms mortal and venial is regarded with considerable jealousy. If the distinction is admitted at all, it is not applied as by the Romanists to different classes of sins, but to different classes of persons.   In the unregenerate no offence is venial, but every one mortal; and in the regenerate no sin can be regarded as mortal, in the full and accurate sense of the term, though in its own nature every sin is so.   It is to be remembered, however, that Protestants do not therefore regard all sins in the regenerate as equal; but every sin in the regenerate is punished in proportion to the heinousness and dangerous character of the offence,—in proportion to the damage which it is calculated to inflict upon the spiritual life of the individual committing it, and in proportion to the scandal it would bring upon the cause of Christ. The object of such temporal punishment is to remove from the heart of the believer that remaining corruption the presence of which disturbs that communion with Christ which it is the purpose of God never will be so disturbed as to be finally broken off. [Winer, *Confessions of Christendom*, xii., gives a clear summary of views on this subject.]

The causes of such falls are here enumerated under three heads. It is evident, however, that these three are resolvable into the incompleteness of the believer's sanctification.   (1.) Temptations,—which can only have power when they appeal to some natural feeling or inclination of the heart. (2.) Indwelling corruption,—which is that within which corresponds or answers to the temptations presented from without. (3.) Neglect of means provided for the preservation of grace,—which is generally the result of the collusion of temptation and inward corruption.

The consequences of such falls are damage to the offender and injury to others. The very essence of such a fall consists in the displeasing of God and grieving His Spirit. (1.) There befalls the offender—loss of the comforts of grace and endurance of some spiritual damage. 'Though the enemies cannot break down the walls of salvation, and kill you, yet if ye look unwarily out over them, some one enemy or other may throw a dart at you, which, though it kill not, may leave blue marks. Though sin cannot dispossess the Spirit entirely, yet it may grieve Him ; and if ye grieve Him, He will grieve you.' (Halyburton, *Works*, p. 628.) We have many instances, too, of sore bodily suffering falling upon undoubted saints in consequence of their sins ; even temporal death may be the penalty of waywardness in believers. We refer for illustration to the case of the man of God at Bethel (see the poem on this incident in Keble's *Christian Year*). Many are inclined to interpret literally what Paul says of many being sickly, and some having fallen asleep, because of carelessness in their approaches to the Lord's table. (2.) Such falls are the occasion of offence and damage to others. How often do we hear the inconsistencies of believers put forward as a plea by those who refuse to identify themselves with the Christian church ! While such taking of offence is inexcusable, he who is the occasion of it must feel it to be a most bitter consequence of his fall.

CHAPTER XVIII.

OF ASSURANCE OF GRACE AND SALVATION.

I.—*Although hypocrites, and other unregenerate men, may vainly deceive themselves with false hopes and carnal presumptions of being in the favour of God and estate of salvation; which hope of theirs shall perish; yet such as truly believe in the Lord Jesus, and love him in sincerity, endeavouring to walk in all good conscience before him, may in this life be certainly assured that they are in the state of grace, and may rejoice in the hope of the glory of God; which hope shall never make them ashamed.*

The false assurance by which hypocrites deceive themselves, being altogether different from the assurance of true faith, should not lead to a depreciation of the doctrine.   The main characteristics of a state of grace are given here : true faith, a sincere love, and a consistent walk.   Edwards, in his excellent *Treatise on the Religious Affections*, has, under the division on Signs of Truly Gracious and Holy Affections, a section entitled, ' Christian Practice is the Chief Sign to Ourselves ' He shows that holy practice is the evidence of the presence of all the Christian graces.   It is the best proof of saving knowledge, true repentance, genuine faith, gracious love, and godly fear.   Not by prying into Divine secrets, but through attention to the duties of the practical Christian life, is the comfort of true assurance to be gained. The following from the *Imitation of Christ* is instructive : ' When one that was in anxiety of mind, often wavering between hope and fear, did once, being oppressed with grief, humbly prostrate himself in a church before the altar, in prayer, and said within himself, "Oh, if I knew that I should yet persevere !" he presently heard within him an answer from God, which said, "If thou didst know it, what wouldst thou do ?   Do now what thou wouldst do then, and thou shalt be secure."   And being herewith comforted and strengthened, he committed himself wholly to the will of God, and his anxious wavering ceased.   Neither had he the mind to search curiously any farther to know what should befall him ; but rather laboured ' to understand what was the perfect and acceptable will of God for the beginning and accomplishing of every good work.'   (Bk. i. chap. xxv. 2.)

II.—*This certainty is not a bare conjectural and probable persuasion, grounded upon a fallible hope; but an infallible assurance of faith, founded upon the divine truth of the promises of salvation, the inward evidence of those graces unto which these promises are made, the testimony of the Spirit of adoption witnessing with our spirits that we are the children of God: which Spirit is the*

H

earnest of our inheritance, whereby we are sealed to the day of redemption.

This Christian assurance has a firm foundation; having a twofold certainty from the presence of the saving graces in the believer, and from the testimony of the Holy Spirit. 'The believer attains to reflex faith,' says Pontoppidan, an old Danish writer quoted by Delitzsch, 'that is, to faith which recognises and experiences itself in the Divine light with joy, partly by proving himself according to God's Word (2 Cor. xiii. 5), and finding himself standing in the faith (*reflexio activa, rationalis vel syllogistica*); partly by receiving without his own agency impressions of the Holy Spirit, which in the ground of his heart give to him the sweet and comforting assurance of his standing in grace, and assure him that he is a child of God (*reflexio mere passiva et supernaturalis*). The reflex faith in this latter sense is separated from the direct faith, just as the repeating echo is distinguished from the voice that calls it forth.' (*Bibl. Psych.* p. 178.) There is a necessity for self-examination in order to discover whether we have those saving graces—those graces which characterize the saved—faith in Christ, love to Him. If we find these really present, although we may have to bewail their feebleness, yet their presence, apart from their development, affords a sure ground of assurance. We believe—then let us remember the promise, 'He that believeth on me hath everlasting life.' We love—then let us not forget Jesus' words, 'If a man love me, my Father will love him.' False confidence trusts to mere subjective emotions; true confidence finds these authenticated by the Spirit which brings assurance of God's love and fatherhood, witnessing convincingly and comfortingly to our position before God. (See *Sermon on the Witness of the Spirit,* M'Laren, 1st series.)

III.—*This infallible assurance doth not so belong to the essence of faith, but that a true believer may wait long, and conflict with many difficulties, before he be partaker of it: yet, being enabled by the Spirit to know the things which are freely given him of God, he may, without extraordinary revelation, in the right use of ordinary means, attain thereunto. And therefore it is the duty of every one to give all diligence to make his calling and election sure; that thereby his heart may be enlarged in peace and joy in the Holy Ghost, in love and thankfulness to God, and in strength and cheerfulness in the duties of obedience, the proper fruits of this assurance: so far is it from inclining men to looseness.*

The distinction is here made between faith and the assurance of faith. Divines have been in the habit of distinguishing the direct act of faith (*actio fidei directa*), by which we lay hold upon or believe in Christ, and the reflex act of faith (*actio fidei reflexa*), by which we gain a comforting experience and assurance of our faith. It is the direct act, the act of faith in Christ, that justifies; not the persuasion that we have of our faith. 'The faith is in its essence,' says Delitzsch, '*fiducia supplex* (assurance of refuge), not *fiducia triumphans seu gloriosa* (assurance of experience). The faith is God's agency, as well in the former state as in the latter: in the one, it is the operation of His grace condescending toward man; in the other, it is the operation of that grace apprehended, and assuring itself, and giving itself to be apprehended by man.' (*Bibl. Psych.* p. 413.) It is highly desirable that we should realize the importance for our comfort and spiritual health of a true and unshaken assurance of our faith and interest in Christ, and at the same time remember that the absence of that assurance may be accounted for without denying the genuineness and sincerity of the faith professed. In his *Trial of a Saving Interest in Christ*, Guthrie shows that it is an error to suppose that every one in Christ knows that he is in Him, or that all who know this have equal certainty in their knowledge, or that assurance is regularly maintained in equal strength, or that real assurance is inconsistent with an inability to answer some objections that may be brought against it. (See chap. i. sect. iii.)

Though in particular cases God may be pleased to give special revelations (see quotation from A'Kempis in the first section), yet it is in the use of the ordinary means that this assurance is to be sought. Compare what is said at the close of the opening section of our Confession. The words of Abraham to the rich man form a suitable warning here. Old practical writers give frequent examples of those who, seeking help from miraculous utterances, were afterwards satisfied with some communication out of the written Word. [Give illustrations of such morbid tendencies from the histories of Swedenborg, Edward Irving, and modern spiritualism.]

IV.—*True believers may have the assurance of their salvation divers ways shaken, diminished, and intermitted; as, by negligence in preserving of it; by falling into some special sin, which woundeth the conscience and grieveth the Spirit; by some sudden or vehement temptation; by God's withdrawing the light of his countenance, and suffering even such as fear him to walk in darkness, and to have no light: yet are they never utterly destitute of that seed of God, and life of faith, that love of Christ and the brethren, that sincerity of heart and conscience of duty, out of which, by the operation of the Spirit, this assurance may in due time be revived, and by the which, in the mean time, they are supported from utter despair.*

This section shows what shakes the believer's assurance of his salvation and takes away for a time its comfort. This is, in short, the presence of sin. There may have been an actual fall into sin. The Spirit is grieved and withdraws His witness; the saving graces are enfeebled, so that the believer is no longer able to grasp the comfort of the promises. Or the mere presentation of sin in sore temptation may occasion discouragement, so that our sense of God's faithfulness and love may be lessened, and our enjoyment of His presence be dimmed. There is danger too of reaction after strenuous spiritual effort, and this reaction leads to loss of spiritual comfort. Christian, after climbing half-way up the hill Difficulty, rests in the arbour and sleeps. Then he loses his roll. He goes on, but soon misses his roll, and sacrifices time and energy returning to find it. 'This roll was the assurance of his life and acceptance at the desired haven.' With the roll in possession again, he was able to face the lions, and all other dangers by the way. [Read *Imitation of Christ*, Bk. ii. chap. ix., 'Of the Want of all Comfort.'] The leading Reformers, in their protest against the Romish view which denied the possibility of assurance by use of the ordinary means, went too far in the direction of identifying faith and the assurance of salvation. This extreme as well as the other is guarded against in our Confession. The statement contained in the latter portion of the above section indicates that while full assurance may be lost, assurance is never wholly lost by the true believer. It is only the hypocrite's hope that is cut off: in the believer, the endurance of the assurance of hope is the earnest of the reawakening in due time of the full assurance of faith.

CHAPTER XIX.

OF THE LAW OF GOD.

I.—*God gave to Adam a law, as a covenant of works, by which he bound him, and all his posterity, to personal, entire, exact, and perpetual obedience; promised life upon the fulfilling, and threatened death upon the breach of it; and endued him with power and ability to keep it.*

A more explicit statement is here made regarding the covenant of works already referred to (chap. vii. 2). The obligation, as we had occasion before to notice, has its origin prior to any covenant agreement. The natural relation of the creature to his Creator obliges him to render obedience, and this was only rendered more evident by the word of promise and threatening expressed in the covenant. Adam possessed, what no man since has had, power sufficient in his own strength to do the works required. By the exercise of his own powers he might have fulfilled the condition and received the blessing of the covenant. [Show the precise meaning of the terms personal, entire, exact, and perpetual, as characterizing the required obedience.] Had Adam rendered the obedience, he would simply have fulfilled an obligation of his nature, without acquiring any merit by his works. Still his righteousness, viewed as his original righteousness confirmed and elevated, would have been secured by his works.

II.—*This law, after his fall, continued to be a perfect rule of righteousness; and, as such, was delivered by God upon Mount Sinai in ten commandments, and written in two tables; the first four commandments containing our duty towards God, and the other six our duty to man.*

The promulgation of the law to Israel is often called the Sinai Covenant. We have certainly scripture authority for calling it a covenant (Ex. xix. 5 ; Deut. v. 2). At the same time we must beware of confusing this use of the word with its use in reference to the two great dispensations—the covenant of works and the covenant of grace. The Sinai Covenant is not to be co-ordinated with these. The question is, What relation does it bear to them? Is it in some way related to both, or is it subsidiary to the one, or to the other? Some appear to regard the Sinai Covenant as neither wholly under the covenant of works, nor wholly under the covenant of grace. It has, they suppose, a tincture of the covenant of grace in the preface to the Decalogue, and in the Decalogue itself there is a simple reproduction of the covenant of works. This would make God the author of confusion. There can be no mingling of the two covenants which are necessarily exclusive of one another. Some, again, view the Sinai Covenant as a peculiar exhibition or republication of the covenant of works. It was the error of legalist Jews so to misconceive the purpose of the Mosaic dispensation, and against this position the apostle argues (Gal. iv. 21, 31). This is not the view of our Confession. For, under the covenant of works the law was not merely a rule of righteousness, such as it remains under the covenant of grace (sec. 6), but rather a rule of judgment according to which those under it were justified or condemned. Some, again, identify the Sinai Covenant with the covenant of grace, regarding it as simply a dispensational form of that covenant. This seems the true and only tenable position. Israel was God's redeemed people, the type of the church ; and it was to this people, as the chosen and redeemed, that the law was addressed. Evidently this is the view of our Confession. That law which to the world is a standard for judgment, is, to those under the covenant of grace, a rule of righteousness. [See for an interesting *resumé* of opinions on this subject, 'The Sinai Covenant,' by Rev. R. G. Balfour, in *British and For. Evan. Review* for 1877. p. 511.]

The latter part of the section describes the contents of the moral law, distributing these contents into two parts—our duty to God, and our duty to man. It is a wise remark of Fairbairn, that as we

know not where one table ended and the other began, so we are not
entitled to make any absolute division between these two parts, but
that we are called rather to recognise the essential unity by which
those two great commandments constitute one perfect law.

III.—*Besides this law, commonly called moral, God was pleased to
give to the people of Israel, as a church under age, ceremonial
laws, containing several typical ordinances; partly of worship,
prefiguring Christ, his graces, actions, sufferings, and benefits;
and partly holding forth divers instructions of moral duties.
All which ceremonial laws are now abrogated under the New
Testament.*

IV.—*To them also, as a body politick, he gave sundry judicial
laws, which expired together with the state of that people, not
obliging any other now, further than the general equity thereof
may require.*

These sections treat of what is mutable in the Divine law. The
confusion between the elements that are immutable and those that
are mutable has been the occasion of many unsatisfactory and
extreme views in regard to the purpose and the present significance of
the Old Testament. Our Confession here very distinctly classifies
under the division of mutable laws—(1) all that were purely ceremonial, and (2) all that were merely judicial,—which are both said to
have been given besides the moral law. [Perhaps the very best discussion of the subject now before us is to be found in Hooker's
Ecclesiastical Polity, where there is a section very ably proving that
neither God's being the author of laws, nor His committing them to
Scripture, nor the continuance of the end for which they were instituted, is any reason sufficient to prove that they are unchangeable.
Book iii. chap. x.]

(1.) Purely ceremonial observances belong to the mutable part
of Divine legislation. They characterized a particular preparatory dispensation, and were peculiarly Jewish. The condition of
those so dealt with under the dispensation of the law is quaintly
described as that of a church under age. (Gal. iv. 1, 2.) As to the use
of such ceremonies, they were partly liturgical and partly ethical.
In correspondence with those uses, they were in their nature preparatory and provisional.

(2.) Judicial laws or political maxims delivered to the Jews are no
longer as such binding. These are in many cases evidently provisional.
In Israel's own history they were modified from time to time as
circumstances required, and the principle was elevated and rendered
purer according as those addressed appeared to the Divine wisdom
able to bear. [Illustrate this by pointing out variations and signs of
development in the revelation of law in Scripture. Compare Ex.

xxi.-xxiii. with Deut. xii.-xxvi. Also, Christ's 'But I say unto you,' Matt. v. 21–48.] It is very evident that the circumstances of modern society demand very different regulations from those which suited national conditions under the Jewish monarchy; and on all hands it is allowed that the increase of enlightenment warrants the application in many directions of a higher standard. Yet whatever principles of eternal justice appeared in those laws are now obligatory, —yet not because found there, but because of their own nature. The adventitious, circumstantial, formal, perishes; the substantial endures. Our Confession is strictly consistent in applying this principle. In chapter xxi. 7, the continued obligation to observe the Sabbath is not made to rest simply on the fact that it formed part of the Jewish law, but rather on the fact that it belonged to the law of natural obligation existing for man from the beginning. The same principle, again, is recognised in chapter xxiv. in regard to the law of marriage.

V.—*The moral law doth for ever bind all, as well justified persons as others, to the obedience thereof; and that not only in regard of the matter contained in it, but also in respect of the authority of God, the Creator, who gave it. Neither doth Christ in the gospel any way dissolve, but much strengthen this obligation.*

This moral law is said to have a twofold binding force—in regard to the matter, and in regard to its author. Yet these two are one; for the moral law is the same as that law originally written on man's heart by his Creator. That moral consciousness which causes us to regard the matter of the law as for ever binding, is itself, as well as the several precepts of the law, from God.

That all men, both unregenerate and regenerate, are under obligation to this moral law, is a principle that ought to be most emphatically maintained. Subjection to law does not characterize any class of men, justified or unjustified. It is characteristic of man as such. Regard for law is demanded by the very nature of man, who is conscious of realizing his true freedom only in submitting to and in applying to himself the terms of the law. (Kant, *Metaphysic of Ethics*, pp. 112, 113.) The universal reference of the binding force of the moral law is meant to mark the inclusion not only of unregenerate persons who may afterward become regenerate, but also that of reprobates. The effects, however, of the law upon these two classes are very different. 'In the elect,' says Rollock, 'the acknowledgment of sin and condemnation which they have by the covenant of works, is unto them a preparative to embrace the covenant of grace; but in the reprobate it is the way to extreme desperation.' (*Effectual Calling*, page 47.)

VI.—*Although true believers be not under the law as a covenant of works, to be thereby justified or condemned; yet is it of great*

*use to them, as well as to others; in that, as a rule of life,
informing them of the will of God and their duty, it directs and
binds them to walk accordingly; discovering also the sinful
pollutions of their nature, hearts, and lives; so as, examining
themselves thereby, they may come to further conviction of, humiliation for, and hatred against sin; together with a clearer sight
of the need they have of Christ, and the perfection of his obedience.
It is likewise of use to the regenerate, to restrain their corruptions,
in that it forbids sin; and the threatenings of it serve to shew
what even their sins deserve, and what afflictions in this life
they may expect for them, although freed from the curse thereof
threatened in the law. The promises of it, in like manner, show
them God's approbation of obedience, and what blessings they may
expect upon the performance thereof, although not as due to them
by the law as a covenant of works: so as a man's doing good,
and refraining from evil, because the law encourageth to the one,
and deterreth from the other, is no evidence of his being under the
law, and not under grace.*

Here are set forth the sense in which believers are under the law,
and the uses of the law to them.   It is not by the law that they are
justified or condemned, but according to its precepts they are guided
in life.   The grand distinction between the unbeliever and the
believer, as related to the law, is that to the one it is a covenant of
works, to the other a covenant of grace.   The unregenerate is under
obligation to keep it perfectly, and to do this solely in his own
strength; and failing this, he must endure its curse.   The regenerate,
again, are required to keep its precepts in order to please God, and
enjoy His unbroken favour; yet this is to be done not in their own
strength, but through grace sought and obtained in fellowship with
Christ.   The works done in the one case, were it possible to do them,
would be works of nature; the works done in the other case are
works of grace, the fruits of the Spirit.

To the believer the uses of the law are these :—1. In general, the
law affords to them a clear discovery of God's will, and, inasmuch
as they are rightly exercised thereby, it awakens and deepens a
sense of their own sinfulness, and recommends to them the perfect
righteousness of Christ's obedience. 2. In particular, the law has a
twofold efficiency by way of threatening and promise. (1.) The
threatening of punishment on account of sin is universal as sin itself.
The regenerate receive punishment in the form of chastisement on
account of their sins, are made to endure bodily, mental, and spiritual
distress, and vividly to realize the desert of their sin.   Those threatenings which imply God's discipline are to the believer very real : so
that while through weakness he sins, he cannot enjoy sin, his after-

thoughts are harassing, because from his spiritual knowledge of the law he knows what sin is. This vivid sense of sin, though they know themselves freed from its condemning power, accounts for the burdened experience of so many true Christians. (Read Owen *On Indwelling Sin.*) (2.) The promises of reward in return for obedience are encouragements, inasmuch as through faith we believe the end is attainable, being dependent not on our own strength but on God's grace, and inasmuch as the recognition of blessed enjoyments as promised rewards gives further assurance of the reality of the union between the believer and Christ.

These uses the law has to the believer for encouragement, because his faith is not perfect : he is urged by them to continue struggling against unbelief.

VII.—*Neither are the forementioned uses of the law contrary to the grace of the gospel, but do sweetly comply with it; the Spirit of Christ subduing and enabling the will of man to do that freely and cheerfully which the will of God revealed in the law requireth to be done.*

The strict requirements of the law, when regarded by the unregenerate man, seem bondage. To him who is under grace, and views the law and its requirements from that point, God's commandments are not grievous. The law does not militate against the gospel, but shows rather to what perfection grace will carry those in whom it works. Hence the presentation of so perfect a rule of righteousness is most happily described as exercising on the regenerate a sweet and attractive influence. Consider the peculiarly affectionate terms in which the Psalmist refers always to the law. This is because it is regarded as the direct expression of God's will : the believer is therefore affected by the law as by the personal presence of God Himself. The Spirit of God within teaches the believer to recognise the Spirit of God in the law.

We may conclude our notes on this whole chapter with the glowing words of Hooker in praise of the law : 'Of law there can be no less acknowledged, than that her seat is the bosom of God, her voice the harmony of the world : all things in heaven and earth do her homage, the very least as feeling her care, and the greatest as not exempted from her power ; both angels and men, and creatures of what condition soever, though each in different sort and manner, yet all, with uniform consent, admiring her as the mother of their peace and joy.' (*Eccles. Polity*, Book i. chap. xvi.)

CHAPTER XX

OF CHRISTIAN LIBERTY AND LIBERTY OF CONSCIENCE

I —*The liberty which Christ hath purchased for believers under the gospel, consists in their freedom from the guilt of sin, the condemning wrath of God, the curse of the moral law; and in their being delivered from this present evil world, bondage to Satan, and dominion of sin, from the evil of afflictions, the sting of death, the victory of the grave, and everlasting damnation; as also in their free access to God, and their yielding obedience unto him, not out of slavish fear, but a child-like love, and willing mind. All which were common also to believers under the law; but under the new testament, the liberty of Christians is further enlarged in their freedom from the yoke of the ceremonial law, to which the Jewish Church was subjected, and in greater boldness of access to the throne of grace, and in fuller communications of the free Spirit of God, than believers under the law did ordinarily partake of.*

This section treats of Christian liberty, showing what it is, and who they are that enjoy its benefits. From its very nature it necessarily belongs to all true believers, but under different dispensations it is enjoyed in varying degrees. That which is essential to Christian liberty is deliverance from the guilt and dominion of sin. The consciousness of this deliverance was not so clear to the Old Testament believers as to those under the New, and hence the joyousness of liberty was neither so full nor so constant in them ; yet the fact of their liberty through Christ was no less a reality. Christian liberty is alone worthy of the name of liberty. ‘ He is the freeman whom the truth makes free, And all are slaves beside.’ The stages of the realization of this freedom are clearly stated. 1. Freedom through justification,—there is no condemnation. 2. Freedom through sanctification,—remaining bonds are gradually broken as the earnest of final emancipation. 3. Freedom through the Spirit of adoption,— the development of the feelings of a free-born child. All this is Christ's gift purchased by Him for believers, and dispensed to them under the gospel.

II.—*God alone is Lord of the conscience, and hath left it free from the doctrines and commandments of men which are in any thing contrary to his word, or beside it, in matters of faith or worship. So that to believe such doctrines, or to obey such commandments out of conscience, is to betray true liberty of conscience; and the*

requiring of an implicit faith, and an absolute and blind obedience,
is to destroy liberty of conscience, and reason also.

This statement has been the subject of very general and hearty
approval.   Its diction is peculiarly felicitous.   It affords a very clear
and satisfactory definition of what is meant by the right of private
judgment as claimed for every Christian man.   This is a fundamental
principle of Protestantism.   The Christian conscience cannot be
coerced.   It may be instructed, it may be appealed to, but it may
not be forced.   All enforced conformity, inasmuch as it does not
recognise the rights of the individual conscience, is firmly repudiated.
God alone, whose image is reflected in the conscience, stands over it
as Lord and superior.   [Read on the right of private judgment, R.
W. Dale, *Ultimate Principles of Protestantism.*]   God speaking in
His Word should direct and rule the human conscience.   When the
Romish Church demands the surrender of the individual conscience,
she puts herself in God's place.   The subjection of conscience to God
secures the freedom of man's whole personality, but subjection to any
other is slavery.   Not only in things directly opposed to God's Word,
but even in regard to things not determined by God's Word, the
individual conscience must have its rights respected.   This was the
plea urged by those who objected to imposing upon the members of
the church conformity in the observance of outward ceremonies.
Gillespie, in his *Dispute against the Ceremonies* (1637), argued that
the imposition of these ceremonies bereft the Christian of his liberty :
1. Because his practice was adstricted ; 2. Because his conscience
was bound ; 3. Because his conscience, which condemned them,
was violated ; 4. Because they were pressed upon them by naked
will and authority, without any reason being given to satisfy the
conscience.   All this will be found in thorough accordance with the
covenant obligation undertaken by each member on entering the
Assembly, to endeavour reformation of religion according to the Word
of God, and the example of the best Reformed churches.

III.—*They who, upon pretence of Christian liberty, do practise any*
    sin, or cherish any lust, do thereby destroy the end of Christian
    liberty ; which is, that, being delivered out of the hands of our
    enemies, we might serve the Lord without fear, in holiness and
    righteousness before him, all the days of our life.

The freedom which belongs to a rational and spiritual creature is
deliverance from all that would hinder the attainment of the end of
his being.   'Man's chief end is to glorify God and to enjoy him for
ever.'   The freedom wherewith Christ maketh His people free consists in the new presentation of this end as the determined and
secured goal of Christian attainment.   Deliverance from the yoke of
bondage, from the slavery and dominion of sin, is simply a means

to the end of holiness and righteousness in the life. Through the
enslaving dominion of sin, law had become a bondage. The
Christian is delivered from this bondage, not that he should be hence-
forth without law to God, but that he should place himself under the
law to Christ. Christian liberty, like every Christian privilege and
grace, must be spiritually discerned. Wanting spiritual enlightenment, outward freedom is mistaken for spiritual freedom. Speaking
of the insurrectionary peasants of Germany, who, in Reformation
times, adopted Anabaptist views, Dorner says : ' The preaching of
Christian liberty had touched them, but only stirred their carnal
nature ; they desired to know nothing of true repentance, but only of
judgment, in their dark hatred against nobles and rulers—a hatred
begotten indeed of long oppression. They sought to draw from the
principle of the Reformation only a Divine sanction for their desire of
temporal freedom.' (*History of Protestant Theology,* i. 135.) Illustrations of the tendency to mistake licence for liberty may be taken
from the histories of any of the Antinomian sects which are invariably developed alongside of Reformation struggles and religious
awakenings.

IV.—*And because the powers which God hath ordained, and the
liberty which Christ hath purchased, are not intended by God to
destroy, but mutually to uphold and preserve one another; they
who, upon pretence of Christian liberty, shall oppose any lawful
power, or the lawful exercise of it, whether it be civil or
ecclesiastical, resist the ordinance of God. And for their publishing of such opinions, or maintaining of such practices, as are
contrary to the light of nature, or to the known principles
of Christianity, whether concerning faith, worship, or conversation; or to the power of godliness; or such erroneous opinions or
practices, as either in their own nature, or in the manner of
publishing or maintaining them, are destructive to the external
peace and order which Christ hath established in the church;
they may lawfully be called to account, and proceeded against
by the censures of the church, and by the power of the civil
magistrate.*

Our Confession here lays down very clearly the position that the
civil power is a Divine ordinance, and that as such it has its own
legitimate sphere. This the Christian in the right use of his liberty
must respect. The general statement made above refers to all regu-
larly-constituted authorities, whether civil or ecclesiastical, and asserts
their rights as against every kind of onesided individualism.

The second part of the section simply explains how the civil and
ecclesiastical authority must in particular cases be exercised. The

main difficulty in connection with this is to determine whether the civil power as well as the ecclesiastical should have any place assigned to it in controversies regarding doctrine and church order. The reference of all the above enumerated offences even to an ecclesiastical tribunal was a subject of a prolonged debate in the Assembly, lasting throughout three days; when it was concluded that all such offenders should be proceeded against by the censures of the church. The debate was then opened as to the power of the civil magistrate in matters of Christian faith and practice. This discussion lasted for six days. Arguments advanced against putting this statement into the Confession were at last held to have been sufficiently answered, and so the section was closed as it now stands. Against this conclusion four somewhat prominent members entered their dissent. It must be admitted that the opening clauses of this section might be so understood as to favour persecuting principles. Yet it is only fair to interpret the phrase, 'practices contrary to the principles of Christianity in faith, worship, or conversation,' by what follows regarding practices destructive of external peace and order. Disorderly practice is often the direct outcome of the dissemination of false doctrine. In regard, for example, to the subjects of the following chapters of the Confession, it is evident that the authority which insists upon the outward observance of the Sabbath, visits the perjurer with punishment, and maintains the sanctity of the marriage bond, deals at once with questions of doctrine and of practice. Further, too, the magistrate must see to it that the contentions of sects do not reach a violation of outward order required by law. (See Professor Mitchell, *Minutes of Assembly*, Introd. p. lxx.) That the Westminster divines as a whole should have had views of toleration such as are now held, it would be unreasonable to expect. In the circumstances of the nation, indeed, toleration as we understand it was practically impossible. People were being educated for liberty, but meantime they had to be restrained from rushing on to licence. Toleration in things indifferent was now proclaimed by members of the Assembly; but certain religious views were so associated with tendencies in the state either to tyranny or to anarchy, that neither divines nor patriotic statesmen could see their way yet to tolerate them. Just while the Assembly was sitting (1644), Milton published his *Areopagitica;* yet even he, in all his enthusiasm for liberty, did not go beyond this in his demands. His plea is that many be tolerated rather than all compelled. 'I mean not tolerated Popery,' he adds in explanation, 'and open superstition, which, as it extirpates all religious and civil supremacies, so itself should be extirpate, provided first that all charitable and compassionate means be used to win and regain the weak and misled; that also which is impious or evil absolutely, either against faith or manners, no law can possibly permit, that intends not to unlaw itself; but those neighbouring differences, or rather indifferences, are what I speak of, whether in some point of doctrine or of discipline, which though they may be many, yet need not interrupt the unity of the Spirit, if we could but find among us the bond of peace.'

It is, however, for the Church now to declare in what sense she accepts any statement in her Confession. In order to obviate all misunderstanding, the American churches, in revising their Standards in 1787, simply struck out the last clause. Our own Church, by an Act of Assembly, 1846, disclaims all intolerant and persecuting principles, and holds that office-bearers in subscribing the Confession do not profess any principles inconsistent with liberty of conscience and the right of private judgment.

CHAPTER XXI.

OF RELIGIOUS WORSHIP AND THE SABBATH DAY.

I.—*The light of nature showeth that there is a God, who hath lordship and sovereignty over all; is good, and doeth good unto all; and is therefore to be feared, loved, praised, called upon, trusted in, and served, with all the heart, and with all the soul, and with all the might. But the acceptable way of worshipping the true God is instituted by himself, and so limited by his own revealed will, that he may not be worshipped according to the imaginations and devices of men, or the suggestions of Satan, under any visible representation, or any other way not prescribed in the Holy Scripture.*

II.—*Religious worship is to be given to God the Father, Son, and Holy Ghost: and to him alone: not to angels, saints, or any other creature; and, since the fall, not without a Mediator: nor in the mediation of any other but of Christ alone.*

In these sections we have a restatement of the two first commandments of the moral law. We have in the first section the second commandment, its precept being decidedly maintained against all Romish and Romanizing tendencies. In the second section we have the first commandment ; the Godhead being now, however, viewed under its Trinitarian manifestation, as Father, Son, and Spirit. The restatement of the first commandment is also made with a reference to Romish error in giving worship to the Virgin, and regarding her and other saints as mediators, whereas Christ alone is Mediator. The formal distinction made by Romanists between worship (*latria*) and reverence (*doulia*) is of no practical importance.

All forms of false worship originate in the breaking of one or other of these two commandments. Romanists worship God by images, and so break the second commandment. Socinians give not worship to the Son as to the Father, and acknowledge not the personality of the Spirit, and thus not worshipping the one God in three persons, they break the first commandment. When once any departure has been made from the purity of worship prescribed by God, it is only possible to keep up the appearance of obedience to the one commandment by manifest disobedience to the other. Compare what Stanley says of Jeroboam—to keep the first commandment he broke the second ; to preserve the belief in the unity of God, he broke the unity and tampered with the spiritual conception of the national worship.

III.—*Prayer, with thanksgiving, being one special part of religious worship, is by God required of all men; and, that it may be accepted, it is to be made in the name of the Son, by the help of his Spirit, according to his will, with understanding, reverence, humility, fervency, faith, love, and perseverance; and, if vocal, in a known tongue.*

IV.—*Prayer is to be made for things lawful, and for all sorts of men living, or that shall live hereafter ; but not for the dead, nor for those of whom it may be known that they have sinned the sin unto death.*

These two sections treat very fully of prayer as a duty and privilege of the Christian. As a duty, indeed, it is incumbent upon all men. It is not limited here, as by some narrow-minded and ill-informed sectaries, who have troubled the church in every age. Note the error of those who, at revival meetings, persistently cry, ' Believe and then pray.' There is to be prayer for faith—prayer for the Spirit. So Peter enjoined Simon Magus, who was in the gall of bitterness, to pray. The prayer of the unconverted for conversion, however, is not without the influence of the Spirit.

True Christian prayer is next described. The Spirit's help has been now consciously obtained. By His presence the understanding has been enlightened, the will subdued, the graces of the soul developed. Christian prayer is offered in the name of Christ. 'In proportion as the prayer offered is really prayer in His name, it will be heard ; for in like proportion it is Jesus who prays the prayer through us.' (Martensen, p. 416.) As to the privilege of prayer in the case of believers, it extends, always subject to the will of God, to all things lawful, and to all persons living or yet to live. The only exceptions are the dead, and those so dead in sin as to be past restoration. Prayers for the dead in the ordinary sense are clearly inconsistent with the doctrine of Protestantism, which regards the destiny of all as sealed by the close of the earthly life. All who deny the theory of restitution must acknowledge the illegitimacy of such prayers. (See further remarks in notes on chapter xxxii. 1.) It had been better, probably, had the last clause not been put into the Confession. It is stated certainly in Scripture language (1 John v. 16), but there is some uncertainty as to its precise meaning. The most satisfactory explanation seems to be that given by the late Dr. Candlish (*Epistle of John*, Lect. xlii.). The sin unto death is not anything so definite and known to us, as to prevent us praying for ourselves or for our brother; but the warning is against the exclusive consideration of the wellbeing of the sinner to the neglect of God's rights and claims. There is a danger lest we view sin as not deadly or as easily excusable. No prayer is inadmissible which puts God first and man second. The two cases excluded by the Confession really stand closely together. Though we do not pray for the dead, we are tempted to indulge a hope sometimes of a less rigorous application of God's law. To ask for a brother grace to repent is always lawful; to ask, or even to indulge the hope, that even apart from repentance mercy should be shown, is not lawful. This last is what our Confession may be regarded as condemning.

V.—*The reading of the scriptures with godly fear; the sound preaching, and conscionable hearing of the word, in obedience unto God, with understanding, faith, and reverence; singing of psalms with grace in the heart; as also the due administration and worthy receiving of the sacraments instituted by Christ; are all parts of the ordinary religious worship of God: besides religious oaths and vows, solemn fastings, and thanksgivings upon special occasions, which are, in their several times and seasons, to be used in a holy and religious manner.*

This section treats of the several parts of religious worship,—ordinary, including the use of the Word and the dispensation of sacraments; and occasional, including the observance of oaths, fasts, and thanksgivings. Prayer is regarded as the condition underlying the profitable use of the Word and the sacraments. These form the ordinary means of grace. It is characteristic of apostolic Christianity and Protestantism to bring the Word to the front. A notion of some magical influence inhering in the sacraments led Romanists to set the Scriptures aside. It was to Paul the great occasion of rejoicing that the Word was preached; and the Reformation struggle has always signalized itself by re-establishing the importance of the ministry of the Word. (See *Shorter Catechism*, Qu. 89, 90.)

The administration of the sacraments, and the lawfulness of oaths and vows, under special circumstances, are treated of in subsequent chapters.

We have here affirmed further the propriety of occasional observance of fasts and thanksgivings. It must, however, be noticed that these are observed truly only where there is a real humiliation of soul, or genuine gratitude among members of the church. In such a case the keeping of those days will prove a spiritual benefit, and will deepen those feelings which first prompted it. Occasions are ever occurring to render such fasts and festivals appropriate. If the churches are not in a state to observe them profitably, it indicates a very low development of spiritual life It should be remarked that the Westminster divines, opposed as they were to all superstitious rites and ceremonies, and to all undue multiplication of holy days, had sufficient breadth of view to recognise and approve such as were seemly and appropriate.

VI.—*Neither prayer, nor any other part of religious worship, is, now under the gospel, either tied unto, or made more acceptable by, any place in which it is performed, or towards which it is directed; but God is to be worshipped every where in spirit and in truth; as in private families daily, and in secret each one by himself; so more solemnly in the publick assemblies, which are not carelessly or wilfully to be neglected or forsaken, when God, by his word or providence, calleth thereunto.*

The early church maintained the doctrine stated in the opening clause of this section. Special places of worship were not essential to worship, which could be as acceptably performed in private houses. At first they were created merely for convenience. The buildings got the name of churches simply because they accommodated the members of the church. As spirituality became less intense, the external began to assert an importance over the internal. Gradually church buildings came to be regarded as sanctuaries in the Jewish sense of the term, and so reverenced as places sacred in themselves apart from the assemblies. (See Pressensé's *Life and Practice in the Early Church*, Bk. ii. chap. iii. § 2.) Our Confession gives here a singularly happy statement, avoiding all ultra-spiritual disparagement of the solemnities of public worship, and at the same time showing that the special solemnity of public worship is not such that acceptable worship may not be rendered in the privacy of home. Each form of worship has a solemnity and significance of its own. The observance of the one will not excuse the neglect of the other.

VII.—*As it is of the law of nature, that, in general, a due proportion of time be set apart for the worship of God; so, in his word, by a positive, moral, and perpetual commandment, binding all men in all ages, he hath particularly appointed one day in seven for a sabbath, to be kept holy unto him: which, from the beginning of the world to the resurrection of Christ, was the last day of the week; and, from the resurrection of Christ, was changed into the first day of the week, which in scripture is called the Lord's Day, and is to be continued to the end of the world, as the Christian Sabbath.*

We have here a statement of the origin and Divine authority of

the day of rest. Its obligation rests on a law of nature, and is therefore immutable. That it belongs to the very nature of man as a
creature to devote a portion of his time to the worship of his Creator,
is the natural basis of the Sabbath law. Besides this, God as
lawgiver was pleased to make that principle of natural law which
demands the worship of the creature, the basis of a positive legislation.
The original appointment of the Sabbath at the close of the creation,
the re-enactment of this precept on Sinai, and the change of the day
to be observed under the Christian dispensation, may be viewed
conjointly as constituting one law,—the positive law of the Christian
Sabbath. We find here mutable and immutable elements. As a
positive law, God could from time to time modify it to suit the
circumstances of His creatures. The change of the day we believe
to have been made under the direct inspiration of God. The early
Christians, guided by apostolic example, observed the first day of
the week; and gradually the real identity of the Sabbath, spiritually
appreciated, and the Lord's day as divinely instituted, was recognised
by the church. The history of the worship of the early church shows
that the Lord's day was by many observed alongside of the seventh-
day Sabbath. While Christian feeling was strong and active, every
morning the earnest Christian enjoyed his short church service and
eucharistic feast preparatory to engaging in the work of the day.
'Sunday,' says Pressensé, 'was to the other days what the bishop
of this age (second century) was to his brethren,—simply *primus
inter pares.*'

VIII.—*This sabbath is then kept holy unto the Lord, when men,
after a due preparing of their hearts, and ordering of their
common affairs beforehand, do not only observe an holy rest all
the day from their own works, words, and thoughts about their
worldly employments and recreations; but also are taken up the
whole time in the publick and private exercises of his worship,
and in the duties of necessity and mercy.*

The Christian Sabbath should be observed as the ideal of the
Christian's daily life. This ideal will be realized not by secularizing
the Lord's day, but by infusing into everyday life a higher spiritual
tone. To a large extent this tone will be the reflection of a heavenly
restfulness from well-spent Sabbaths. The ideal striven after in
Christian practice is such an observance of our Sabbaths as will
make them days of heaven upon earth. Yet Sabbath exercises should
be such as aim at the formation of such tempers and habits of the soul
as may practicably be developed in the world. They should be such
that we might reasonably expect to find on the following Sabbath
that we had not been retarded but advanced by our life in the world.
Views of unearthly virtue are mere dreams,—not devout imaginations,
but vain imaginings. If we spend our Sabbaths in framing such

airy fancies, the week day will find us less capable than before of work for God in the daily life. Our religious meditations must be of such a nature as will help us to be more religious in life and conversation in the world. Too often they are pietistic reveries about an unreal state which we call spiritual and heavenly, but which only exists in our imaginations. Much of the generally approved Sabbath reading fosters this tendency, and is therefore thoroughly unhealthy in tone. The statement of the Confession as to the way in which the Sabbath should be sanctified is moderate and wise. The devotional and the practical are not sundered. The obligation of the second great commandment is recognised as well as that of the first, the worship of God and the duty owing to our fellow-men. The religious and secular theories of the day are apt to overlook one or other. The secularist professes to worship by the simple discharge of relative duties. The extreme religionist sometimes gives us the impression that he is inclined to minimize the claims of necessity and mercy.

CHAPTER XXII.

OF LAWFUL OATHS AND VOWS.

I.—*A lawful oath is a part of religious worship, wherein, upon just occasion, the person swearing solemnly calleth God to witness what he asserteth or promiseth; and to judge him according to the truth or falsehood of what he sweareth.*

The New Testament prohibition of swearing is to be understood of the unnecessary and frivolous use of oaths. In all the ordinary affairs of life the precept of Jesus and of the apostles holds good,— 'Let your yea be yea, and your nay, nay.' That in special circumstances an oath for confirmation, or to render an important statement more impressive, is warrantable, may be shown from the example of Paul. An oath necessarily and solemnly taken is a religious act. It takes the form of a confession of our faith in God's power, righteousness, and holiness. When we make an assertion of fact on oath, we honour God by declaring that what may be beyond the reach of human knowledge is known to Him. When we make a promise on oath, we declare that in our heart we regard God as the ultimate ground of all truth and faithfulness. When we, in the oath, invoke God's judgment according to the truth or falsehood of that to which we swear, we must as Christians realize the awfulness of the doom which perjury involves.

II.—*The name of God only is that by which men ought to swear, and therein it is to be used with all holy fear and reverence; therefore to swear vainly or rashly by that glorious and dreadful name, or to swear at all by any other thing, is sinful, and to be abhorred. Yet as, in matters of weight and moment, an oath is warranted by the word of God under the New Testament, as well as under the Old; so a lawful oath, being imposed by lawful authority, in such matters, ought to be taken.*

Here we have asserted the sanction and solemnity of a lawful oath. Our Lord in the Sermon on the Mount, and also the Apostle James, clearly repudiate distinctions which the quibbling casuists among the Jews sought to make between different oaths as more or less binding. The appeal in a truly religious oath is to the heart-searcher. The use therefore of any other name than that of God implies that he who uses it, either is giving God's glory to another, or is swearing rashly and frivolously. Christ shows that those who swear by other names than that of God will be held guilty of profanity. That no other name than God's is allowed in an oath must render all who reverence that great and terrible name particularly careful to use an oath only in cases of strict necessity, and under circumstances the most solemn and impressive.

III.—*Whosoever taketh an oath, ought duly to consider the weightiness of so solemn an act, and therein to avouch nothing but what he is fully persuaded is the truth. Neither may any man bind himself by oath to any thing but what is good and just, and what he believeth so to be, and what he is able and resolved to perform. Yet it is a sin to refuse an oath touching any thing that is good and just, being imposed by lawful authority.*

Limits within which an oath may be taken and kept. No oath should be taken in regard to anything of which one has any reason to believe that he is not in possession of all the truth. An oath is absolute in contrast to a simple assertion. We may declare that to the best of our knowledge it is as we affirm, and then show the grounds of our confidence. But when under oath we dare only state that of which we have no doubt, nor can conceive the possibility of error. Hence the oath must relate to matters of fact, or to undertakings which we have the power to fulfil. The second clause evidently applies to cases in which he who takes the oath is free from compulsion. In matters morally indifferent there is to be no oath taken. The decision must therefore be made between the alternatives, good or bad, right or wrong. All this refers to promissory oaths, as the previous clause to assertory oaths. One on oath must promise to do only what he knows to be right and good; and he may only promise what he believes himself capable of performing. The last clause excludes the error of the Quakers, who refuse to take oaths to the civil magistrate. It was probably originally directed against the Anabaptists, who declared oaths illicit.

IV.—*An oath is to be taken in the plain and common sense of the words, without equivocation or mental reservation. It cannot oblige to sin; but in any thing not sinful, being taken, it binds to performance, although to a man's own hurt; nor is it to be violated, although made to hereticks or infidels.*

The obligation of an oath cannot be escaped by attaching to the words used a meaning that would not naturally have been given them by the party interested. Paley tells of Temures, who promised the garrison of a besieged city that if they would surrender no blood should be shed, and on their surrender he had them buried alive. Many such acts of treachery are told in history. The actual breach of an oath in such a case is aggravated by mockery. Notorious instances of the violation of oaths have been excused and approved of by Roman casuists. [On the Romish doctrine of Mental Reservation, read Pascal's *Provincial Letters*, ix.] Similar to this are lies of omission; Paley instances the case of a writer on history who, in a book professing to tell the story of Charles I., would suppress all allusion to the king's despotic measures. (*Moral Phil.* Bk. iii. chap. xv.) If something sinful has been promised by oath (as Herod unguardedly promised what included that which he had no lawful right to give), the sinful oath should be repented of. To perform it, is to add sin to sin. This second clause touches on a difficult point. It deals with the question of the binding obligation of oaths when made under error or compulsion. That one should only swear to that which he is able and resolved to perform, is evidently true. The question, however, is, Should this statement rule absolutely? One may by force be compelled to swear to do what he may regard as unjust. For example, a robber may allow his prisoner to go free under promise on oath to send a sum of money for ransom. Bishop Sanderson, who is a great authority on these questions, determines that this should be done. 'If the matter required, by force or sad fear, be not unlawful or injurious to any, but only somewhat disadvantageous to the swearer,—as, if one travelling should fall among robbers that with drawn swords would threaten his life unless he would promise them such a sum of money with an oath; in this case it is lawful both to promise the money and to confirm the promise with an oath. I say, such an oath doth oblige.' The unlawfulness lay with him who imposed the oath; the condition is not unlawful to him who took it.

According to the Romish doctrine, the church must determine what oaths are to be kept, and what not. As superior, the church undertakes to free the individual conscience. Protestantism in the spirit of Apostolic Christianity, while it gives the dignity of true liberty to the Christian conscience, makes the individual conscience answerable for all personal acts. Hence the sacredness of the oath depends not on the character to whom the oath is sworn, but on the

individual assurance given in the great name of God.   Abundant
illustrations may be found in the history of Romish persecutions of
the use made of the infamous maxim, ' No faith with heretics.'

V.—*A vow is of the like nature with a promissory oath, and ought to
be made with the like religious care, and to be performed with
the like faithfulness.*

VI.—*It is not to be made to any creature, but to God alone : and that
it may be accepted, it is to be made voluntarily, out of faith, and
conscience of duty, in way of thankfulness for mercy received, or
for the obtaining of what we want; whereby we more strictly
bind ourselves to necessary duties, or to other things, so far and
so long as they may fitly conduce thereunto.*

Much of what was said regarding the oath applies to the vow.
Its use is moral and subjective,—for some result in the individual
life, and must not be regarded as extending farther.   The most
satisfactory and most thoroughly religious vow is that of more complete consecration as an expression of thankfulness for experience of
God's mercy.   Thus often in the Psalms.   Jacob's vow is a good
example of one made in view of obtaining something.

VII.—*No man may vow to do anything forbidden in the word of
God, or what would hinder any duty therein commanded, or
which is not in his power, and for the performance whereof he
hath no promise of ability from God.   In which respects, Popish
monastical vows of perpetual single life, professed poverty, and
regular obedience, are so far from being degrees of higher perfection, that they are superstitious and sinful snares, in which no
Christian may entangle himself.*

An evil practical result of the misuse of vows is the inevitable
collision of duties which follows.   If the letter of the vow is fulfilled,
the performance of some evident duty may be prevented.   Vows
made consciously, for such an end, are anathematized by Jesus as
hypocritical pretences.   Illustration : the Jewish custom of saying,
Corban.   The second clause refers to vows such as are made by
Romanists in fulfilling the so-called Counsels of Perfection.   That
these are worthy of the description given above, the history of
Christendom under the Romish *régime* abundantly proves.

CHAPTER XXIII.

OF THE CIVIL MAGISTRATE.

I. —*God, the supreme Lord and King of all the world, hath ordained civil magistrates to be under him over the people, for his own glory, and the publick good; and, to this end, hath armed them with the power of the sword, for the defence and encouragement of them that are good, and for the punishment of evil-doers.*

The Christian recognises magisterial authority as of God. This recognition, however, imposes a limit, while it yields a peculiar sanction to that authority. It is not only his appointment that is acknowledged as from God, but also the special end for which this appointment is made. The ancient Apologists for Christianity, such as Tertullian and Origen, very clearly seized this principle. 'That which thus exalts the dignity of the state,' says Pressensé, reporting the views of the early church as to its relations with the state, 'is at the same time that which limits its power; for as it is appointed by God, it forfeits its claim when it fails to fulfil its end. If the prince makes use of his authority, not to uphold justice, but to gratify evil passions, he becomes a tyrant, and consequently places himself in opposition to the very idea of the state as instituted by God.' (*Life and Practice of Early Church*, p. 452.) The recognition of magisterial authority given in our Confession is carefully guarded, so that it lends no countenance to despotic absolutism. The power is acknowledged only while the duty of the office is discharged. The distinction between a tyrant and a wise constitutional ruler is admirably shown by George Buchanan in his *Rights of the Crown in Scotland.*

II.—*It is lawful for Christians to accept and execute the office of a magistrate, when called thereunto : in the managing whereof, as they ought especially to maintain piety, justice, and peace, according to the wholesome laws of each commonwealth; so, for that end, they may lawfully, now under the New Testament, wage war upon just and necessary occasions.*

The history of the Reformation supplies us with illustrations of the mischievous results of error in regard to the duties of Christians in relation to the state. Romanists and Anabaptists, holding in some respects views diametrically opposed to one another, were agreed in denying all independent importance to the state. The Romanist, regarding the state as simply a department of the church, was quite ready to take civil offices, not, however, as our Confession puts it, 'when called thereunto.' The churchman claimed the right

of addressing the call, and taking to himself the civil office, or be-
stowing it as he pleased.   The Anabaptist, again, would refuse
formally to take any office in the state, or to recognise in any way
civil and military arrangements ; but that very force which he
declines to acknowledge in civil government, he does not scruple
himself to use.   (Compare Dorner, *History of Protestant Theology*,
i. 140, 141.) This confusion, tending either to absolutism or to
anarchy, so evident in Romanism and in Anabaptism, was avoided
by the Reformers, in their enunciation of the duties of the Christian
citizen.   The office of the magistrate is fully recognised as of Divine
appointment.   Our Confession speaks of a call to such an office
being indispensable to the legal occupancy of such a position.   It
does not expressly declare who the party is by whom such a call
may be addressed.   Very enlightened and advanced views will be
found maintained by Rutherford in his *Lex Rex* (1644), published
during the sitting of the Assembly, of which he was a member. ' The
power of creating a man a king is from the people.'   He holds that
inferior magistrates are not under the king so far as the discharge of
their particular duties is concerned. ' The servants of the king are
his domestics, the judges are *ministri regni, non regis ;* the ministers
and judges of the kingdom, not of the king.'
Compare the history of the Burgher and Antiburgher controversy.
The stricter party refused to take office or show any sympathy with
the government of the country, lest a general approval of the British
constitution might be supposed to involve approval of prelatical and
Erastian principles.   [The lawfulness of war is asserted against the
Anabaptists.   Quakers now decline military service and disapprove
of war.]

III.—*The civil magistrate may not assume to himself the administration of the word and sacraments, or the power of the keys of the
kingdom of heaven: yet he hath authority, and it is his duty,
to take order, that unity and peace be preserved in the church,
that the truth of God be kept pure and entire, that all blasphemies
and heresies be suppressed, all corruptions and abuses in worship
and discipline prevented or reformed, and all the ordinances of
God duly settled, administered, and observed.   For the better
effecting whereof, he hath power to call synods, to be present at
them, and to provide that whatsoever is transacted in them be
according to the mind of God.*

Erastians seldom claim for the civil magistrate the right of dis-
pensing the sacraments and preaching the Word, and Mr. Coleman
expressly repudiated this notion.   Erastus himself, however, did not
scruple to say that even this belonged to the jurisdiction of the civil
magistrate.   There is no doubt that Erastian principles consistently

carried out will not admit any such exception ; for if it be allowed, there is a distinction thus made between the functions of the church and the state, which requires the anti-Erastian position of co-ordination of jurisdictions. (Compare *Aaron's Rod Blossoming*, Book ii. chap. iii.)

The first entire sentence in the above section indicates the Westminster doctrine of the relation of civil and ecclesiastical authorities in regard to the maintaining of a profession of religion in the world. The words employed are certainly capable of a harsh interpretation, if, for example, the suppression of heresies be understood in the more rigorous and vulgar sense. Brown of Wamphray, writing in 1660, quotes a declaration of James VI., uttered in 1585, as quite expressing the claims of the Puritan and Covenanting party. The king had said that he, for his part, should never, and that his posterity ought never, to cite, summon, or apprehend any pastor for matters of doctrine in religion, salvation, heresies, or true interpretation of Scripture, but avoucheth it to be a matter purely ecclesiastical, and altogether impertinent to his calling. (*Apologetical Narration*, sect. v.) In light of such a statement as this, which fairly represents the mind of the Westminster divines, the deliverance of the Confession must be understood of moral support and encouragement to ecclesiastical officers in the administration of doctrine and discipline. This at least is the sense authoritatively attributed to the passage by an Act of the Free Church Assembly which disclaims all intolerant and persecuting principles. (Act xii. Assembly 1846.) The American Confession has, in the revised form of this section, limited the duties of the civil magistrate in reference to the church, to protecting members of ecclesiastical assemblies in the discharge of their special duties, and abstaining from all interference in such processes. [An admirable statement and argument in favour of the anti-Erastian and tolerant character of this chapter is to be found in Dr. Cunningham's *Discussions on Church Principles*, chap. viii., 'The Westminster Confession on the Relations between Church and State.' The view that this chapter maintains intolerant and really Erastian principles is keenly expressed in Dr. Marshall's *Principles of the Westminster Standards persecuting*, chap. v.]

The right of the magistrate to call synods is limited by Act of Assembly, 1647, to kirks not constituted and settled ; at other times the magistrate is free to advise with synods of ministers and elders, who meet upon delegation from their churches. The right of ordinarily calling synods is thus reserved to the church ; only in peculiar circumstances and emergencies is it allowed to the civil magistrate. (See chapter xxx. 1.)

IV.—*It is the duty of people to pray for magistrates, to honour their persons, to pay them tribute and other dues, to obey their lawful commands, and to be subject to their authority for conscience sake.*

Infidelity, or difference in religion, doth not make void the magistrate's just and legal authority, nor free the people from their due obedience to him : from which ecclesiastical persons are not exempted; much less hath the Pope any power or jurisdiction over them in their dominions, or over any of their people; and least of all to deprive them of their dominions or lives, if he shall judge them to be hereticks, or upon any other pretence whatsoever.

In this section the errors of Levellers and Ultramontanes are alike condemned.   Notwithstanding the keen dislike and well-grounded jealousy entertained by the Reformed Church against all forms of Erastian encroachment, they were careful to avoid the contrary extreme.   Those holding civil offices have rights which should be recognised and respected.   Sectaries are not to be encouraged in refusing the lawful commands of rulers, who may in religious opinions differ from themselves.   In a particular direction this was the Ultramontane practice.   Especially from the time of Hildebrand (eleventh century), the spiritual power centred in the Pope assumed absolute supremacy over the state.   The prince had to acknowledge himself and his treasury as at the disposal of the Roman pontiff, who could relieve the people of their oath of allegiance, and, by placing a refractory civil ruler under excommunication, could remove him from the protection of the laws.   The Cardinal's words, when threatening King John with excommunication, illustrate the terrible assumption denounced in our Confession :—

'Meritorious shall that hand be called,
Canonised and worshipped as a saint,
That takes away by any secret course
Thy hateful life.'   (*King John*, Act iii. Scene 1.)

CHAPTER XXIV.

OF MARRIAGE AND DIVORCE.

I.—*Marriage is to be between one man and one woman : neither is it lawful for any man to have more than one wife, nor for any woman to have more than one husband at the same time.*

II.—*Marriage was ordained for the mutual help of husband and wife; for the increase of mankind with a legitimate issue, and of the church with an holy seed; and for preventing of uncleanness.*

The rule of monogamy laid down here is now, in every civilised land, regarded as a fundamental principle, about which there need be no dispute.   In certain quarters an attempt is made to disparage the Old Testament morality by referring to the polygamy of several of its prominent and well-approved characters. The answer that now most commends itself to Christian apologists is that the morality of the Bible is, like that of the race, regularly progressive. What did not offend the conscience in earlier days, would offend the conscience now; and what was allowed, though not expressly approved, in earlier times, may without any inconsistency be now expressly forbidden. Further, it is notorious that in all cases on record in Scripture, polygamy was the fruitful source of domestic misery. By this, men are taught the folly, as by express command they are taught the offensiveness before God, of such practices.

The statement of the second section guards against a danger that showed itself in the reaction from pagan licence. In the exaltation of the spiritual side of human nature, there was a temptation to ignore or unduly repress the corporeal. In the early Christian church, however, there was much done for the elevation and purification of domestic life. The Christian family contrasts beautifully and strikingly with the pagan family. In the days when pure doctrine prevailed, members of the same family were taught to recognise the special duties they owed to one another. 'We can walk in the footsteps of Christ,' says Clement of Alexandria, 'when our wife and children walk with us. A family is no hindrance to progress in the Christian course when all follow the same guide. The wife who loves her husband learns to walk with him step by step.' (See Pressensé, *Life and Practice in the Early Church*, p. 412.) It would have been well for the church and society generally had such true and ethically beautiful sentiments continued to prevail.

III.—*It is lawful for all sorts of people to marry who are able with judgment to give their consent: yet it is the duty of Christians to marry only in the Lord. And therefore such as profess the true reformed religion should not marry with infidels, Papists, or other idolaters: neither should such as are godly be unequally yoked, by marrying with such as are notoriously wicked in their life, or maintain damnable heresies.*

Lecky remarks that mixed marriages may do much to assuage the rancour and asperity of sects, but only after a considerable measure of tolerance has been already attained. Now if this were said merely of differences of sects, implying only lesser denominational divergencies,—differences on matters not essential to salvation,—we might indeed accept it as a true position. As intended, however, it must appear only as the recommendation of indifferentism. The writer's real meaning appears from the following sentence : 'In a union in which each partner believes and realizes that the other is doomed to an eternity of misery there can be no real happiness, no sympathy. no trust ; and a domestic agreement that some of the children should be educated in one religion, and some in the other, would be im possible when each parent believed it to be an agreement that some children should be doomed to hell.' (*European Morals*, ii. p. 354.) It is just with differences of this sort that our Confession deals. Earnest and conscientious believers in the Reformed doctrine are heartily convinced that infidel opinions and Romish superstitions, inasmuch as they interfere with or prevent reliance upon Christ for salvation, involve condemnation and eternal loss. The practical result of such marriages is either a domestic life embittered in the way described above, or the growth of an indifference, commendable in the eyes of such as Mr. Lecky, but in the view of all evangelical spirits, most deplorable. Observation may convince any one of the truth of the words of Thomas Adams : ' One religion matching with another not seldom breeds an atheist, one of no religion at all.' We should, however, carefully note, that not only false views, but also faults in life and character, are regarded by our Confession as a bar to Christian marriage. In a worldly age like the present, where so much is sacrificed to position and wealth, the warning cannot be too eagerly urged against the marriage of such as profess godliness with those who are notoriously wicked in their lives. It should be observed, too, that our Confession is very moderate and cautious in its statements prohibitory or dissuasive of marriage, and carefully guards against the dangerous extreme of undue restriction. There is danger in insisting upon a full maturity of Christian character in young persons as a condition to Christian marriage. Thoroughly incompatible religious views, an evident indifference to religion, and manifest wickedness in life,—these may be laid down as universal grounds upon which Christian friendship will feel entitled to urge objection. Beyond this, the Christian friend or the church counsellor may not feel called upon to go, and to more than this the individuals interested may not be required as Christians to yield obedience. We may sum up these remarks with the wise words of Harless : ' Instead of wishing to recognise in outward behaviour the presence of the grace of God, one will at once proceed in God's name to the bond of wedlock, where no actual evidence is given in word or deed, in sentiment or mode of behaviour, that the object of our choice has consciously abandoned the grace of that kingdom in whose community he has been planted by the sacrament of Baptism.' (*Christian Ethics*, p. 436.)

IV.—*Marriage ought not to be within the degrees of consanguinity or affinity forbidden in the word; nor can such incestuous marriages ever be made lawful by any law of man, or consent of parties, so as those persons may live together as man and wife. The man may not marry any of his wife's kindred nearer in blood than he may of his own, nor the woman of her husband's kindred nearer in blood than of her own.*

We have here affirmed very strongly and distinctly the principles which those maintain who oppose what is known as the Marriage Affinity Bill. The Free Church of Scotland has by the resolutions of her Assemblies very determinedly taken up this position, and this has been argued on precisely the same lines as our Confession. The arguments that have generally been employed in support of this thesis are these :—1. That it is in accordance with the express requirement of Scripture ; the well-known passage in Leviticus being regarded as the only direct statement, but others being referred to as involving the same principle. 2. That the assertion of this position is essential to the maintenance of social morality ; any change here, it is held, would seriously affect the present freedom and purity of family life. 3 That any alteration of the present law would be the abandonment of the principle on which alone any prohibition can consistently rest ; inasmuch as prohibition on any other ground would be arbitrary, and could not appeal to the natural convictions of mankind. [This whole subject is ably treated by the late Professor Gibson in a publication entitled *The Marriage Affinity Question ;* see also another by the late Professor Lindsay.]

V.—*Adultery or fornication committed after a contract, being detected before marriage, giveth just occasion to the innocent party to dissolve that contract. In the case of adultery after marriage, it is lawful for the innocent party to sue out a divorce, and, after the divorce, to marry another, as if the offending party were dead.*

VI.—*Although the corruption of man be such as is apt to study arguments, unduly to put asunder those whom God hath joined together in marriage ; yet nothing but adultery, or such wilful desertion as can no way be remedied by the church or civil magistrate, is cause sufficient of dissolving the bond of marriage : wherein a publick and orderly course of proceeding is to be observed, and the persons concerned in it not left to their own wills and discretion in their own case.*

The Romish Church, consistently with her view of the sacramental character of marriage, pronounces the marriage tie absolutely indissoluble ; yet, the facilities given for effecting separation, and the ingenuity exercised in devising proofs of nullity of marriage, have rendered the Romish practice as lax as its doctrine is severe. Hodge, quoting from Dens, mentions sixteen causes that render marriage null Our Confession, in conformity with most Protestant Confessions, allows divorce on either of the two grounds of adultery or wilful desertion. The law of divorce differs in England and Scotland. In the former, only adultery, and that in the case of the husband aggravated by cruelty or desertion, is valid ground for divorce ; in the latter, the law is precisely in accordance with that laid down in our Confession,—wilful desertion being also recognised as affording good ground for divorce. [A good *resumé* of laws is given in Chambers's *Encyclopædia*, art. Divorce.   See also a clear and very summary statement of the position taken up by the early church against the unbounded liberty of divorce prevailing at Rome, in Lecky, *European Morals*, ii. p. 352.]

CHAPTER XXV.

OF THE CHURCH.

I.—*The catholick or universal church, which is invisible, consists of the whole number of the elect that have been, are, or shall be gathered into one, under Christ the head thereof; and is the spouse, the body, the fulness of him that filleth all in all.*

II.—*The visible church, which is also catholick or universal under the gospel (not confined to one nation, as before under the law), consists of all those throughout the world that profess the true religion, together with their children ; and is the kingdom of the Lord Jesus Christ, the house and family of God, out of which there is no ordinary possibility of salvation.*

The word church (kirk) is from the Greek *kuriake*, and means the Lord's house.   This corresponds with the expression in the close of the second section.

These sections treat of the church as visible and invisible.   This distinction may be traced in the practice of the early church, though it had not then received formal expression.   When a member had suffered a second excommunication for any fault, there was no restoration allowed.   Yet it was admitted that such a one might on repentance receive forgiveness from Christ.   He might thus be restored to the membership of the invisible church, or rather, if, notwithstanding his falls, he were a real Christian, he continued throughout a member of the invisible church, though he could no longer claim membership in the visible church.   Thus the distinction was recognised. (Comp. Pressensé, *Heresy and Christian Doctrine*, Bk. ii. chap. iv. § 5.)   The express statement of the distinction properly belongs to the Reformation.   When this question came to be generally discussed, the Romanists did not hesitate to declare the church at once a community of believers, and an organization for the dispensation of Word and sacraments.   With them, however, the idea of a saintly fellowship was quite subordinate to that of an outward organization. This view is reversed by the Protestants. With them, the church is first the fellowship of the saints, and secondly, an institution. Here the idea of the invisible church first gained any real importance.

The statement made in the first section regarding the Catholic or universal church, that it is invisible, should not be so understood as to imply that the idea of the invisible church is something entirely separate and distinct from that of the visible church. These are simply two aspects under which the church is viewed. The church, as distinguished from the church of to-day, must necessarily be regarded as invisible. Statistics cannot be applied to it. Of this ideal community there are members in glory, and there are members still unborn. It is not, however, without relation to the visible church, inasmuch as it includes all on the earth who are members of Christ, the Head. In the invisible church, the idea and the reality perfectly correspond. There is a portion of the invisible church which belongs to the visible,—that portion presently existing on the earth. This and nothing more constitutes the real membership of the visible church according to its idea. In it, however, the idea and the reality do not perfectly correspond, as in the invisible church. Profession of religion, as something of which man can judge, and not the actual presence of religious principles, which can be perfectly known only to the searcher of hearts, is the condition of membership in that outward organization which we call the visible church. Those professing religion constitute together the kingdom of Jesus Christ. To such as profess themselves members of this community, Christ as king addresses the laws of His kingdom. Those who do not yield themselves to His rule, and obey His laws, are cast out. Their excommunication shows that they have never been truly in communion. (1 John ii. 19.) Those who truly belong to the kingdom of God (as distinguished from those who are only not far from it), are members in common of the visible and of the invisible church.

When we say that out of the visible church there is no ordinary possibility of salvation, we guard against the error of supposing that connection with the church as an institution necessarily secures salvation, and equally against the notion that God regards the use of His own appointed means of grace as of slight importance. By sovereign power He can work savingly apart from those means, but ordinarily He does not. Cyprian said, 'He who has not the church as his mother has not God as his Father.' When the church is viewed primarily as an institution, such a maxim leads to an ecclesiasticism at once formal and exclusive.

III. — *Unto this catholick visible church Christ hath given the ministry, oracles, and ordinances of God, for the gathering and perfecting of the saints in this life, to the end of the world; and*

*doth by his own presence and Spirit, according to his promise
make them effectual thereunto.*

This section describes the end for which the church and its
ordinances have been appointed. In Christ as the God-man the
church has its origin. Its final end also is in Him, and church
membership is meaningless unless it is understood of a fellowship
with Jesus which finally effects a real communication of His own
character to us, so that we may be said to be partakers of the Divine
nature. (2 Pet. i. 4.) Between this beginning in Christ, and ending
in Him, there lies the course of the visible church in the world. In
this the human and Divine elements are variously mingled. No
saint in that church is wholly free from sin, and yet in it there is
evidently a power that is a Divine power working for righteousness,
and that righteousness is the righteousness of God.

It belongs to this visible church to administer the ordinances of
grace. These owe their authority to the appointment of God, and
are by Him designed for the conversion of sinners and the edification of true members of the church. Because these means of grace
have been committed to the church, there is ordinarily no salvation
out of it. To the sinner the church addresses in God's name the
gospel invitation ; and to the believer, the church, through the promised presence of the Spirit, brings nourishment, and affords the
means of growth. The preaching of the Word, and the dispensation
of sacraments, constitute the external notes of the church.

IV.—*This catholick church hath been sometimes more, sometimes less
visible. And particular churches, which are members thereof,
are more or less pure, according as the doctrine of the gospel
is taught and embraced, ordinances administered, and publick
worship performed more or less purely in them.*

V.—*The purest churches under heaven are subject both to mixture
and error; and some have so degenerated as to become no
churches of Christ, but synagogues of Satan. Nevertheless, there
shall be always a church on earth to worship God according to
his will.*

This statement may be easily and profitably illustrated from the
history of the church : that the church is sometimes more, sometimes
less visible, from the story of Pagan persecution and attempted
suppression ; that it is sometimes more, sometimes less pure, from
the story of Romish persecutions, the corruptions that prevailed in
the church during pre-Reformation times, and the state of various
sects in the present day. No absolute perfection in doctrine and
practice is admitted of any church. 'The church is absolutely
faultless as regards her *principle* and her *beginning;* absolutely
faultless also as to her *final aim;* but in the interval between these

extremes, in her historical and free development, her relative fallibility lies. The historical development of the church is not, as Catholicism asserts, normal; it is subject, like a ship on the billows, to the undulations of the times.' (Martensen.) The notion that perfect purity of communion is attainable in the visible church has led to most injurious errors of sectarianism. The various forms of Plymouthism are irreconcilable with our Lord's teaching in the parable of the Tares of the field. The degree of purity more or less in a church depends on the purity of her Confession of Faith, and on the exactness with which the faith confessed is put in practice; as Calvin : *fidei professio et vitæ exemplum.* 'That church which has most power with God, and then, next, the most sympathetic power with men, is the truest church.' (Beecher.) Stanley eulogizes the tolerance of this article. (See *Macmillan's Mag.* for 1881, pp. 290, 291.)

VI.—*There is no other head of the church but the Lord Jesus Christ : nor can the Pope of Rome in any sense be head thereof; but is that antichrist, that man of sin, and son of perdition, that exalteth himself in the church against Christ, and all that is called God.*

This is an important doctrine of Protestantism. It is the belief of all Christians, out of the communion of Rome, that the church has no visible head. The one head of the church visible and invisible (which is one), is the Lord Jesus Christ. It was usual with the Puritans, in their opposition to Episcopalian Erastianism, to maintain a twofold headship of Christ,—over the church, as Son of man ; over the nations, as Son of God. This distinction was practically applied :—'In the church as man He hath officers under Him, which officers are ecclesiastical persons.' The use of the term Head of the Church as applied by the Church of England to the sovereign, though not intended as in Rome, shows how incomplete the Protestantism of that church is, and how confused her notion of the relation of the church to Christ. (See Hooker, *Eccles. Polity,* Bk. viii.) When Cranmer was questioned about the headship of the church, he showed that he intended to make the king head of ecclesiastical persons as well as civil, but not head of the church. This is what our Confession clearly affirms. It condemns alike all Hierarchical and all Erastian tendencies.

CHAPTER XXVI.

OF COMMUNION OF SAINTS.

I.—*All saints that are united to Jesus Christ their head by his Spirit, and by faith, have fellowship with him in his graces, sufferings, death, resurrection, and glory. And being united to one another*

K

*in love, they have communion in each other's gifts and graces;
and are obliged to the performance of such duties, publick and
private, as do conduce to their mutual good, both in the inward
and outward man.*

The fellowship of believers with one another is made to rest on
the reality of their fellowship with Christ. By means of those
graces which are gained through a saving relation to Christ, individual believers are enabled and constrained to maintain a new
relation with each other. Those graces have been bestowed on
them not merely as individuals, but as members of a family,—the
household of God,—and must therefore be exercised for the common
good. The advantage of the individual is inseparably connected
with that of the community. 'Rendering blessing, knowing that ye
are thereunto called, that ye should inherit a blessing.' (1 Pet. iii. 9.)

II.—*Saints, by profession, are bound to maintain an holy fellowship
and communion in the worship of God, and in performing such
other spiritual services as tend to their mutual edification; as
also in relieving each other in outward things, according to their
several abilities and necessities. Which communion, as God
offereth opportunity, is to be extended unto all those who in every
place call upon the name of the Lord Jesus.*

Here we have the mutual offices of members of the church
enumerated under two classes, spiritual and temporal. The general
principle is that each member should seek the other's benefit, as
he is able, in all things. The range of this obligation is not to be
restricted by narrowing the circle of our denomination. This communion is not limited to the members of the sect to which we may
belong, but the offices of such Christian fellowship are to be extended, as opportunity is given, to all who by profession acknowledge
the name of Jesus.

An interesting statement was made by the covenanters Henderson
and Dickson, in reply to the charge of the Aberdeen opposers of
the covenant, that out of their own parishes they exercised their
gifts. 'Even he who is not universall pastor of the kirk is pastor of
the universall kirk; and the apostle hath taught us that we are
members one of another.' The special attention that is claimed for
our Christian brethren (Gal. vi. 10), does not in the least conflict with
any properly-conceived philanthropy. Scripture precepts are equally
remote from inculcating a cosmopolitanism, whose vagueness and
generality deprive it of all efficiency, and from approving a sectarian
spirit, even should profession of Christianity be that sect. A Christian, who is a father, is required to be tender and helpful toward all
children as he has opportunity, but he may not make the calls of

this general affection an excuse for overlooking the special duties which he owes to his own family

III.—*This communion which the saints have with Christ, doth not make them in any wise partakers of the substance of his Godhead, or to be equal with Christ in any respect · either of which to affirm is impious and blasphemous. Nor doth their communion one with another, as saints, take away or infringe the title or property which each man hath in his goods and possessions.*

This section indicates a further parallel between the fellowship of believers with Christ and their fellowship with one another. There is in neither case any confusion of personalities. Though believers are said to be one with Christ, yet He is ever distinct from them, and He has over them, as members of His body, the pre-eminence of the head. Even so, individual believers have their several endowments to conserve and cultivate, and their several functions to perform. Each one, using his own gifts, will profit himself and the church at large ; failing to use them, he will have personal loss and further condemnation because of the loss which the church sustains by his neglect. The Communism condemned in the latter clause has no place in Scripture. Renan (*Life of Jesus*, chap. x.) seeks to represent Jesus as denouncing all possession of property. He denounces covetousness and oppression, and riches only as they may foster these sins. The Communism of the early Jerusalem church (Acts iv. 32–37) was only temporary, and determined by local circumstances. It was suited to the condition of a church, still small in membership, which could be modelled after the pattern of the apostolate, with its treasurer and common purse. This plan was not tried again or elsewhere even in the apostolic church.

CHAPTER XXVII.

OF THE SACRAMENTS.

I.—*Sacraments are holy signs and seals of the covenant of grace, immediately instituted by God, to represent Christ and his benefits, and to confirm our interest in him ; as also to put a visible difference between those that belong unto the church and the rest of the world ; and solemnly to engage them to the service of God in Christ, according to his word.*

The name sacrament here given to certain symbolical ordinances observed according to Christ's appointment in the church is not a biblical word. The early Fathers applied the word *sacramentum* to rites and doctrines which were at once peculiarly sacred, and involved in some degree of mystery. Gradually its use was restricted to symbolic ordinances, though opinions differed as to the number of these. Our Confession takes here a thorough and comprehensive view of the significance and purpose of the sacraments. They are first of all means of grace, representing Christ's benefits, and confirming our interest in them, setting forth and emphasizing the grand vital truths of Christianity—regeneration, and the forgiveness of sins. They are, secondarily, signs of a religious profession, marking off the church from the world. [See Candlish, *The Sacraments*.]

II.—*There is in every sacrament a spiritual relation, or sacramental union, between the sign and the thing signified; whence it comes to pass, that the names and effects of the one are attributed to the other.*

The false notion of baptismal regeneration, so prevalent both in Lutheran and in Anglican churches, results from overlooking the principle of interpretation laid down in this section. What is said of the elements used in the sacrament, and generally of the sacramental action, is strictly true only of that which the action represents. The washing with water is not regeneration, but has a sacramental relation to the receiving of the Holy Ghost, which constitutes the principle of regeneration. The partaking of bread and wine is not the securing of the gift of forgiveness, but has a sacramental relation to that saving act of Christ. To identify the sacramental elements and the spiritual blessings would be to confound the sign with the thing signified.

III.—*The grace which is exhibited in or by the sacraments, rightly used, is not conferred by any power in them; neither doth the efficacy of a sacrament depend upon the piety or intention of him that doth administer it, but upon the work of the Spirit, and the word of institution; which contains, together with a precept authorizing the use thereof, a promise of benefit to worthy receivers.*

The efficacy of the sacraments is here described negatively and positively. (1) The power does not lie in the sacrament viewed *per se*, nor is it conditioned by the character of him who administers it. The Romish theory makes the sacrament efficacious in itself, *ex opere operato*, and thus gives what may be called a magical view of the sacrament. (Candlish, *The Sacraments*, p. 35.) The notion that all depends upon the intention of the officiating priest, *ex opere operantis*, led to great abuse in the Romish Church, and left it ordinarily uncertain whether one had at any time received the communion or not. (2) The Protestant doctrine places the efficacy in the observance of the acts prescribed in the institution, and in the fulfilment of the condition of faith on the part of the receiver as therein implied. 'All receive not the grace of God, which receive the sacraments of His grace. Neither is it ordinarily His will to bestow the grace of sacraments on any but by the sacraments ; which grace also, they that receive by sacraments, or with sacraments, receive it from Him, and not from them.' (Hooker, *Eccles. Polity*, Bk. v. ch. lvii.)

IV.—*There be only two sacraments ordained by Christ our Lord in the gospel, that is to say, Baptism, and the Supper of the Lord ; neither of which may be dispensed by any but by a minister of the word, lawfully ordained.*

The Romish Church recognises seven sacraments. This was attained after various proposals had been put forward. At different times we find four and six suggested as the proper number ; then twelve ; once even as many as thirty ; but finally Petrus Lombardus secured the general approval of the church for seven, as the perfect number ; though besides these there are many sacramental acts— *sacramentalia*—recognised. Protestants rightly renounce Confirmation, Penance, Orders, Marriage, and Extreme Unction, inasmuch as they do not conform to the strict idea of a sacrament. They are sacred acts, and may be viewed as symbolical of spiritual truth, but they are not institutions of Christ in the same sense as Baptism and the Lord's Supper. They may be all grouped as secondary under the two proper sacraments as primary. It may be noticed, too, that certain of those so-called sacraments refer only to special epochs and peculiar relations of life,—Marriage and Orders,—whereas the true sacraments recognise no distinction of rank, sex, or calling. (Comp. Martensen, *Chr. Dogmatics*, sect. 248.) The question has been elaborately discussed (Hooker, *Eccles. Polity*, Bk. v. ch. lxi), whether a layman or female may not in an emergency baptize. To assert that this may be done is essentially Romish, and is based on the idea, whether consciously entertained or not, of the absolute necessity of the sacraments to salvation.

V.—*The sacraments of the Old Testament, in regard of the spiritual things thereby signified and exhibited, were, for substance, the same with those of the New.*

It is very evident that there is a close resemblance between circumcision and baptism (only the exigencies of controversy caused some Baptists to deny this), and between the Passover and the Lord's Supper. Scripture passages may be collected which express, imply, or suggest these parallels. The statement of our Confession is moderate and guarded. It does not say that the New Testament sacraments are simple reproductions of the Old Testament sacraments, but that they are substantially the same. In the new dispensation they occupy the same place as those others did in the old. To both Old and New Testament sacraments the twofold description given in the first section will apply ;—they are means of grace and tokens of adherence to the church.

CHAPTER XXVIII.

OF BAPTISM.

I.—*Baptism is a sacrament of the New Testament, ordained by Jesus Christ, not only for the solemn admission of the party baptized into the visible church, but also to be unto him a sign and seal of the covenant of grace, of his ingrafting into Christ, of regeneration, of remission of sins, and of his giving up unto God through Jesus Christ, to walk in newness of life : which sacrament is, by Christ's own appointment, to be continued in his church until the end of the world.*

Here we have the twofold character of the sacrament attributed to Baptism. It is not, as Socinians describe it, merely an initiatory ceremony, but it is also a sign and seal of spiritual benefits and a means of grace. If we regard Baptism as simply an initiatory rite, we make it either a merely formal act, as indicating something like a hereditary religious status, or a magical operation, working effectively of itself apart from moral conditions. (See Pressensé, *Life and Practice in the Early Church*, Bk. i. ch. i. sect. 2.) Baptism is primarily the sacrament of regeneration, and some have limited it to this, and objected even to the mention of remission of sins. However, regeneration cannot be conceived of, nor can the sign of regeneration be conceived of, apart from the remission of sins. Regeneration is potential sanctification, the initiation of a spiritual process which has for its end complete deliverance from sin. We cannot think of this process begun or carried on apart from the revelation of the Divine forgiveness. It is no contradiction to make Baptism the initiatory rite, and at the same time, the sign and seal of those blessings of the covenant of grace afterwards to be developed.

II.—*The outward element to be used in this sacrament is water, wherewith the party is to be baptized in the name of the Father, and of the Son, and of the Holy Ghost, by a minister of the gospel, lawfully called thereunto.*

Only water is recognised as the element to be used. Besides this in the Romish Church an elaborate ceremonial was introduced ;

comprising—the sign of the cross, salt, touching ear and nose with spittle, anointing with oil, dressing in a white robe and carrying a burning torch. All these, as unordained, whatever their symbolical suitability, must be regarded as at least unessential to the administration of the sacrament. Three things essential are enumerated here : (1) The simple use of water as the element in the sacrament ; (2) The use of the name of Father, Son, and Spirit ; (3) The administration of the ordinance at the hand of one lawfully ordained. Where these conditions are observed, the baptism must be regarded as valid.

III.—*Dipping of the person into the water is not necessary ; but baptism is rightly administered by pouring or sprinkling water upon the person.*

The position here taken in regard to the mode of baptism is extremely moderate. There is no denunciation of immersion ; no denial of the validity of baptism so administered. It is simply said that such a form is not necessary. The mode is rightly regarded as immaterial, because not strictly determined by any express injunction. When this is granted, then the most convenient mode will be preferred, as the more troublesome has nothing special to recommend it. In controversy with Baptists, we should content ourselves with showing that no clear example from Scripture can be adduced in favour of immersion, without claiming any such in favour of sprinkling. [On this and following sections, read Witherow, *Scriptural Baptism, its Mode and Subjects.*]

IV.—*Not only those that do actually profess faith in and obedience unto Christ, but also the infants of one or both believing parents are to be baptized.*

This section refers to the subjects of baptism. It is the chief contention of Baptists that the ordinance should be granted only to those who can profess personal faith. Now our Confession claims the rite of baptism for infants, not on the ground of personal faith. It is conferred because of their parents' faith, but as a sacrament it has reference to an expected development of faith in the baptized. Faith in any proper sense cannot be predicated of children who receive baptism. The position above stated rests on the inclusion of children in the covenant promises of God, the analogy from the practice of circumcision among the Jews, Scripture references to the baptism of whole families, without any hint that in all these cases there were none but adult members, etc.

V.—*Although it be a great sin to contemn or neglect this ordinance, yet grace and salvation are not so inseparably annexed unto it, as*

*that no person can be regenerated or saved without it, or that all
that are baptized are undoubtedly regenerated.*

While God is free according to His sovereign grace to confer
salvation as He pleases, with or without the observance of any
ordinance, it is always incumbent upon the believer and the church
to observe the ordinances enjoined. Baptism cannot be neglected
without sin, but the sin is his who neglects to seek or confer the
sacrament. That the unbaptized must be regarded as unsaved is a
notion which results only from the false view of Augustine, that
baptism alone and efficiently removes original sin. On this theory
the unbaptized infant dying has still the guilt of original sin, and for
that must suffer. Compare the old canon in opposition to this : *non
privatio, sed contemtus sacramenti damnat.* Luther says : ' God has
not bound Himself to the sacraments so as not to be able to do
otherwise without the sacrament. So I hope that the good and
gracious God has something good in view for those who, not by any
guilt of their own, are unbaptized. What He will do with them, He
has revealed to none, that baptism may not be despised, but has
reserved to His own mercy; God does wrong to no one.' (Comp.
Dorner, *Hist. of Prot. Theology*, vol. i. p. 172.) The doctrine of the
absolute necessity of the Sacraments involves the twofold error
repudiated above—the destruction of all the unbaptized, and the
actual regeneration of the baptized. Our view of the necessity of the
sacrament is that this necessity is *non absoluta sed ordinata.*

VI.—*The efficacy of baptism is not tied to that moment of time wherein
    it is administered; yet notwithstanding, by the right use of this
    ordinance, the grace promised is not only offered, but really
    exhibited and conferred by the Holy Ghost, to such (whether of
    age or infants) as that grace belongeth unto, according to the
    counsel of God's own will, in his appointed time.*

The grace of baptism may not be conferred when it is administered, yet it will prove efficacious at any time when the grace is
bestowed. ' The Protestant doctrine of the Efficacy of Baptism, as
held by the Westminster divines, does not imply that, even in cases
in which baptism is not only valid but effectual, its effect must take
place at once. But, on the other hand, in such cases the grace is as
really connected with the sacrament as if it had been given at the
very moment of its administration.' (Candlish, *The Sacraments*,
p. 73.) The word ' exhibited ' is here used in an old sense to mean
' conferred.'

VII.—*The sacrament of baptism is but once to be administered to any
    person.*

Even the Church of Rome admits the validity of heretical baptism, and refuses to rebaptize. So careful are Romanists in this, that in any case where it is uncertain whether a party has been baptized or not, they use the formula : ' If thou hast been baptized, I baptize thee not ; if thou hast not been baptized, I baptize thee.' In the early church it was common to baptize those who were admitted from heretical sects ; and this was proper, because those sects generally denied the doctrine of the Trinity, and thus their baptism, wanting an essential part, was invalid. The rule of administering baptism only once to a person, results from the very meaning of the sacrament.

CHAPTER XXIX.

OF THE LORD'S SUPPER.

I.—*Our Lord Jesus, in the night wherein he was betrayed, instituted the sacrament of his body and blood, called the Lord's Supper, to be observed in his church unto the end of the world, for the perpetual remembrance of the sacrifice of himself in his death, the sealing all benefits thereof unto true believers, their spiritual nourishment and growth in him, their further engagement in and to all duties which they owe unto him, and to be a bond and pledge of their communion with him, and with each other, as members of his mystical body.*

We have here what may be called the simple biblical doctrine of the Lord's Supper. This holy sacrament is described as to—(1) Its institution by Christ immediately before His death ; (2) Its continuance in the church provided by the words of institution unto the end of the world ; (3) Its significance and purpose,—a commemoration and communion,—a memorial of Christ's death, and a seal of spiritual benefits, involving the intensifying of Christian obligations.

II.—*In this sacrament Christ is not offered up to his Father, nor any real sacrifice made at all for remission of sins of the quick or dead; but only a commemoration of that one offering up of himself, by himself, upon the cross, once for all, and a spiritual oblation of all possible praise unto God for the same; so that the Popish sacrifice of the mass, as they call it, is most abominably injurious to Christ's one only sacrifice, the alone propitiation for all the sins of the elect.*

The sacrament of the Supper is not a sacrifice, as is represented in the mass. (The name mass is supposed to be derived from the form of dismissal—*missa est*).[1] If we use the term sacrifice at all in connection with the sacrament, we only mean that it is a sacrifice of praise for the one sacrifice offered up once for all on Calvary. This constitutes a fundamental difference between the Romish and Protestant doctrines of the sacrament. At the same time (see sect. v.) we are not prevented from speaking of the signs in the sacraments in terms strictly applicable to that which the signs signify. The bread and wine as sacramental elements do not form a sacrifice, but they represent the great sacrifice. ' So great, so new, and so joyful ought it to seem unto thee, when thou comest to these holy mysteries, as if on this same day Christ first descending into the womb of the Virgin were become man, or hanging on the cross did this day suffer and die for the salvation of mankind.' (*Imitation of Christ*, Bk. iv. 11. 6.) The author of the Wisdom of Solomon, referring to the incident of the brazen serpent, says that the people had in it ' a sign of salvation, to put them in remembrance of the commandment of the law ; for he who turned himself toward it was not saved by the thing that he saw, but by Thee, who art the Saviour of all' (chap. xvi. 6, 7).

III.—*The Lord Jesus hath, in this ordinance, appointed his ministers to declare his word of institution to the people, to pray, and bless the elements of bread and wine, and thereby to set them apart from a common to a holy use; and to take and break the bread, to take the cup, and (they communicating also themselves) to give both to the communicants; but to none who are not then present in the congregation.*

The first part of this section indicates what is meant by the consecration of the elements in the administration of the communion. It is to be noted that the consecration applies to the elements as *used.* Romanists consider the elements as consecrated apart from their use, as having a certain physical sacredness independent of the spiritual state of the recipient.

Further, this section describes the symbolical acts, breaking the bread, giving the poured out wine ; and the giving of both elements to all communicants. Each of these acts is necessary to the right dispensation of the ordinance. Each has its own symbolic import, and the benefit of the sacrament consists in the enjoyment of all those spiritual realities which these acts symbolize.

The sacramental elements are only to be given where the communion is publicly dispensed. This injunction is given because of

---

[1] 'But it is at least an ingenious explanation that it is a phrase taken from the food placed upon the table, *missus*, or possibly from the table itself, *mensa*, and thence perpetuating itself in the Old English word " *mess* of pottage," " soldier's mess," and in the solemn words for feasts, as Christ*mas*,' etc. (Stanley's *Christian Institutions*, p. 44) ; or may it not simply be derived from *massa*, the dough or paste used in the form of loaf or wafer?

the danger attending the reservation of communion elements for the use of the sick and the dying. Such a practice would be likely to foster the notion that the communion is necessary to salvation, that the elements have a magical influence, and that the partaking of the sacrament before death will procure an entrance into glory. If this danger could be guarded against, we can quite appreciate the desire, which many express, to gratify afflicted saints, who have been long deprived.

IV.—*Private masses, or receiving this sacrament by a priest, or any other, alone; as likewise the denial of the cup to the people; worshipping the elements, the lifting them up, or carrying them about for adoration, and the reserving them for any pretended religious use; are all contrary to the nature of this sacrament, and to the institution of Christ.*

The first portion of this section gives a more explicit statement of matters referred to in the previous section. Notice here particularly, the objection to withholding the cup from the communicants. The doctrine of the church in regard to the consecration of the sacramental elements was that the receiver enjoyed the real presence of Chiist. The Romanists explained their view of the real presence by the theory of Transubstantiation ; the Lutherans, by the theory of Consubstantiation,—the actual presence of Christ's body and blood in, with, and under the substance of the elements ; the Reformed Church, by the doctrine of Christ's Spiritual Presence, real to those who exercise faith. The Romish theory was further in need of explanatory theories to account for the wonderful change in the substance of the elements. That which was finally accepted was proposed by Thomas Aquinas, *concomitantia,*—the body has the blood, the whole Christ is present in the consecrated bread. Taking this view, the Romish ecclesiastics, superstitious and scrupulous in their care over the elements which they supposed to be now really the body and blood of Christ, lest a crumb of bread should fall, had it made into tiny wafers, each communicant receiving one ; and lest the wine should be spilt in passing from one to another, withheld the cup, comforting the communicants with the assurance that in the bread they partook of a whole Christ. For Protestants, all that is important here is covered by the apostolic injunction, ' Let all things be done decently.'

V.—*The outward elements in this sacrament, duly set apart to the uses ordained by Christ, have such relation to him crucified, as that truly, yet sacramentally only, they are sometimes called by the name of the things they represent, to wit, the body and blood of Christ; albeit, in substance and nature, they still remain truly and only bread and wine, as they were before.*

Much confusion has resulted from not attending to the distinction laid down here between a sacramental relation and a substantial identity. Luther insisted on the words, 'This is my body,' and refusing all explanations, never quite rose above the fundamentally Romish conception. Lutherans call this a simple child-like faith ; others have called it dogged obstinacy. Because of this elementary position, the Lutheran mysticism is essentially materialistic. The notion of the real presence in the Reformed Church is purely spiritual.

VI.—*That doctrine which maintains a change of the substance of bread and wine into the substance of Christ's body and blood (commonly called Transubstantiation) by consecration of a priest, or by any other way, is repugnant not to scripture alone, but even to common sense and reason; overthroweth the nature of the sacrament; and hath been and is the cause of manifold super-stitions, yea, of gross idolatries.*

The doctrine of Transubstantiation is here rightly regarded as at the basis of all those Romish errors about the sacrament condemned in the previous sections. If it be so that consecration of the elements converts these into the very body and blood of Christ, then it is right that we should pay adoration to the elevated host, and that we should regard the sacramental action—the breaking and pouring out—as a renewed sacrifice. This doctrine crept gradually into the church. The foundation of it was laid in the mystical expressions of certain of the Greek Fathers. It had so taken hold of the church before the middle of the eleventh century that Berengarius of Tours was con-demned for denying it. Formal church sanction was given to the doctrine in 1215 at the Fourth Lateran Council, and from that time it has been a central and characteristic dogma of Rome. It is repudiated by our Confession on a threefold ground—(1) Being irrational in the exact sense that involves being unscriptural; (2) Con-tradicting the idea of a sacrament, because it identifies the sign and the thing signified ; (3) Occasioning many superstitions and idolatries —adoration of the host, and signs of reverence due only to God.

VII.—*Worthy receivers, outwardly partaking of the visible elements in this sacrament, do then also inwardly by faith, really and indeed, yet not carnally and corporally, but spiritually, receive and feed upon Christ crucified, and all benefits of his death: the body and blood of Christ being then not corporally or carnally in, with, or under the bread and wine; yet as really, but spiritually.*

present to the faith of believers in that ordinance, as the elements themselves are to their outward senses.

Here we have an express repudiation of the Lutheran doctrine of Consubstantiation According to this Lutheran theory, the substance of the bread and wine is not destroyed, as in the theory of Transubstantiation, but really continues, while in, with, and under these substances,—bread and wine,—when consecrated as sacramental elements, there are presented the actual body and blood of Christ. This is, if possible, less satisfactory than the Romish theory. Like most attempts at compromise, it only introduces a new difficulty. The main objection to Transubstantiation is that it destroys the idea of a sacrament—identifying the sign with the thing signified. The same objection applies to Consubstantiation. It so joins sign and thing signified that both together are taken in the hand, both together are eaten by the teeth. That this is so, is apparent from the Lutheran doctrine that the body and blood of Christ are present in the sacramental elements, in consequence of their consecration, independently of any faith on the part of the recipient. Our Confession, on the contrary, emphasizes the necessity of faith in order to secure the real presence, which is therefore conceived as a spiritual presence. There is a true relation—a sacramental relation—between the sign and the thing signified. Just as the bread and wine are present to the outward senses, so the body and blood of Christ, as spiritual nourishment, are present to the spiritual apprehension of those who receive the outward elements in faith.

VIII.—*Although ignorant and wicked men receive the outward elements in this sacrament, yet they receive not the thing signified thereby, but by their unworthy coming thereunto are guilty of the body and blood of the Lord, to their own damnation. Wherefore all ignorant and ungodly persons, as they are unfit to enjoy communion with him, so are they unworthy of the Lord's table, and cannot, without great sin against Christ, while they remain such, partake of these holy mysteries, or be admitted thereunto.*

The distinction between the sign in the sacrament and the grace which is the thing signified is very clearly stated by Calvin, that is, the distinction between partaking of the elements of the sacrament and enjoying the benefits of the sacrament. In his treatment of this point he has closely followed Augustine. *Sacramentum* is distinguished from *res sacramenti;* the benefit of the sacrament is only for the elect ; for while, as in the case of the Jews, the sacrament may be common to all, the grace which constitutes the efficiency of the sacrament is not common ; and when we partake of the outward elements, the sacrament is one thing, and the efficiency of the sacrament another : the elements partaken of may be life to one, and death to another; but the very substance of the sacrament,—that of which the elements are a sacrament,—ministers life to all who partake of it, and death to none; he dies not who partakes, but the partaking must be of the real substance of the sacrament, not of the mere visible sacrament, not outwardly with the teeth, but inwardly with the heart. (See Calvin, *Institutes*, Bk. iv. chap. xiv. § 15.) That which is appointed by God does not indeed suffer change, yet what is really presented may not be that which is actually received; or, to use the words of Augustine, 'If you receive it carnally, it ceases not to be spiritual, but it is not so to thee.' The reality of the sacrament is in no way affected by the unworthy failing to obtain the blessing, or rather to share in the substance of the sacrament. Just as the gospel invitation is addressed to all, so is the sacrament presented or offered to all; but, as in the one case, so in the other, while the reality of the power to bless is fully maintained, this blessing—the actual presence of Christ in grace and forgiveness—is communicated only to those who exercise faith. Any number of unbelieving guests at the table cannot so affect the reality of the sacrament, that one believer there will fail to enjoy for himself the very presence of Christ.

The closing passage regarding unworthy communicating is carefully expressed. Ignorant and ungodly persons, while remaining such, cannot come forward without great sin—that is, such a rash and irreverent approach is an aggravation of their sin of ignorance and ungodliness; and they cannot be admitted—that is, the admission of those known to be ignorant and ungodly will be reckoned a sin to the church so admitting. Too often, however, abstaining from communicating is put in place of the discontinuance of the life and practice inconsistent with that holy action. Such abstaining is itself the sign of a further sin, inasmuch as it indicates the absence of that penitence which would have rendered profitable communion possible.

CHAPTER XXX.

OF CHURCH CENSURES.

I.—*The Lord Jesus, as king and head of his church, hath therein appointed a government in the hand of church-officers, distinct from the civil magistrate.*

This statement is singularly well conceived, and has been the subject of very general approval. The position of the Westminster divines was a delicate one. In opposition to the violent and tyrannical prelatic party that had just been removed, there was a temptation to give expression to a one-sided anti-hierarchical tendency, and thus to neglect the claims of the great Head of the church. Or, in their opposition to the proud and dictatorial worldly statesmen then in power, there was a danger of their putting their anti-Erastian views in such a form as would seem irreconcilable with the orderly conduct of national government. Notwithstanding their decided opposition to all hierarchical pretensions and to all Erastian encroachments, the divines succeeded admirably in giving to each its due,—rendering to Cæsar the things that are Cæsar's, and to God the things that are God's. It was a favourite argument with those who wished to have either the civil or the ecclesiastical power supreme, that otherwise there would be an *imperium in imperio*, and that the two jurisdictions would inevitably clash with one another. The possibility of recognising the full import and jurisdiction of both ecclesiastical and civil power is admirably illustrated by Gillespie. A prince, during a sea voyage, though still a prince, and in this respect supreme governor of all on board, does not assume the government of the ship, which is exercised by one who is the prince's subject. ' And as the governor of a ship acknowledgeth his prince for his only supreme governor even then whilst he is governing and directing the course of the ship (otherwise while he is governing her course he should not be his prince's subject), yet he doth not thereby acknowledge that his prince governeth his action of directing the course of the ship (for then should the prince be the pilot); so, when one hath acknowledged the prince to be the only supreme governor upon earth of all ecclesiastical persons in his dominions (see *Conf.* chap. xxiii. 4), even whilst they are ordering and determining ecclesiastical causes, yet he hath not thereby acknowledged that the prince governeth the ecclesiastical causes.' (*The English Popish Ceremonies*, chap. viii. 4.) This is precisely the spiritual independence claimed by the Free Church. Presbyterians are loyal subjects according to the principles of their church government. The orderliness of their self-government in ecclesiastical and spiritual matters should rather be regarded as a promise and assurance of like behaviour under the civil government which they acknowledge. The danger of seeking to blend spiritual and temporal power in one may be shown from the history of the Papacy. There is an instructive passage in Dante, which illustrates this. Marco Lombardo speaks of two suns, the Emperor and the Bishop of Rome, who had shed their lights respectively on the world's way and on God's; but the one had quenched the other,—the sword had been grafted on the crook,—and for want of mutual restraint both grew worse.

' The Church of Rome,
Mixing two governments that ill assort,
Hath missed her footing, fallen into the mire,
And there herself and burden much defiled ' (*Purgatorio*, xvi. 129-132.)

Though objecting to the statement of this section, Stanley claims the Westminster Confession as an Erastian document. (See *Macmillan's Magazine* for 1881, p. 291.)

II.—To these officers the keys of the kingdom of heaven are committed, by virtue whereof they have power respectively to retain and remit sins, to shut that kingdom against the impenitent, both by the word and censures; and to open it unto penitent sinners, by the ministry of the gospel, and by absolution from censures, as occasion shall require.

Those church-officers for whom the former section claimed a special jurisdiction, have here their special duties laid down. The power which they exercise is called the Power of the Keys (Matt. xvi. 19), to distinguish it from the Power of the Sword—a ministerial as distinguished from a magisterial power. These officers exercise this power, not as individuals, but as ranged in their official positions, though the Confession does not particularly determine the form and constitution of church judicatories. Church discipline is essentially an act of the church as such (1 Cor. v. 4). The divines distinguish between magisterial power, as one delegated by God as supreme ruler to kings and princes as His deputies on earth, and ministerial power, which is no delegation of authority, but a commission as to servants given by the God-man, the Mediator, not authorizing the making of laws, but simply the making of them known. [Read on this subject, Rutherford's *Lex Rex*,—especially chap. xlii.] This section makes it clear that the Power of the Keys is not understood exclusively of the employment of church power in retaining and remitting sins, but rather of the exercise of the general ministerial functions, the ministry of the Gospel,—that is, the preaching of the Word, the dispensation of the sacraments, and the administration of discipline. When rightly understood, the power of binding and loosing, opening and shutting, here intended, is not different from the full declaration of the Gospel, which denounces doom upon the impenitent, and gives assurance of forgiveness to the penitent.

In the Romish Church, excommunication was converted into an engine of tyranny and extortion. Dante denounces the avarice of Popes who made war not with the sword, but by 'taking the bread away,' and who wrote ecclesiastical censures just to be paid for cancelling them. (*Paradiso*, xviii. 123–132.)

III.—*Church censures are necessary for the reclaiming and gaining of offending brethren; for deterring of others from the like offences; for purging out of that leaven which might infect the whole lump; for vindicating the honour of Christ, and the holy profession of the gospel; and for preventing the wrath of God, which might justly fall upon the church, if they should suffer his covenant, and the seals thereof, to be profaned by notorious and obstinate offenders.*

The end for which church discipline is to be exercised is the salvation of souls: the power is given to edification and not to destruction. (2 Cor. xiii. 10.) It is only when its gracious intention is frustrated that destruction ensues. According to our Confession, this power is committed to the church in order that the knowledge of this may deter from sin, or strengthen endeavours at resistance among those who are tempted. If, notwithstanding the knowledge of this power committed to the church, members of the church still fall into sin, the power must be positively exercised for a threefold purpose · (1.) To do what is possible to arrest at the earliest stage, what might become a serious and widespread defection ; (2.) To protect Christ's honour by repudiating the sin in His name, and showing that He will give no favour or countenance to sin ; (3.) To save the church as a whole from that just visitation of God which is denounced not only against the original offender, but also against all who are partakers in the sin. Familiar illustrations : Achan in the camp ; Jonah in the ship.

IV.—*For the better attaining of these ends, the officers of the church are to proceed by admonition, suspension from the sacrament of the Lord's Supper for a season, and by excommunication from the church, according to the nature of the crime, and demerit of the person.*

This section lays down the method to be pursued as most likely to attain these ends   We have here three stages in the exercise of discipline. (1.) Simple admonition in cases where it may seem that solemn words of warning and counsel may be helpful in checking the beginning of declension. (2.) Temporary suspension from the communion, if a member has been walking in an unseemly way, and his approach just then to the table might give just offence and cause scandal. (3.) Regular excommunication, the removal of the name from the communion roll,—in case the offence be a special, serious, and notorious one, or the person dealt with have aggravated his guilt by repeated falls. No evangelical church regards excommunication as final ; the end in view is ultimate restoration of the individual, strengthened and purified by the discipline.

CHAPTER XXXI.

OF SYNODS AND COUNCILS.

I.—*For the better government, and further edification of the church, there ought to be such assemblies as are commonly called Synods or Councils.*

The word synod originally means simply an assembly, and is so used in this place. The divines, careful not to render their formulary sectarian, avoided such close determination of the form of church government as might render the Confession, otherwise suitable, unacceptable to some. In those Scottish Presbyterian Churches whose supreme court is a General Assembly, 'Synod' means a subordinate provincial assembly of ministers and elders. We have here simply the assertion of the right of the church to have ecclesiastical assemblies to provide for good government and the general welfare of the church.

II.—*As magistrates may lawfully call a synod of ministers, and other fit persons, to consult and advise with about matters of religion; so if magistrates be open enemies to the church, the ministers of Christ, of themselves, by virtue of their office, or they, with other fit persons upon delegation from their churches, may meet together in such assemblies.*

This section determines the question as to the parties in whom the right of calling such synods is vested.

The first part of the section has been objected to as countenancing Erastianism. When we consider the general tenor of the passage, we may be assured that no such view was intended. To prevent misunderstanding, however, the Assembly of the Scottish Church which adopted the Confession (A.D. 1647) distinctly stated that this clause was understood to refer only to kirks not settled or constituted in point of government, and affirmed that in kirks constituted and settled a synod should not be called merely by magisterial authority, nor without a delegation from the churches to the ministers so to convene.

The latter part of the section shows clearly how advanced and liberal the views of the divines were in regard to legitimate popular control exercised over monarchs. No more satisfactory statement of the case can be given than that which we have from Rutherford. He entitles one of his chapters, 'Whether or no the convening of the subjects without the king's will be unlawful.' 'Convention of the subjects, in a tumultuary way, for a seditious end, to make war without warrant of law, is forbidden; but not when religion, laws, liberties, invasion of foreign enemies, necessitateth the subjects to convene, although the king and ordinary judicatures, going a corrupt way to pervert judgment, shall refuse to consent to their conventions.' (*Lex Rex*, p. 233.) And he goes on to say that refusing the liberty would be as foolish as to require people to wait for an express Act of Parliament before going to quench a fire or to pursue a wolf. This principle was immediately applied to religious assemblies; and it was a saying among our covenanting forefathers, that if denied the liberty of calling religious assemblies and meeting in these, they might as well be denied the Gospel. Those Aberdeen professors of divinity and ministers who refused the covenant, vigorously opposed Henderson and Dickson, who had been sent as delegates to persuade them to sign that document, maintaining that all manner of leagues apart from royal sanction were forbidden, and clinging to the statement of a civil enactment on that point. 'In this you will so precisely adhere to the letter of the law,' answered the covenanters, 'that you will have no meetings without the king's consent, even in the case of the preservation of religion, of his majesty's authority, and of the liberties of the kingdom, which we are sure must be contrary to the reason and life of the law : since the safety of the people is the sovereign law.'

III.—*It belongeth to synods and councils ministerially to determine controversies of faith, and cases of conscience; to set down rules and directions for the better ordering of the publick worship of God, and government of his church; to receive complaints in cases of maladministration, and authoritatively to determine the same : which decrees and determinations, if consonant to the word of God, are to be received with reverence and submission, not only for their agreement with the word, but also for the power whereby they are made, as being an ordinance of God, appointed thereunto in his word.*

This section states the functions of synods and the authority belonging to their legislative decrees. Ecclesiastical synods may legitimately take cognizance of three different orders of cases. 1. The settling of disputes and uncertainties in matters of faith,— determining in cases of suspected heresy, whether the statements challenged are in accordance with the expressed doctrinal positions of the church Standards. (The reference to cases of conscience indicates the right of the church by means of her assemblies to resolve doubts and explain difficulties ; this, however, should ordinarily be left to pastoral dealing, and only when difficulty in determining a point has become general in the church, should the superior courts deal with the question.) 2. The maintenance of church order,—if in details any modification seems desirable in regard to the form of conducting worship, or managing the affairs of the church. 3. The hearing of appeals and reviewing the decisions of the inferior courts. Our General Assembly reviews proceedings of presbyteries and synods, when these have been appealed against. and may reverse or confirm the decisions of these courts ; and parties must receive its sentence as final.

All this is done ministerially,—the members of Assembly acting as ministers, servants of God; but such decisions, when agreeable to God's Word, are to be received for a twofold reason : (1) because consonant with God's Word ; (2) because the ministerial authority is itself an ordinance of God.

IV.—*All synods or councils since the apostles' times, whether general or particular, may err, and many have erred; therefore they are not to be made the rule of faith and practice, but to be used as an help in both.*

Ecclesiastical councils are not infallible. The Romish Church for a time maintained that, while particular or provincial synods had erred, Œcumenical or general synods had never erred. It was afterwards asserted that infallibility belonged to decisions of Œcumenical councils only when they had the sanction of the Pope, and only when they referred to matters of faith and morals, and not to mere details of discipline. The Vatican Council in 1870 decreed the Pope's infallibility, and so authoritatively settled the question as to the relative importance of Pope and General Council. Even before this, Hefele, the historian of church councils, wrote : ' To appeal from the Pope to a council, an authority usually very difficult to constitute and to consult, is simply to cloak ecclesiastical insubordination by a mere formality.' Our Confession repudiates the doctrine of human Infallibility unreservedly. The Westminster divines were far from claiming this to themselves ; and their work in the Confession they do not offer as a rule of faith and practice (which the Bible alone is), but only as a guide and directory to the meaning and truth of Scripture.

V.—*Synods and councils are to handle or conclude nothing but that which is ecclesiastical; and are not to intermeddle with civil affairs, which concern the commonwealth, unless by way of humble petition, in cases extraordinary; or by way of advice for satisfaction of conscience, if they be thereunto required by the civil magistrate.*

While claiming liberty of meeting and discussion for ecclesiastical courts, our church is careful to show that the charge of danger to government, as in the case of an *imperium in imperio*, is unfounded. Synods are to limit their deliberations as far as possible to purely ecclesiastical matters, and to avoid the domain of politics. In times of persecution, the members of ecclesiastical courts had of necessity to express their views on rulers and acts of government, because these tyrannically interfered with ecclesiastical causes. (See Brown of Wamphray's *Apologetical Narration*, sect. vi.) It was the error of the Papacy to interfere with and seek to dominate civil affairs by their ecclesiastical decisions. The Reformers, and after them our Puritan and Covenanting forefathers, sought carefully to avoid this error.

CHAPTER XXXII.

OF THE STATE OF MEN AFTER DEATH, AND OF THE RESURRECTION OF THE DEAD.

I.—*The bodies of men after death return to dust, and see corruption; but their souls (which neither die nor sleep), having an immortal subsistence, immediately return to God who gave them. The souls of the righteous, being then made perfect in holiness, are received into the highest heavens, where they behold the face of God in light and glory, waiting for the full redemption of their bodies; and the souls of the wicked are cast into hell, where they remain in torments and utter darkness, reserved to the judgment of the great day. Besides these two places for souls separated from their bodies, the scripture acknowledgeth none.*

In this section there are three doctrinal positions laid down. (1.) The Immortality of the Soul. The state of the soul after the death of the body is described in Scripture figuratively as a sleep (1 Thess. iv. 14). The idea of the sleep of souls, however, is rejected as inconsistent with passages that speak of departed spirits as active, and describe the scene of their activity as the immediate presence of Christ. The notion of the sleep of souls was entertained by sects in the third century opposed by Origen, and again by certain sects in the sixteenth century against whom Calvin wrote a treatise. It is still maintained by Delitzsch and a few others. (2.) A State of Rewards and Punishments. The doctrine of Immortality, as applied to all souls, contradicts the annihilation theory. Those who hold that theory speak of immortality as not natural, but conditional. While we hold that Scripture clearly teaches that man as man is immortal, we are careful to distinguish, against Restitutionists of all kinds, that immortality is not synonymous with eternal life. It is the express doctrine of Revelation that there are different destinations for the souls of men: Heaven for the righteous, into which, as a fixed condition of bliss, the souls of the just immediately pass,—Hell for the wicked, into which, without hope of reprieve, the souls of the unjust are immediately driven. (3.) No Intermediate Condition. When we speak of an intermediate state of souls, we do not mean a probationary state, but simply the condition of those souls intermediate between the periods of their own death and of the final judgment. The idea of purgatory appears in the writings of the early Fathers. Later, by the school divines, divisions were supposed in this region :—*Limbus Infantium*, the place of unbaptized infants, practically hell, as there is no release, though there is absence of actual pain ; *Limbus Patrum*, the place of the Old Testament saints, where they waited the completion of Christ's work.

II.—*At the last day, such as are found alive shall not die, but be changed; and all the dead shall be raised up with the self-same bodies, and none other, although with different qualities, which shall be united again to their souls for ever.*

III.—*The bodies of the unjust shall, by the power of Christ, be raised to dishonour; the bodies of the just, by his Spirit, unto honour, and be made comformable to his own glorious body.*

These sections affirm—(1.) The resurrection of the body; (2.) The different destinations of the bodies raised up.

The essential identity of the resurrection body and that which had been laid in the grave is clearly stated. The expression 'the self-same bodies' does not necessarily imply that those several material atoms which make up our present body will be gathered up and placed together. That such material identity is not intended is seen from the use of the apostle's expression regarding those who remain alive on the earth at the period of the judgment, that they shall be changed. The substance, too, of bodies is constantly changing, yet our bodies from infancy to old age are regarded as the self-same bodies. The identity of the resurrection body and the body laid in the grave may be similar to that of the body of our earthly life in all its stages. The identity is like that of the seed-corn and its fruit. The qualities of the resurrection body will be such as will fit the conditions of the risen life. Our only hints regarding those modifications are such as may be gathered from what is told us of our Lord's body after His resurrection; yet even on this there would be a certain change when He had ascended unto His Father.

As to whether any real change of place or condition will occur after the judgment, Scripture is silent. Dante indulges in speculations as to a change of condition at the judgment, in the case of those who, in the other world, wait the coming of that day. (Read *Inferno*, vi. 102–117.) Cary appends this quotation from Augustine:—'At the resurrection of the flesh, both the happiness of the good and the torments of the wicked will be increased.'

CHAPTER XXXIII.

OF THE LAST JUDGMENT.

I.—*God hath appointed a day wherein he will judge the world in righteousness by Jesus Christ, to whom all power and judgment is given of the Father. In which day, not only the apostate angels shall be judged, but likewise all persons that have lived upon earth shall appear before the tribunal of Christ, to give an account of their thoughts, words, and deeds, and to receive according to what they have done in the body, whether good or evil.*

The statement above given runs very closely on scriptural lines : a day of judgment appointed by God, judgment committed to the Son, angels and men to be judged, and judgment to be given according to deeds done,—thereby the two classes, already separated at death, being now even more conspicuously distinguished. The points here emphasized are the reality, the certainty, and the principle of the judgment. The imagery employed in Scripture is not to be pressed and interpreted literally, inasmuch as the precise form and method of procedure on that day are among the secret things of God. 'Even in the Middle Ages,' says Oosterzee, referring to Thomas Aquinas, 'it was readily granted : *totum illud judicium, et quoad discussionem et quoad sententiam, non vocaliter sed mentaliter perficietur.*' (*Christian Dogmatics*, p. 802.) 'The wicked,' says Matthew Henry, 'took up with left-hand blessings, riches and honour ; and so shall their doom be.'

II.—*The end of God's appointing this day is for the manifestation of the glory of his mercy in the eternal salvation of the elect, and of his justice in the damnation of the reprobate, who are wicked and disobedient. For then shall the righteous go into everlasting life, and receive that fulness of joy and refreshing which shall come from the presence of the Lord; but the wicked, who know not God, and obey not the gospel of Jesus Christ, shall be cast into eternal torments, and be punished with everlasting destruction from the presence of the Lord, and from the glory of his power.*

The chief end or purpose of this judgment is to assert the truth and holiness of God,—His mercy in the case of the righteous, and His justice in the case of the wicked. Conspicuously in regard to the righteous, He shows Himself at once a just God and a Saviour. Fulness of joy on the one hand, actual eternal torments on the other hand, are not ignored ; yet refreshing and destruction are regarded as determined by the presence or absence of the Lord. 'The blessed strike the root of their life in the eternal life of God. . . . Their present is God. To be deprived of this present, and still to subsist without end—this in itself alone is a torment of hell for the condemned.' (Delitzsch, *Bibl. Psych.* p. 557.)

III.—*As Christ would have us to be certainly persuaded that there shall be a day of judgment, both to deter all men from sin, and for the greater consolation of the godly in their adversity ; so will he have that day unknown to men, that they may shake off all carnal security, and be always watchful, because they know not at what hour the Lord will come; and may be ever prepared to say, Come, Lord Jesus, come quickly. Amen.*

The end of the judgment as concerns men, subordinate to that of the Divine glory, is to deter from sin, and encourage to works of holiness. Terror may paralyze or it may restrain from evil courses, just according to the spirit of the subject of it, gracious or reprobate. This twofold result from a view of the judgment day is vividly depicted in the *Pilgrim's Progress.* In the Interpreter's house Christian is brought to see a man shaking with fear because of a vision he had of this great day, being himself unprepared ; and the Interpreter in sending Christian away says to him that he must keep in mind the things he had seen—' that they may be as a goad in thy sides to prick thee forward in the way thou must go.'

The apostle (2 Pet. iii. 3) shows that denial or forgetfulness of the coming judgment is intimately connected with careless and sinful walking, and that (vv. 11, 12) thoughtful anticipation of that day is helpful in securing godliness and holiness of conversation.

INDEX.

—o—

Acceptilatio, theory of, 77.
Adoption, a Christian grace, 92.
,, its nature, 93.
,, its privileges, 93.
Antinomianism, 100, 108
Apocrypha, uninspired writings, 34.
Apostasy, 111.
Apostles' Creed, incompleteness of, 5.
Assurance, from the Spirit's witness, 114.
,, not of the essence of faith, 114.
,, what disturbs, 115.
,, what warrants it, 113.
Authenticity of original Scripture texts, 39.
Authority of Scripture, 35.

Baptism, doctrine of, 150.
,, mode of, 151.
,, subjects of, 151.
,, not necessary to salvation, 152.
,, to be administered only once, 152
Body, resurrection of the, 165.
,, state of, after death, 165.
Bondage of the will, 79.

Calvinism of the Confession, 21.
Canon of Scripture, 32.
Canonicity, test of, 33.
Censures of the Church, 158.
Church as institution, 144.
Church buildings, idea of their sacredness, 129.
Church, salvation ordinarily in the, 143
,, visible and invisible, 142.
Churches, their relative perfection, 144.
Communicatio idiomatum, 76.
Communion of saints with Christ, 146.
,, ,, with one another, 146.
Community of goods not enjoined, 147.
Conditional decree, 47.
Confession of Aberdeen, 10.
,, of Knox, 7.
,, of Westminster, 11.

Confessions of Faith, their relation to Scripture, 1.
Confessions of Faith, what acceptance of, implies, 3.
Confession of Faith should be definite, 4.
Confession of sin, 103.
Conflict of believers with sin, 97.
Consubstantiation, Lutheran theory of, 157.
Counsels of perfection, 107.
Counter-imputation, 88.
Covenant, general idea of a, 65.
,, of grace, 67
,, ,, conditions of, 68.
,, of works, 66.
,, uses of a, 66.
Creation, the biblical doctrine of, 52.

Death, the wages of sin, 64.
Decree, God's eternal, 46.
,, ,, ,, relation of, to free dom, 47.
Decree, not conditional, 47.
Discipline in the Church, 136, 160.
Dispensations of the covenant of grace, 69.

Effectual calling, 82.
Elect infants, 85.
Elect only redeemed, 49.
Election in Christ, 49
Erastian controversy, 15.
Erastianism condemned, 136, 158.
Eternity of punishment, 165.
Eutychian view of person of Christ, 71
Everlasting life, 165
Excommunication, 160.

Faith a saving grace, 97.
,, necessary to worthy communicating, 157.
Faith not the ground but the fruit of election, 49.
Faith, the increase of, 98.
,, the instrument in justification, 88.

Faith, reason or ground of, 98.
,,   varying degrees of, 99.
Falls of believers, 111.
     ,,   causes of, 112.
     ,,   consequences of, 112.
Fasts, observance of, 128.
Fœderal theology, 65.
Foreordination and predestination, 48.
Forgiveness of sins of believers, 91.
Freedom of the will, 78.

God, attributes of, 43.
,,   tripersonality of, 44.
,,   unity of, 42.
Good works rewarded, 108.
     ,,   their relation to faith, 88, 108.
Grace, extent of meaning, 90.
,,   growth in, 96.
,,   irresistible, 85.
Grundtvig's plea for a short creed, 5
Guilt of sin, 64.

Heaven, the place of souls of righteous, 165.
Hell, the place of souls of wicked, 165.
Hereditary guilt, 62.
Humiliation, state of, 74.

Identity of resurrection body, 166.
Image of God in man, 53.
Immortality of the soul, 165.
Imputation an element in justification, 87.
Imputation of Adam's sin, 62.
Inability, doctrine of, 63.
Independent controversy, 17.
Indwelling sin, 64, 81.
Infallibility of Church councils denied, 164.
Infant baptism, 151.
Infant salvation, 85.

Judgment-day, 167.
     ,,   why the time of, concealed, 168.
Judgment-day, certainty of, 168.
Judgment, principle of the, 167.
Justification by application of the Spirit, 90.
Justification by faith, 88.
     ,,   doctrine of, 87.
     ,,   of Old Testament saints, 75, 91.
Justification, Romish doctrine of, 89.
     ,,   through merits of Christ, 88.

Keys, power of the, 136, 160.

Law of God at Sinai, 117.
,,   to Adam, 116.
Law, relation of, to believers, 120.
Laws, what mutable, 118.
,,   what immutable, 119.
Liberty, doctrine of Christian, 26, 122.
Licence distinguished from liberty, 123

Magistracy open to Christians, 135.
Magistrate, limits of his jurisdiction, 136.
Magistrate owes his authority to God, 135.
Magistrate's power to call synods, 137, 162.
Magistrates, Christian's duty toward, 138.
Man in the image of God, 53.
Marriage affinity question, 140.
Marriages, mixed, 139.
Mediate imputation, theory of, 63.
Mediatorial work of Christ, 70.
Mental reservation, 133.
Ministerial power, 163.
Ministry of the Word, 128.
Miracles, possibility of, 56.
Monogamy, 138.

Natural religion, insufficiency of, 29, 30, 86.
Nestorian view of person of Christ, 71.

Oaths, meaning of, 131.
,,   obligation of, 133.
Oaths, only to be made in God's name, 132.
Oaths, when warrantable, 132.
Obedience of Christ, active and passive, 73, 75.
Offices of the Redeemer, 70.

Papal claims as to jurisdiction, 138.
Perfection, Christian doctrine of, 64.
Perfection of Scripture, 37.
Perseverance, doctrine of, 110.
,,   on what it depends, 110.
Person of Christ, 71.
Perspicuity of Scripture, 38.
Prayer, the duty and the privilege, 127.
Predestination and foreordination, 48.
Predestination, how expressed in Confession, 22.
Predestination to be handled with care, 51.
Private judgment, right of, 123.
Providence as care for the Church, 60.
,,   in relation to evil, 57.
Providence in relation to judicial hardening, 59.
Providence in relation to temptation, 58.

Providence, relation to human freedom, 55.
Providence, upholding and disposing, 55.
Punishment, eternal, 165.
Purgatory, introduction of the idea of, 165.

Reason of faith, the, 98.
Redemption, extent of, 25, 77.
  ,,   only of the elect, 49.
Regeneration and justification, 90.
Repentance, doctrine of, 100.
  ,,   its range, 102.
  ,,   necessity of, 101.
  ,,   of particular acts of sin, 103.
  ,,   relation to faith, 100.
Reprobation, 50.
Resurrection body, identity of, 166.
Resurrection of the dead, 165.
Revelation, 29.
Righteousness, original, 61.

Sabbath, law of the, 129.
  ,,   sanctification of the, 130.
Sacraments, doctrine of the, 147.
Sacraments, no magical power in the, 148.
Sacraments of Old Testament same as those of the New, 149.
Salvation only through Christ, 86.
Sanctification, doctrine of, 94.
  ,,   imperfect in this life, 96.
  ,,   relation to justification, 95.
  ,,   the work of the Spirit, 95.
Scientia media, 47.
Scripture, authenticity of original texts of, 39.
Scripture, authority of, 35.
  ,,   interpretation of, 40.
  ,,   perfection of, 37.
  ,,   perspicuity of, 38.
  ,,   revelation written, 30.
  ,,   translations of, 39.
  ,,   uses of, in controversy, 41.
Sin, nature and origin of, 61.
Sin, original, 24, 62.
Sinai covenant, 117.
Sinlessness of Jesus, 72.
Sins of believers, 64.
Six days of creation, 52.
Soul, immortality of the, 165.
Soul, sleep of the, 165.
States of humiliation and exaltation, 74.
Subordinate Standards, 1.
Subordinationism, 45, 73.
Subscription, what it implies, 3.

Supererogation, works of, 106.
Supper, the Lord's, doctrine of, 153.
  ,,   elements continue unchanged, 156.
Supper, the Lord's, not a sacrifice, 153.
  ,,   relation to word and prayer, 154.
Supper, the Lord's, to be publicly observed, 155.
Supralapsarianism, theory of, 23.
Synergism, 63.
Synods, calling of, 162.
  ,,   fallibility of, 164.
  ,,   uses and functions of, 163.

Testament in sense of covenant, 68.
Thanksgiving-days, observance of, 128.
Toleration, necessary limits to, 124.
  ,,   principles of Christian, 26
Translations of Scripture to be used, 39.
Transubstantiation, Romish theory of, 156.
Trinity, attempted illustrations of the doctrine of, 45.
Trinity, doctrine of the, 44.

Unworthy communicating, 157.

Voluntariness of Christ's suffering, 73.
Vow compared to the oath, 134.
Vows, when illegitimate, 134.

War, when lawful, 135.
Westminster Assembly, arrangements for meeting, 11.
Westminster Assembly, composition and membership of, 14.
Westminster Assembly, controversies of, 15.
Westminster Confession, 18.
  ,,   its doctrines characterized, 20.
Will, bondage of the, 79
Will in the glorified, 81.
Will of man in innocency, 79.
  ,,   natural liberty of, 78.
Will, state of, in the converted man, 80, 84.
Word, reading and ministry of the, 128.
Works, good, the fruit of the Spirit, 105, 106.
Works of supererogation, 106.
  ,,   of unregenerate man, sinful, 109.
Works, what are good, 88, 105.
Worship due to God only, 126.
Worthy communicating, 157